# Skeletal Marriage

## Jim Kohl

*This book is dedicated to all my family and friends that stuck with me through my sickness, and to my Beautiful Susan who came to me after.*

# Acknowledgments

This book would not have been possible had I not hated myself so completely for such a long time, so thanks to me for that. Thanks also to me for loving myself enough to write it all down and put it on paper forever so that I no longer have to be a self-destructive anorexic. Thanks to Susan, my girlfriend, for editing this for me and for the support she shows for my writing every day. Thanks to Peggy, without whom I might be dead. Thanks to certain members of the LeyVa staff that bad mouthed Noble Poverty so much that it sold well—that was LONG overdue. Thanks to Shadows & Light Magazine for publishing my short story this year. Thanks to Shift Magazine at San Jose State University, especially Heidi, for seeking me out to write a piece on poverty for them. Thanks to Willow Glen Books for holding the only book signing for When Colors Run. That bookstore always supports the unknown writers, and we all owe them a debt of gratitude. Thanks to those that came to that book signing, especially, Susan, Brighid, Josh, Martin, Kristin, Bernhard, Dominique, Lorenzo, David G (guitar player extraordinaire), Justin and his girlfriend, whose name I don't remember. Thanks to my family that I have not yet mentioned Diane, Mark, Baby Makena, Grandma Reilly, Mom and Dad, and Ernie.

And super special thanks to Sandi, Susan's mom, who once said—and I quote—"Tell Jim if he ever quotes me in a book, he's dead meat."

# *Introduction*

This isn't my first memoir. In 1999, I wrote a memoir about my teaching experiences. One of the criticisms of that book on Amazon.com was that it was too much about me and not enough about the corrupt educational system in California. If you picked up this book looking for a be-all-end-all, definitive book about anorexia, then find another one—but good luck.

This book tells my story of anorexia. More specifically, this book spans the time when the weight loss started to the time when I was again approaching a healthy weight. I'll show you what I know about my anorexia, and I'll show you what it did to me, to my family, and to my friends. That's really the best anyone can do.

Anorexia is as individual as a fingerprint. Although fingerprints are similar, there are subtle differences among them. If someone tells you they have the definitive book on anorexia, they may as well say they have the definitive book on fingerprints and snowflakes.

All the events and emotions portrayed in this book are real. All the people in this book are also real. Anorexia in men is real too. I was lucky in that I postponed my own death, but anorexia really never goes away. As I type this, I see my "healthy" gut in front of me and want to do something about it. I know that sounds innocent enough; we all want to lose weight, but in my head, there is never enough weight loss.

I apologize to anyone I hurt and to those that are hurt by the telling of this story, mostly my ex wife and now very good friend, Kristin. We both got ugly, but this is my story, and I was sick. She knows that now. Honesty is everything. If this book can bring about awareness to anyone with anorexia or can help anyone who loves someone with anorexia, then it has done its job.

# *Chapter 1*

My boss's voice droned about the project I had been assigned to write about. I had a legal pad in front of me at the Thursday morning meeting. I had scribbled the date of the meeting at the top and waited for something pertinent to my job to be mentioned with my pen at the ready position. Not too much followed the date on my paper.

About five of us sat around the table in the conference room in the trailer where we worked behind the secure gates of Lawrence Livermore National Laboratory. I had been up since 4, wrote fiction, got my daughter ready, helped my wife Kristin figure out which shoes looked best with the 3$^{rd}$ outfit she'd tried on that morning, got myself ready, made the 50 mile drive from Modesto with my daughter, and dropped her off at daycare, so I could start work at 7 am.

Lots of days I couldn't wait to get to work so I could rest.

Ron was still talking, so I had to listen. This was the status meeting, after all, and God help me if I didn't know what the status was. Hurry up and wait was usually the status, and that Thursday was no exception.

I felt myself nodding off right there at the oval conference room table. The only thing keeping me awake was the fear of my forehead crashing against the table. Each time gravity woke me when my head lolled forward, I looked around the table to see if anyone noticed.

Ron was still talking, Heather was taking the minutes, and no one was looking at me. Wait...Sandie, the new administrative assistant, gave me a knowing smile from across the table. She had seen. Dammit!

She seemed pretty cool though. I didn't think she'd rat me out to Ron about being less than thrilled with the status of things. Plus, I was tired. I sipped at the travel coffee cup I had on the table to try and play it off that I had been attentive the whole time.

Karen, her hair prematurely silver, tapped her pen on her own legal pad.

Ron was saying how there was a delay, again, in the delivery of the units we needed to send the excess waste we had onsite to its final resting place. "Los Alamos still has one of the units, and the other two could conceivably be here on time, but DOE won't send them until we have the other unit anyway…"

It was the same old story. I doubted whether we'd ever get the equipment, but to say so would come off as being a pessimist. Plus, what did I care really? My job was really just to write about the process that the alleged equipment would allow us to follow if it ever showed up, and my position in this part of the lab only lasted until it did show up.

The room blurred for me again. I saw the green border that protected the walls from the tops of the chairs spread and fuse with the white of the walls as my eyelids fluttered and my head got heavier.

POP!

A white flash woke me. It was like the room had a power surge. Slowly, the room faded from Heaven white back to normal. Confusing…

but not entirely…

unpleasant.

Ron was still talking, Heather still scribbled notes, and the others in the room still had the interested look of good meeting attendees.

"So if there are no questions, I guess that's it for today," Ron said.

Ron looked around the room to each of us, and when no one said anything, we all said thank you and climbed from our chairs to return to our offices.

I sat in front of my computer and looked over the sparse notes I took in the meeting. Not too much for me to do based on what was said in there, and it was just as well seeing as my head was killing me. My phone rang. "This is Jim."

"Hey Bubba." It was my wife, Kristin.

"Hey Honey, what's going on?" At the time, Kristin worked in San Jose where we used to live—a full 100 mile commute. I never complained about my 50 mile drive in front of her.

"Not much. Just seeing how you are doing?"

"Actually, things are kind of weird. I have a huge headache." The light from my office was making it worse.

"Really? Do you have anything to take?"

"No, I don't think I do, but it was really weird. I was in a meeting and dozing off…"

Kristin gasped, "Did anyone see you?"

"This one lady, but she's cool." I said, "But anyway, it was like I saw this flash and heard a pop sound, and after that my head was killing me."

"So does anyone there have anything to take?"

"Are you listening?"

"Oh, sorry, Hon, I was reading something. What now?"

"I said there was this flash of light and a loud popping sound." I was used to repeating things to her on the phone when she was at work. "Maybe I'm getting migraines or something."

"Is the headache that bad?"

"Yeah, the lights in here are killing me." I twirled the phone cord in my fingers. "I'm thinking of going to the doctor maybe."

"Well, if you think you have to."

"I don't know. Maybe it'll go away."

"All right, baby, well I hope you feel better."

"Thanks."

But it didn't go away. The computer screen was burning straight through to my optic nerve. I squinted and pushed my fingertips against my temples, but I couldn't get a break.

My sister had migraines. I remembered a time when we were younger, and I had to keep her awake all night for some sort of test the next morning. We went to see the movie *The Doors,* had lots of coffee at Denny's, and watched movies on video when we got home. By 5 am, she was so pissed at me, but I was duty-bound to make sure she stayed awake.

How was I supposed to stay up all night? I had a 4 year old that counted on me.

I pulled a document up on my government-issue Mac and scrolled through the pages.

On the Internet, I was part of a message board called the BBQ Basement. Those guys combined had had every health problem known to professional medicine. I posted:

Hey Everyone:
   I had this weird thing happen to me today where I saw a white flash of light and heard a loud pop. Now my head is hurting like crazy, and it has been for a good hour or so. Could this be migraines?

Now all I had to do was wait for an answer, but that wasn't helping my head at all.

I could ask Heather for Tylenol, I thought. I decided not to because I didn't want to have to tell the story of the pop at work and have everyone think that I was going insane. Insanity was frowned upon in the conservative lab environment, and I was in the process of getting my Q clearance, which would allow me to work on confidential documentation. They didn't want a nut job looking at that stuff.

Each hour, I checked back at the message board, and some people answered me, mostly describing their own experiences with migraines or the experiences that their friend's cousin's brother's had. Flashing lights were part of it, so I decided that must be what I had.

I called the doctor and talked to the Kaiser advice nurse. I explained the pop, the flashing light, and the headache again.

"What do you mean a pop?" The nurse said.

"Like it..." the more time that passed after it, the harder time I had explaining. "It was like I heard a pop, and saw a white flash of light, and then the room came back."

"I've never heard of this." She sounded like every mechanic that ever worked on the '68 Mustang I had as a teen. "I think you better come in. Let me transfer you to the appointment desk."

I waited while the recording played soothing music interrupted with reminders to get my flu shot and with advice on what to do to ease the symptoms of my allergies. "What do I do for a pop in the head?" I asked the recording to amuse myself.

When the line went live again, I explained that I was developing migraine headaches, and I needed to come in and get some pain medicine.

"Can you come in today?"

"No, I'm at work." I never felt good telling a boss that I had to leave in the middle of the day. I liked to give at least a day's notice.

"How bad is the pain?"

I saw where this was going. "It's bad."

I made an appointment for later that afternoon.

# *Chapter 2*

Ron was cool about my leaving an hour early so I could make the appointment. All was great—with the exception of the pain in my head. "I know I have a bad headache. Why can't they just prescribe a pain killer and be done with it?"

I turned that thought around in my pounding head as I headed down East Avenue toward Storyland Daycare where Brighid was.

I showed up in the middle of naptime. The floor was lined with little blue cots filled with kids in different states of sleep.

Ms. Annette, the director of Storyland met me at the door. "You're early," she said.

"Yeah, I have a doctor's appointment." Kneeling by Brighid's cot, I rubbed her back and shook her awake. She rolled onto her back and rubbed her eyes with her little fists. "Brighid," I said.

Her eyes popped open. "Daddy?"

"Yeah baby. C'mon we gotta go."

"Go?"

"Daddy has a doctor's appointment," Ms. Annette said, handing me Brighid's backpack.

"Yeah," I added, "And on the way, we are gonna get Jack in the Box."

"Mmmmm," Carolyn, the co-director, said.

"Lucky girl," Ms. Annette said, "We'll see you tomorrow, okay?"

I helped fold up her blankets and took Brighid's hand to lead her to the car.

"I wanna do it," she said as we got to the green wooden gate that separated the kids from the actual door. She reached over and worked the latch. The kids were forbidden from touching the gate's latch unless their parent was there, and I smiled at her desire for independence.

We got to the drive through window at Jack in the Box, and I ordered one of the biggest burger meals they had—not knowing that it would be my last fast food for nearly a year and a half.

Brighid and I had a car picnic on the 50 mile drive back to Modesto and the doctor's office. Jerry Garcia's *Not Just for Kids* CD played in the background as we drove up the Altamont freeway. "There ain't no bugs on me," Jerry sang with David

Grishman doing the harmony. The sun shined, and I handed Brighid her french fries as she ate her car picnic in the confines of her car seat.

"Why you going to the doctor, Daddy?"

"Cause I have a headache."

"Headache?" her 4-year old mind didn't wrap around the idea right away.

"Yeah. It's when your head hurts."

"You gonna get a shot?"

*Of tequila? I wish.* "I don't know. I doubt it. I just need some headache medicine." Some mystery sauce slopped from my burger to the lump of my shirt stretched thin around my huge gut. "Dammit," I said too quiet to be heard over Jerry.

"Will you keep me safe?" This was the standard deal we had whenever one of us had to go to a doctor.

"Mmm hmm." In the rearview mirror, I saw her carefully eating one french fry at a time. I felt safer already.

There was no line at the Kaiser doctor's office that afternoon. Brighid and I showed my card, paid my co-pay, and took a seat in the waiting room to read books. Twenty minutes went by, and we were running out of kids books.

My cell phone rang. "Hey Bubba."

"Hey honey, how's it going?"

"Pretty good. Just working. Did you see the doctor yet?"

"Nah. Still sitting in the waiting room."

"Ah...Hey listen. Do you think you could run by the store and get..." It doesn't matter what she asked me to get—it was always something. I never got to go straight home from work. She had that carpool and the drive from San Jose, so it was my job. I got it. "...and get me a surprise."

"At the grocery store?"

"Thanks Bubba." She was gone.

Nurses called in other patients, and Brighid and I played "Baby," a game we invented where we used our hands as naked sock puppets and had them talk to each other in deep voices.

"How you doing, Baby?"

"Pretty good, Baby."

"Don't call me 'Baby,' Baby."

"James Kohl," said the nurse. She held my chart in one hand and held the door open for us with the other. "How are we doing today?"

"I'm all right. Just have a bad headache."

"I'm Brighid."

"Hi, Brighid! I'm Marissa."

Brighid beamed.

"Mr. Kohl, if I could get you to step up on the scale, please."

I got up on it, but not before taking off my denim jacket that was filled with car keys and other random junk that would make me seem heavier than I was. I didn't need help being heavier. It was bad enough my Doc Martens were on.

The nurse adjusted the small weights on the scale until it balanced, and all I knew was that it was well above 200 pounds. She wrote down the number, and I stepped from the scale. My ignorant bliss shattered. Scales were bad news, and I didn't own one.

"Roll up your sleeve, please, so I can get your blood pressure."

All this was a waste of time. I needed some pain pills for my head so I could be on my way. That's it—just a headache. The nurse had a job to do though, and so I unbuttoned my shirt sleeve and rolled it up as far as I could.

She wrapped the band around my arm and fastened the Velcro. She turned on the machine, and air tightened it even more.

"Does it hurt?" Brighid said, her huge brown eyes looking up at me.

"No, Honey. Not at all."

Brighid had doubt on her face.

"Hmmm," the nurse said. "Let's try it one more time."

"What's wrong?"

"Well, it's a little high. Have you had high blood pressure before?"

"Not really, no." This wasn't exactly true. The previous October, I had pneumonia, and when I went to the doctor they had told me the same thing.

Marissa repositioned the band and fired the machine up one more time.

"How is it?" I asked as the armband exhaled.

"It's 167 over 125. I'll mention it to the doctor."

"Can high blood pressure cause headaches?" I mean, it's great that they check these things, but just the pain pills please.

"Maybe. I'll mention it to Dr. Moraga."

The nurse led us to an examination room, settled us in, and Brighid immediately had to use the bathroom. "Crap, Brighid! Why couldn't you have said something before we got in here?"

"I don't know."

The back of my throat burned with the spicier parts of the cheap hamburger I ate on the way here. "What am I supposed to do? I need to see the doctor."

"I'm sorry." Her shoulders slumped and she looked at the floor.

"Fine," I said through gritted teeth. I knew deep inside she didn't do this to sabotage me, but at the same time I wondered why Kristin, her mother, never had to take her to the doctor when she went.

We stepped into the hall and I found a nurse. "My daughter here has to use the bathroom, and I don't want to miss my doctor." I tapped Brighid on the top of her head with the end of my index finger.

"Dr. Moraga?"

"I think so, yes."

"I'll make sure she knows. It's down that hall on the left." She pointed.

I had Brighid's hand, and we walked fast. She dragged behind me like a can behind a newlywed's car. Kaiser wasn't customer oriented to the point where the doctor would wait for you. If I missed my window, she'd probably go see some other patients and get to me when she had time or forget me all together. Kristin should find a job closer. I cussed and spit to myself the whole time Brighid sat on the toilet for what seemed like the longest bathroom experience in all of human history.

The heat built in my head and added to the pain as she sat there not doing anything. "C'mon, Brighid. Daddy has to see the doctor."

She just looked at me from the toilet seat, pants around her ankles. All I needed were the pain pills. This whole trip was so unnecessary, and now I was going to miss the doctor. I paced the small floor of the bathroom with my throat burning and my head getting heavier.

She finished, and I helped her clean up, pulled her pants back up, and dragged her down the hall back to the examination room. There was a body-mass index chart on the wall that showed how much you should weigh based on height. I looked at the colored squares until they went out of focus.

"Wanna read a book, Daddy?"

*No! I have no idea if I already missed the doctor or not. Why do you even have to be here?* I immediately hated that thought and myself for having it. "Sure, honey."

She chose a small picture book and sat next to me in the examination room chairs. We were barely into seeing what the animals were doing on the farm when the knock came on the door and the doctor came in.

"Hello Mr. Kohl."

*Was I really Mr. Kohl? Did I look that old to a doctor?* "Hi."

"I'm Brighid."

"Hi, Brighid! I'm Dr. Moraga." It wasn't as cute this time. I was ready to go. Give me the pain pills so I can get on with my life. "So the chart said you are here for a headache?"

"Yeah, I've had it since this morning." The story of the pop came next, along with my self-diagnoses of migraines.

"Anyone in your immediate family have migraines?"

"My sister."

The doctor nodded and laid my chart on the counter near the sink. "I'm concerned about your blood pressure. Let's take it again," she said.

"Okay. But I'm really here for…"

"A headache, I know." She had me sit up on the vinyl bed covered with that same paper they use to make toilet seat covers for public restrooms. "Roll your sleeve up, please."

Again the machine tightened the armband and hissed out the air when it was finished. The doctor didn't look pleased. "I want you to lie back on the bed," she said, "I want you to relax yourself as much as you can. Then I'm going to come back and take your blood pressure again."

I didn't have time to relax. Dominique and Lorenzo, my stepchildren, would be home by now and I needed to get the prescription, drop by the pharmacy to get the pills, pick up the stuff Kristin asked me to get, go home, help with homework, cook dinner, and get Brighid ready for bed. Relaxing wasn't on the schedule.

The cheap paper crinkled beneath me as I lay back on the bed.

"I'll be back in about 10 minutes," Dr. Moraga said.

"Daddy, why did she turn the lights off?"

"Because I need to relax. Shhhh."

"That was mean!"

"Brighid, I need to relax. We need to be quiet, okay?"

Even in the dim light of the room, I could see her pouting. Normally, she was quiet when she was pouting, so that was a good thing. I needed to hurry up and relax. God knew what drama the kids would have in store for me when I got there. Dominique was 13, and every day was a new crises.

I closed my eyes and lay as still as I could. The slightest movement on the paper sounded like the guy in the movies with the loud candy wrapper. I hated doctors. I shouldn't have even come in. I tried to see the ceiling of the room, but the darkness was punctuated with little specks of light that zigged and flashed at the edge of my vision. I'd been seeing those a lot lately, now that I thought about it.

Okay, I was relaxed now. Where was the doctor?

A few minutes later, she returned. "I'm hoping this will lower your numbers, Mr. Kohl. Some people have white coat syndrome, and get nervous at the doctor's office. That can raise the blood pressure."

"I just have a headache."

"Mmm hmmm," she said. My sleeve was still rolled up and she wrapped my arm again.

"Does it hurt, Daddy?"

"No, baby."

Dr. Moraga nodded and unwrapped the armband with a rip of the Velcro. "You have high blood pressure. Do you have a family history of that?"

"My grandmother has it. My grandfather died of a heart attack. Both of them actually. I think my mom has it too."

"I think there are some things we need to do. I'm going to prescribe Atelenol. Also, you should cut fats and salts out of your diet. Do you exercise?"

"Not really."

"Smoke?"

"No."

"Well, that's good. You should also probably cut caffeine. Do you drink a lot of coffee?"

"Constantly."

Another nod from Dr. Moraga. Her lips tightened as she pulled her prescription pad from the pocket of her white coat. "I'm also going to take you down and run an EKG on you. With the history of heart disease in your family, it's just not worth the risk."

"What about my headache?" It sounded stupid now. The rest of this couldn't be real though. I was only 34. She's talking about things that happen to people in their 60s. I looked from the doctor to Brighid, who sat on the blue chair in the examination room looking at the pictures and diagrams on the wall.

"Also," the doctor continued as if I hadn't heard enough already, "Your BMI is in the high risk range."

"BMI?"

"Body mass index. It's this chart." She spread her fingers across the colored squares that I noticed when we first came into the room. "It's a weight guide based on height that we use to determine a healthy weight. Once you cut the salt and fat from your diet, and exercise—like a half hour walk a day—you should start to be closer to the healthy area." She traced the healthy white diagonal that was the goal weight, but I didn't even look at the number.

Too much came at me too fast. I knew I shouldn't have come to the doctors. Tylenol or Aleve would have been just fine. Now, all of a sudden, I'm dying. My eyes met Brighid's. I couldn't die now.

"So let's get you hooked up to the EKG machine."

She may as well have said electric chair. I grabbed my denim jacket and Brighid's hand. We followed Dr. Moraga to the cardiologist section of Kaiser. Was I going to have to spend the night in the hospital? Who would ask Brighid what her favorite part of the day was when she went to bed?

The double doors opened for us when Dr. Moraga hit a panel on the wall, and she had me take my shirt off and lay down on another bed. The technician came and attached felt pads to different areas of my chest. "I'll be back at the end of the test," Dr. Moraga said, clipboard tucked beneath her arm.

11

Wires stretched from my chest to a machine and Brighid stood next to me, looking smaller than she had in her life. She held my hand. "I will keep you safe." The two of us were isolated by the blue medical curtains made of dentist bib material.

Thirty four is too young to be having an EKG test in front of your 4-year-old daughter. As a matter of fact, I can't think of a good age for that to happen. Her big brown eyes held mine. The lines blurred between parent and child. Who was supposed to protect whom?

The test ran, and my at-rest heart rate was far above the normal number. My heart worked so hard to get blood to me that it was exhausting me, the doctor said.

"What about that pop and all that?"

"You may have had a near stroke experience. I cannot emphasize enough that you must eat better and take your medicine." She gave me a pamphlet for a class Kaiser offered that showed you how to eat well. I was to enroll in that class.

"Stroke?"

Dr. Moraga nodded. My mom had had something like that happen.

The blue curtain was pulled back and a heavyset man with a gray beard was face to face with me. "Hey man, I heard what the doctor was saying to you. I'm a heart patient too. Let me just tell you one thing that they forgot to tell me. Stay away from those energy drinks like Red Bull. Oh man, I had one of those…Whew! Knocked me for a loop."

"Right on." The words barely passed my lips. *Heart patient too?* I came in for a headache.

# Chapter 3

The light turned to a green arrow for us to turn left on Briggsmore, but the line of traffic didn't move. I pressed my lips against each other and pounded on the steering wheel. What the hell was the delay? Did they think it could get greener if they waited? I never used my horn because Robert Fulghum wrote that interrupting daydreaming at a traffic light could be dangerous because the daydreaming driver could be a biochemist whose daydream is bringing them within seconds of discovering the cure for cancer. I had no mind for that sort of optimism today, but I still didn't use the horn.

"Are we going home now, Daddy?"

"No. We need to stop by the grocery store."

"Grocery store?"

"Yes." I know she was language delayed, but some days the repeating half of what I said just wasn't cute. I had a life sentence of pills to lessen my blood pressure. Safeway was the last thing I wanted to do, but the call had already come from the wife. The crap I'd get for not going was more than I could stand.

My chest tightened and the taste of hot metal nagged at the back of my mouth. If I called my sister, maybe I would feel better. Someone had to know about this blood pressure thing. Telling Diane was the dress rehearsal for telling my Mom.

"Hey kiddo." Diane was about 29 at the time, but I always called her that.

"Hey!"

"Dude. I just got out of the doctor's office and it turns out I have high blood pressure."

"Oh no," she said. "I'm so sorry. So what does that mean?"

"It means I have to take some pills. Probably for the rest of my life. And I have to exercise and whatever. We have a treadmill though, but no one has ever used it."

"Daddy, I want to go home!"

"Just a second kiddo." Pulling the cell away from my ear, I turned my head far enough to see Brighid in her car seat from the corner of my eye. "We can't right now, honey."

"I want to go home!"

"Not right now!" My face heated, and my voice cracked for the yelling. With the phone back by my ear, I said, "Jesus Christ, no wonder I have high blood pressure."

Brighid started crying.

"I'm sorry," Diane said. "So like what does this mean? Less fats and stuff?"

"That and salt. And the real killer is caffeine."

"Oh!" It came like a groan as my passion for coffee was no secret.

"I guess I'll have to switch to decaf. I gotta pick up some stuff from the store for Kristin anyway, so I may as well get some of that." I turned my head again as I waited to turn left into the Safeway parking lot. "Stop crying."

"I can't" Brighid said, her face glazed with tears.

"You already have the medicine?" Diane said.

"Yeah. I got it right there at the Kaiser after the appointment. Dude, they hooked me up to the heart machine and everything. I'm at Safeway now though, so I better go. I'll talk to you later."

"Take care of yourself."

"Yeah," I said.

Brighid accepted my apology for yelling, and eventually calmed herself. There is nothing more embarrassing than dragging a crying kid through the grocery store. Few things in life make you feel like you are in such a spotlight. *Yeah, my kid's crying. I beat her senseless, which takes all of 2 seconds.* As crappy as the day was going, at least I didn't have to be that spectacle.

The cell phone sang out Beethoven's Ninth again, a tune I had chosen because of the *Clockwork Orange* connection. "Hello?"

"Hey sweetie."

"Hey babe."

"Are you at the store yet?"

"Just got here."

"How did it go at the doctors?"

"Bad. I'll tell you when you get home."

Kristin was not one for patience. "What do you mean bad? Tell me now."

"My blood pressure is high, and that pop thing this morning was a near stroke experience." Tears welled in my eyes.

"Oh my god. So they didn't give you pain pills?"

Brighid and I reached the sidewalk in front of the Safeway, but I still held onto her hand. Right then I realized that I no longer had the headache. "No. Some pills for the blood pressure though." I dabbed at my eye with my shirtsleeve. "I'll tell you all about it later."

"Hey, can you get me some tampons while you're there? I'm starting."

"Okay."

"And don't forget my surprise."

"Okay." In one motion, I snapped the cell phone shut and clipped it back on my belt.

"Let's go schmooger." I used my nickname for Brighid.

The day had really kicked my ass, and I needed to relax and take it all in. Everything had to change, and I had to go through the whole grieving process in a night. I pulled into our driveway with what we needed from Safeway in the trunk, including Kristin's surprise, and my new prescription on the passenger seat beside me.

Dominique had the music blaring when I got home and was cleaning the kitchen. "Jesus!" she said as Brighid and I walked into the kitchen to put away the groceries. "I didn't hear you come in."

"No kidding," I said.

She went into the dining room where the stereo sat on my parents' old TV stand and turned down her CD. "How was your day?"

"Crappy," I said. "I have high blood pressure. I have to take pills now and eat better. How was yours?"

She told me the latest in the drama that went on between her and her friends and I half listened while I made Brighid a Kid's Cuisine in the microwave. "Is your homework done?"

"Almost." I knew this was an exaggeration at best, but I didn't have it in me to fight it today.

"Where's Lorenzo?"

"Up in his room."

I nodded, knowing that the X-Box was whirring away up there.

The microwave beeped, and I got Brighid's meal for her and set it on the table. I climbed the stairs to our room and changed out of my work clothes. Beethoven's Ninth screeched to life again. "Hello?"

"Hey sweetie."

"Hey."

"What's the matter?"

Did she really not know? I sighed. "Nothing."

"How are the kids?"

"They seem all right. Dominique cleaned the kitchen."

"Did she do a good job?"

"Let me check." I bounded down the stairs and examined the kitchen from the bottom. "I guess so. It seems okay to me."

"Tell her it better be clean to my standards when I get there. I'm on my way home right now."

"Right on." I moved from the kitchen's doorway to the living room couch to finish the conversation. "So what, you think you'll be here about 7?"

"Probably 7:30. Why?"

"It's just I'm...I don't know. I'm really bummed out about this high blood pressure thing."

"I will help you," she said, "We all should be eating better anyway."

I smiled. "I just want to curl up in bed with you."

"Move your ass, jackass!"

"Huh?"

"Not you, honey. This dude had to get in front of me and now he's going like 30 miles an hour."

"Oh," I said.

"Anyway. My Tia Mary and my cousins are coming over."

"Tonight?" My tone was less than excited.

"Yeah. Why?"

"Well, babe, I was sort of hoping it could just be us tonight. I need to get used to this whole thing."

"You need to learn to go with the flow," she said, and I knew that arguing the point would just make her mad and her aunt and cousins would still come over, so there was no point.

"All right."

She asked me a couple more things about what I had taken care of, what I had bought at the store, and gave me a couple things she'd like me to have done before her family got there. We hung up, and I melted into the couch with my cell in my hand, knowing it would ring again soon.

# Chapter 4

Kristin showed up that evening about ten minutes after I put Brighid down for the night and a few minutes before her aunt and her cousins, Netty and Raquel, showed up. "Come upstairs with me," she said.

I followed her up and sat on the bed while she tore off her work clothes and released her hair from the clip that held it since 4 am. She tossed the clip to the side and pulled on her long pajama pants and an oversized T-Shirt.

By the time I was in my Lucky Charms pajama pants and my robe, the doorbell rang.

Tia Mary, Raquel, and Netty came in and I offered them drinks. They all sat in the living room. "Kristin will be down in a second," I said. I went to the kitchen and poured them each some Pepsi. Soda with caffeine was off limits to me, so I pulled a glass of water from the Alhambra cooler.

"How have you been, Mijo?" Tia Mary asked, as I handed her and Raquel a soda and went back to the kitchen for Netty's.

"I've had better days. I just found out I have high blood pressure."

"You?" Tia Mary asked.

"Yeah." My tears fought to come, but I didn't want to wreck their visit and make it about me. I swallowed hard as I returned with Netty's soda and my water. "So I have to watch what I eat and stuff. Plus, they gave me some pills. No more caffeine," I said, tapping my water glass.

I got a chair from the kitchen table for myself, saving the living room chair for Kristin. She came down the stairs. "Hey guys."

"What's up girl?" Raquel said.

"Can I get you a drink, baby?" I said.

She looked the room over. "Pepsi would be fine, sweetie."

I sprang from my chair and set the water glass on its seat. Hugs were exchanged in the living room as I found a clean glass and poured Kristin a Pepsi. The women talked, but the voices meant nothing to me. In my mind, I saw the felt tabs all over my chest and Brighid looking small by the bedside.

An empty house would have been ideal tonight, but Kristin said I had to learn to go with the flow. The flow seemed to go the way she wanted it, but damned if I would say that out loud. I was married and marriage was about compromise. Being a good husband meant keeping your mouth shut. Kristin always told me I couldn't let my anti-social feelings run my life. She was waiting for her Pepsi. I had to get back in there.

"Thanks, Bubba," Kristin said as I handed her the drink. I mustered a smile and took a seat on the wooden chair.

I didn't add to the talk, but they got on fine with my silence. I was the chair I sat in, occasionally sipping the water even though I wasn't thirsty. This was Kristin's family, so my part was to stay here and make sure that all their needs were met.

Turkey and chicken breast were low in fat. I could eat those. I'd have to make sure I bought chicken breast that didn't have the skin on it. Even if you peeled the skin off after it was cooked, there was more fat in it than if you bought it skinned. My mother taught me that when my dad was diagnosed with high cholesterol. Jesus, I was only 34. Wait, Kristin was talking to me. "What babe?"

"Bubba, Netty's allergies are bothering her. Can you go upstairs and get her a chloritrimitron?" Kristin said.

"No, he doesn't have to do that," Netty said.

"It's not a problem," Kristin said, "Bubba, can you do that?"

"Sure."

I climbed the stairs, grateful for the escape. I lay on the bed for a couple minutes before I looked through the basket in the bathroom cabinet where we tossed all the medicine bottles.

"Can you find it?" Kristin called to me.

"Just a second."

I dug through the Tylenol and the kids goopy grape stuff, which only had a sip left in it. I tossed aside an inhaler before I finally found the right bottle.

Downstairs, the women laughed about something that was worlds away from me and my near stroke experience. Maybe I was too self centered. I would work on that. I handed Netty the little yellow pill and returned to my station on the kitchen chair.

They were saying something about our nephew, Paul, who was shipped to Iraq in the first wave of the movement to topple Saddam Hussein and his weapons of mass destruction. They reassured each other that there was nothing to worry about because Paul was crazy enough to take out anyone. Nervous laughter followed.

Netty took her pill and said, "Does this thing make you tired?"

"Yes," I said. Did that sound too eager? I checked Kristin's expression. Hard to tell, really. I might have messed up.

"Mom, we better go." Netty said, checking the time on her cell phone. "I don't want to be falling asleep on the ride home. Plus, you guys get up early." She looked at me and then at Kristin.

"Oh that's right, they do." Tia Mary said. There was a round of goodbye hugs, and the three of them went out the door. I got their glasses and put them in the sink.

"I'm going to bring my car in," Kristin said.

"I'll go with you." I'd been waiting all night for a few minutes alone with my wife, and I had my chance. Soon after she put the car away, she'd want to go to bed, so this was it. She climbed into the driver's side of the SUV in the driveway, hit the lock button, and I got in the passenger's seat.

"Babe," I said as she slid the key into the ignition, "This is really bumming me out."

She didn't turn the key. Her silhouette in the moonlight made me want to kiss her. She didn't speak.

"I'm freaking out about this. I mean, having a near stroke experience and all that. Plus..." tears formed in my eyes, and I hated them because Kristin hated weakness. "I don't want to take pills for the rest of my life."

"You might not have to," she said.

"But I might."

"You can either lay down and let this kill you, or you can fight it. Part of fighting it is the pills, but you also have that treadmill in the garage. I'll teach you how to cook so we don't have to have fast food so often."

"I can never have it."

"Fine, whatever you want. But this is not the end of the world unless you let it be."

"But it's just such a major thing."

"Everything to you is a major thing."

I sat quiet. She hit the garage door opener and started the car. We rode into the garage, went back inside, and climbed the stairs for bed.

# Chapter 5

It was Friday, the day that I always met Emmeline and Caroline in the cafeteria at work for lunch. The main cafeteria sat by a man-made lake in the center of the lab's 2-square mile campus. One of the things I really like about the lab was that it was more like working for a college than a big company.

The University of California system, which also boasted UC Berkeley and UCLA, ran the Lab. There were hundreds of orange community bicycles spread throughout the grounds. I took one and headed down the path toward the cafeteria.

I loved these Friday lunches. All of us were editors that had started at the lab about the same time. Caroline was single, I was married with kids, and Emmeline was married without kids. We joked that we were the entire human experience when we got together. Recently, Gabrielle had joined our lunches. She was the newest editor at the lab, but Emmeline had worked with her before.

I coasted to a stop near the cafeteria door and parked the bike. "Stay," I told it in the hopes that I would still have a bike to ride back to my office. The cafeteria's automatic door opened for me, and I walked through, smiling at my own dorkiness.

Normally, I would get a double cheeseburger and some onion rings on these Friday lunches. Today, I got in line at the salad bar. I filled my plate with iceberg lettuce and spinach leaves. Adding some broccoli and mushrooms, I topped it off with a sprinkling of fat-free Italian dressing. The croutons looked tempting, but that Atkins guy crossed my mind and I left them.

"A salad?" Emmeline said as she found my table and set her purse down.

"Yeah," I said, nodding with my lips pressed together.

"You're going on a diet?" Emmeline stood by the table with her ATM card in her hand.

"Sorta. I'll tell you all about it when you get your food."

Gabrielle arrived next looking frazzled, but that was normal. "This annual report is so impossible," she said. "Well, the report's not, but the people I have to work with. They want an editor, but they don't want to take any of my suggestions. Is Emmeline here yet?"

"Yeah, she's getting her food," I said, motioning toward the register lines with my plastic fork.

"I brought my lunch. I just have to heat it up in the microwave. Can you watch my purse?"

I nodded with my mouth full of salad.

Emmeline came back to the table first, which was good because of the three of them I felt most comfortable with her. She sat across from me and waited for me to talk. We started with how things were in general and how work was going.

"I went to the doctor yesterday, and I found out I have high blood pressure." I said. My eyes got watery.

"What does that mean for you?"

I went through the whole story—the pop, the headache, the EKG with Brighid by my side, the prescription, and the new way of eating. "And I can't have coffee."

"Oh my gosh, Jim," Emmeline said, "Coffee is your life."

"I know." Emmeline and I spent about 3 weeks in neighboring cubicles in the lab's TID building. She'd seen my constant flow of coffee from the start of my shift to 11 am each day. "This morning, I brought in a thermos of decaf."

"How did that work for you?"

"It was better than having nothing."

"I am sorry, Jim. What did Kristin say?"

"She's being really supportive. She said we'd all eat better as a family. I'm starting up on the treadmill this weekend. It's about time we did more with it than pile stuff on it in the garage."

Emmeline laughed. "Our exercise bike is like that."

I nodded. "Hang laundry on it?"

"Exactly."

Gabrielle sat at the table with the stress of work tensing her face. "Hey guys." She went on about how the project she was working on was really hard to put together and how the deadlines they gave her were impossible to meet.

"Jim has high blood pressure."

Gabrielle paused and her blue eyes met mine. "I was wondering about the salad, but I didn't want to say anything. When did you find this out?"

"Yesterday," I said.

"Well, at least you are doing something about it. A lot of people have it and don't do anything. It can cause all sorts of complications."

"I had a near stroke experience yesterday. That's how I found out about it." One more time with the story of the pop, but I abbreviated it since Emmeline had already heard it.

"Well, good for you for going to the doctor, lots of men wouldn't do that."

"I have kids. I can't just let myself go," I said, but I didn't really mean it. My kids had nothing to do with it. You can't do things like this for someone else, you have to do them for you.

There was more talk about high blood pressure and what it can do if it goes untreated. Then there were some anecdotes about how people have beaten the disease.

"I just don't want to have to take pills the rest of my life. I'm only 34."

The topic changed, and then Caroline showed up when the rest of us only had about 10 minutes left on our lunch.

"Jim has high blood pressure," Emmeline announced.

She looked at me and the empty plate in front of me. "I'm not surprised," she said.

I swallowed hard and smiled through the pain. What she meant exactly, I'll never know. But maybe she wasn't looking at the plate in front of me. Maybe she was looking at my stomach, stretched to an unnatural state from too many double cheeseburgers and onion rings. The table was crushed silent, and I wished to God someone would say something.

I checked the clock on the wall by the TV that was never loud enough to hear over the hum of conversation. "I gotta head back," I said.

"I probably should too," Gabrielle said, "I'm supposed to meet with another author for the annual report at 1:15, and I still have to prepare my notes for that." I wasn't the only one looking for a parachute from the awkward crash the conversation took.

I saddled up on one of the orange bikes, grateful that even a short ride like this counted as exercise and knowing I was going to have to work to fix my body inside and out.

# Chapter 6

My morning routine started a half hour earlier, so I could use the treadmill. I was able to walk at about 3.5 miles per hour at first, but I knew that if I stuck with it I'd be able to go faster. I couldn't wait to be able to go faster. The treadmill also kept track of how far I went and how many calories I burned doing it—all within the privacy and comfort of my garage.

To pass the time, I listened to books on tape. Stephen King said that books on tape did the same thing to your mind that reading does. I got a library card from the Livermore library so I could go and get these books on my lunch break from work. The idea of exercising my mind and body simultaneously was deliciously Zen.

After the treadmill, I would write for an hour before eating my Special K with berries for breakfast—skim milk, of course. Then I'd shower, get dressed, get Brighid up and start her on her morning rituals of bathroom, shower, clothes, hair, and cartoons.

In between, I'd give my opinions on which of the outfits Kristin took from the closet looked the best and which shoes would be better with whatever choice she finally made. I was Daddy, fashion expert, hair stylist, writer, and health nut all in one.

Last, I'd pile Brighid into the car with her backpack, 2 stuffed animals, Jerry Garcia's kids' CD, and my thermos of decaf. These were all essential for our 50-mile commute. Weekends were great just because I didn't have to deal with the driving part.

At night, I'd pop my pill. It was the 20 milligram reminder that I could die, and nightly I faced that fact alone. I probably made too much of a big deal about it, but I couldn't take one without hearing Dr. Moraga's voice echoing in my head: "Near stroke experience."

My friend Nazih had sent me an e-mail when I confided in him that they had discovered I had high blood pressure. He said that he had had it as well, but that through diet, he had it under control. Diet was the key. Nazih didn't even have to take the pills anymore.

From work one day, I called Kaiser to see about the healthy eating class that Dr. Moraga recommended I take.

"The classes are Wednesday afternoons from 2 until 3," the Kaiser advice nurse said.

"You guys never have them later in the evening?" Modesto was a good hour drive if traffic was perfect. The older kids would still be in school at 2 pm, so not only would I have to leave work early but Brighid would have to sit with me in a class about eating. To expect a 4-year old to do that would be asking too much.

Did I really need this class? I grew up eating low-fat foods because of my Dad's high cholesterol. What could they tell me in that class that I didn't already know? Stick to poultry breast meat, fat free cheese, skim milk, Mrs. Dash instead of salt and I'd be fine. How could I go wrong?

"Thanks, but I really can't make that class."

"Do you want me to put your number on a list in case they ever have one in the evenings? They sometimes do; there just isn't one on the calendar now." She sounded like she thought it was a really good idea, but that was probably just her job talking. The phone calls were monitored, and if she let a co pay go without a fight, she might get reamed.

"No, but thanks though."

"Are you sure?"

"Yes, thank you."

That moment may have been, as Elvis Costello might say, one of my most brilliant mistakes.

We were watching one of those shows about surgery on a Saturday afternoon. These shows weirded me out. Doctors cut and stretched skin in ways that didn't seem human all the while working over the open patient with the routine look of a mechanic changing oil. Kristin loved them.

"I've been thinking a lot lately, and I've made a decision," she said during a commercial break.

"Really? About what?" I sat on the opposite end of the couch from her.

"About the gastric bypass surgery. I want it."

"Honey, you don't need that kind of surgery. You are beautiful." The horror stories of the stomach stapling surgery flashed across my mind. My wife wanted to be that wide open car with the nonchalant mechanic hovering over her.

"I know you think so, and I love that," she said. "But I have never been thin. I want that—to be thin. I want to be more active and be able to keep up more with you and the kids. You're losing weight now."

"Not yet," I said.

"But you are working on it. I can't lose weight like you can. I don't have the discipline, and you know I don't have the patience either. Remember when we both joined 24-Hour Fitness?"

She worked really hard for about a month that time. She ate the way the nutritionist told us to for the most part. In a month's time, she was so disheartened with her progress that she gave the whole thing up.

I hated the idea of the surgery though. "What if you die, honey? There are all sorts of complications that that surgery can bring."

"They've gotten better at it. It's not as dangerous as it used to be."

"How do you know that? And don't tell me it's because you saw it on here," I said, pointing to the TV where the doctors were slicing a woman's face and pulling it tight as a snare drum against her skull.

"My friend Alex at work's cousin had it done. She came in and talked to me about how it changed her life and how much better she feels."

I sat silent, listening for what would come next. Alex was addicted to exercise and obsessed with her weight. The cousin was probably the same monster now.

"She lost over 200 pounds."

"You don't have 200 pounds to lose, sweetheart."

"Maybe not," she said, "but I am heavier than I want to be, and this will at least help me get to a place where I can start being more active and keep the weight off."

"Why don't you just diet and exercise?"

She sighed, and I knew from experience I was testing her patience too much. "We've been over that," she said.

I knew of a woman that had that done that I e-mailed with on occasion. She told me she lost a lot of her hair and had to go in each month to have vitamin B shots. "What if your hair falls out?" I was grasping now, but appealing to her vanity might work.

"Alex's cousin said that can happen at first, but once you get your protein intake regulated, it grows back."

Damn that cousin of Alex's. "What about getting all the vitamins and stuff?"

"The only vitamins I'd have a problem absorbing are B12 and calcium. As long as I take B12 sublingual vitamins, that won't be a problem. There's also some sort of solution for the calcium problem, but I don't remember what it was."

"You're all just going on what Alex's cousin said?" All I could picture was Kristin's funeral—me sitting ringside to the casket, wearing a black trench coat with a pack of cigarettes and a bottle of Jack Daniels.

"I looked up a lot of stuff on the Internet too."

She was serious. Normally, if she wanted something researched, she came to me and asked me to do it for her. "You'll never be able to eat more than a mouthful of food again. You really want to live the rest of your life like that?"

"I really want this, honey."

It was time to give up. Marriage was about compromise and understanding the other's point of view. She had broached this subject before, though never with this intensity and with her facts all in line. Those were whims, and there was a chance this was too, but from the look on her face and the sound of her voice, I doubted it. "I don't like it," I said, "Not at all. But I will back you in whatever decision you make."

"Thanks, Bubba." She came to my side of the couch and cuddled against me.

# Chapter 7

I did the grocery shopping with Brighid each week. I bought fat free and low fat everything. These days, the low fat and nonfat chips tasted the same as regular. The standard fat free cheese and low-fat turkey would do for sandwiches. Ground turkey or chicken took the place of ground beef. There were pre-made turkey burgers that just had to be seasoned and thrown on the grill. Lean Cusines were the perfect frozen meal to take to work, with little more than 8 grams of fat in the whole tray. Special K with berries and skim milk made the perfect breakfast.

Spaghetti sauce posed a problem. It was hard to find a completely fat free spaghetti sauce. Kristin showed me how to make my own sauce using Roma tomatoes and spices. I learned how to cook a low fat version of spaghetti, turkey burritos, a chicken stir fry, and turkey burgers. The kids were sick of the weekly menu within a month, but my low fat, low sodium diet was well on its way.

Kristin looked into the gastric bypass more, and I looked at the websites she had been to. I also spoke with a few more people that had had the operation, but my fears stayed the same.

Her doctor said she had to lose 32 pounds before they would perform the surgery. She ate better and walked at lunch. Sometimes she used the treadmill in the evenings as well. In the mall one day, she made a decision that would shape my life for the next year and a half.

"I want to buy a scale," she said.

I was all for it. We picked out a digital one. I knew I had lost some weight, and I felt confident enough to get on a scale and track my progress from here.

On the treadmill, I was the happiest. No one could tell me what to do or how to do it. I could survive a day of doing the laundry and having the way I folded towels criticized by spending a half hour with the speed cranked as fast as I could make it. Throughout the session, I would reach behind me and feel how much sweat had accumulated on my lower back. Sweat was good. Sweat was progress.

I pictured the fat melting off me with every step. The books on tape kept my mind busy, but not so busy that I wouldn't make a note of the treadmill's lap, calorie, and mileage count. Those red digital numbers added up, and the higher the number the lower the number on the scale and the lower my blood pressure would be.

In the morning before the treadmill, I would use the bathroom, and go to the dining room where we kept the scale. I'd drop my walking shorts and stand naked on the scale to see the number. 225. I hadn't lost that much yet.

I had just returned to my desk one afternoon at the Lab, excited that my belt was now one notch tighter than it had been, when Sandie came by my office. "Jim, do you want to try some of these nuts?" she said. She held out a can of nuts bathed in some sort of special seasoning.

"I really can't," I said, "but thanks. I just found out a few weeks ago that I have high blood pressure, so I have to stay away from fat and salt."

"Ah. I understand," she said.

People did understand, and I loved the support I got. I hated the disease though, and in an attempt to battle it on all fronts I gave Michael Pencher, the protagonist from my novel *Through the Fog,* high blood pressure.

Taking the pills didn't bother me as much anymore. It became just something I had to do like taking out the trash, cooking dinner, doing laundry, cleaning house, or paying bills.

I called Kristin. "Hey babe, my belt is one notch tighter today."

"Good for you, honey!"

"The scale doesn't show too much though."

"That's okay. You've always been a belt loop kind of guy."

Yeah I had.

My friend Renee, whom I e-mail with, said that it's how your clothes look on you that counts. "As long as things fit and you look good in the mirror. That's how I judge it. Weight doesn't matter."

I didn't buy that for a second. Weight was important. It was another way of measuring success in this battle against high blood pressure. The BMI chart had a white section for my height, after all, and I had to be in that white section to be considered a healthy weight. That's what this was all about—health.

Belt loops aside, the mirror showed me a fat guy. The scale was important because it could show you slight improvement while the mirror could only show drastic improvement. I hated the mirror.

A couple weeks later, people started to notice the difference in me. Karen, the woman that worked as an equal to my boss came by one day. "Are you doing Atkins?" she said.

"No. I'm doing low fat and low salt. It's a high blood pressure thing."

"Well, it's working. I can see it in your face."

"Thanks." What a great feeling!

"You're really looking good. I've been trying the Atkins for about a month now."

"Right on. I've been doing this for a couple months at least. It takes time," I said, turning my swivel chair to face her.

She nodded. "What I had no idea about before I started this was the amount of carbs that are in fruit. I used to have orange juice every morning, and that is so high in carbs. Because you know, carbs turn to sugar, which then turn to fat."

"No kidding?" I said. This information was dire. I was having a glass of orange juice each day. I decided right then to cut down to half a glass.

I felt better too. The fact that I could get up in the morning and power walk for a half hour was a huge accomplishment. Everything was easier, and I even stopped dozing off in meetings.

The strict food regimen went out the door on Saturday. Whatever I felt like having I had. This usually included a big fat chorizo and egg burrito for breakfast and whatever other evils I found appetizing throughout the day. The treadmill was a constant though. The guilt from skipping it was far worse than the 30 minute sacrifice of doing it. Also, the treadmill was all mine. It was 30 minutes where no one would say "daddy" or "Bubba" or "Jim."

## *Chapter 8*

We visited my parents when my belt had made a 2-notch advancement. We only went to San Jose for birthdays or holidays. This was my father's birthday.

"Hello my darling!" my mom sang to Brighid as the door opened. She bent down and took Brighid's soft cheeks in her hands. "How is my girl?"

"Good," Brighid said.

"Did you come here to see me?"

Brighid nodded. Kristin, the older kids, and I squeezed past the greeting and turned into the family room where my dad stood a few feet from the door. "Happy birthday, Dad," I said.

"Why thank you," he said.

"Happy birthday, Dick," Dominique said.

"Thank you!" he said. "Hello Lorenzo."

"Hey." Lorenzo was a kid of few words, unless the words had to do with video games, music, or shows and movies he was interested in.

We all took seats in the family room around the coffee table where a variety of crackers and fat free cheese were laid out.

"Can I get you guys anything to drink?" my dad asked. "We have beer, wine, soda, margaritas..."

My dad makes the best margaritas in the world. He got the recipe from a bartender one time when he and my mom had a margarita out. "Margaritas would be great," I said.

"Kristin?"

"Yes, please," she said.

My dad went to the closet that used to be the toy closet for me and my sister when we were kids and grabbed the necessary bottles. He went to the kitchen and got out the pitcher and the ice. My mom and Brighid finished helloing in the hallway and joined the rest of us around the coffee table.

Dominique knelt in front of the snacks like a monk at prayer. I was holding back from joining in quite yet.

My parents asked the kids about school, and they each said it was going well.

"Honey, do you want a margarita?" my dad called from the kitchen.

30

"Yes please. Diane will want one too. She should be here soon."

"I can always make more," my dad said.

"No Mark today?" I asked. Mark was my sister's long-term boyfriend. They'd been seeing each other for at least 5 years at this point, and were certain to get married.

"He has to work," my mom said.

"Really?" I said. "Selling cars?" That was his normal gig, but his ambition was to be a studio drummer. He had the talent, but the opportunities for that were few in the Bay Area. He always said he'd have a better chance of that in Southern California, where he and Diane planned to eventually settle down.

"I guess so," my mom said.

My dad delivered the margaritas and the first sip was magic in my mouth with the cold tangy bite and the ice against my upper lip. Margaritas were fat free. I held the glass in my hand and thought of Karen—what was the carb count in this lime-green glass? *Carbs turn to fat.*

I had to watch how many of these I drank anyway in case Kristin wanted me to drive home. The one would be okay, right? I could work it off on the treadmill probably. I already used the treadmill today. Maybe tomorrow, I could go an extra couple minutes or something.

Diane showed up and Brighid met her at the door with a hug.

"Margarita, Diane?"

"Yes. Thank you! Happy birthday!" Diane sat a small bag with a card and tissue paper protruding from the top on the kitchen table.

"Well thank you!" My dad always sounds like he's surprised people know it's his birthday even though my mom invited us all for this occasion.

"Hey," Diane said to me. "Hi Kristin."

"Hi." Kristin said.

Dominique sang out her greeting, and Lorenzo grunted his.

About three margaritas into the afternoon, we all went into the dining room where my mom had her best dishes waiting complete with a table cloth and matching napkins. Candles stood in the center of the table. Brighid sat on one side of me and Kristin sat on the other.

I knew I didn't have to worry about the food we ate because my mom always cooks low fat even though my dad's high cholesterol problem is nowhere near where it was when he was diagnosed. I scooped some of the casserole-type entree onto Brighid's plate and then my own. "Do you want some salad, Honey?"

She nodded, so I scooped her some of that as well. My mom makes the best salads.

Even though I knew it was low fat, I took only the one helping. There was no reason to eat all that much. It was good, but why take any chances? One plateful is enough for any human for a meal.

"Let me just say, Jim," my mom said at one point, "That you are already looking so much better. Your face has lost that bloated look, and you have your color back."

"Yes, absolutely," Diane said.

"He's been working pretty hard on it," Kristin said. "I taught him how to cook a few things."

"Well, he's starting to look like himself again. I was really getting worried there for a while. You look really good."

"Thanks." I smiled. It felt good that people noticed my efforts. It was all mine. Even though Kristin chimed in with how she was supporting the efforts, she wasn't around to feed me all day. The discipline and self control were mine to be proud of and looking like myself again was my accomplishment alone.

Cake time was next. "Just a small piece for me, please." Tasting the cake would be enough. There was no reason to ever feel full after a meal.

"Take Brighid to the bathroom, Bubba," Kristin said.

"Okay." I left the table and took Brighid's little hand to walk the familiar hall to the bathroom that was right across the way from my childhood bedroom. I heard them all talking out there as I stood by Brighid while she took care of things on the toilet. Kristin was saying something about her surgery, and I was glad that I didn't have to sit for that.

Not long after the table was cleared Kristin and I gave each other the look and announced we were going to head back. It was a 2-hour drive, after all.

Once we were on the freeway, Kristin started in. "Did you see how your mom was so careful not to say anything about Mark and how he's not working?"

"I guess."

"That guy is such a bum, and no one will say anything to Diane," Kristin said.

"What would be the point of bringing it up?"

"It's just so fake. They are so afraid of saying something that would hurt her feelings because they know if they piss her off, she'll never talk to them again. But your mom had no problem saying that you looked bloated."

"She said I used to."

"Still," Kristin said looking over at me now and then from the driver's seat, "Do you seriously think that your mom would ever tell Diane that she looked bloated at any time in her life?"

"I don't know." There was some dust on the air conditioning vent that I stared at as we drove.

"Of course she wouldn't. You can't upset the princess, but they have no problem saying horrible things about you. And that's because you never tell them anything." Kristin shook her head and huffed, exhaling against the steering wheel. The kids were in their own world of music in the backseat. "Did you see how your mom made sure that your dad had enough margaritas made for your sister?"

"Yeah, well…she knew Diane would want one," I was confused by this talk, but not surprised. It was common every time we left my mom's house.

"Do you think she would have made such a point to reserve one for you? Or for me?"

"I don't know."

"Of course she wouldn't. Diane is the golden child and you are just a side thought, and that is because you never tell them anything."

"Okay." Agreeing was better than having this conversation continue.

"But do you really see my point?"

"Yeah."

"Are you sure you're not just saying that?"

"I don't know, Kristin. I have no idea. I just don't want to complain."

"You just have no balls to stick up for yourself or me. I bet they say all kinds of things about me though. Because you need to strap some on and stick up for us, but you never do."

Diane was much more vocal when things didn't go her way than I was. It was a difference in our personalities. I didn't feel attacked, and I didn't feel the need to defend myself. Even if I did feel attacked, I'd just internalize it. I dealt with it my way. But maybe I needed to let people know when I felt attacked.

Luckily, I had Kristin to let me know when I felt attacked.

# Chapter 9

Food labels became as important to me as any of the literature I studied in college. They were the key to health. I wanted off the pills—that was my goal.

My friend Martin also had high blood pressure. He'd been diagnosed long before I was. We would swap medication stories on the phone.

"They have me on 10 milligrams of such and such a day."

"Does it make you dizzy?"

"A little, but I take it at night," I said.

"Good idea. They had me on that for a while, but then they moved me over to whatchacallit. I like that one a whole lot better."

"You know, dude," I said, "This is a conversation that two guys in an old-folks home should be having."

He laughed.

"Seriously. I think if I keep dieting and exercising, I'll probably get off these meds. I hate the idea of taking a prescription forever," I said.

"Are you watching your salt?"

"Not as much as I am the fat," I said, "I've been looking at all the labels and having less than 10 grams of fat a day."

"You have to watch the salt too. That's what always messes up my dad." Martin was trying to help, but I hated hearing diet advice. I knew what I was doing.

"I've just been hitting that treadmill hard too. Thirty minutes a day."

"That's cool," Martin said.

"And I only allow myself junk on the weekends. I pretty much eat whatever I see on the weekends if it looks good. Except coffee. That's been the shittiest thing about this."

"Wow, giving up coffee." Martin paused as if knowing the loss I felt. "See you're lucky that you don't have the food addiction. That's my problem."

I didn't know what to say to that.

Kristin lay on the bed waiting for me while I stared in the mirror. It had been a few weeks now, and I still looked fat to myself. How long would it take? I remembered reading somewhere that it can take up to 12 weeks before you notice a difference in yourself.

"You look really good," she said.

"Really?" I looked at my naked body in the mirror. "You think so?"

"I mean, you always looked good to me," she qualified, "But you are looking really good. That ass..."

I blushed. "Seriously though, you notice a difference?"

"Absolutely."

I checked it again. Maybe other people could see it easier on you than you could see it on yourself. The middle of my body was the hardest area to lose from. "Look at this," I said, pinching the roll of fat that was my middle.

"You should do crunches if you want to get rid of that," Kristin said.

"Along with the treadmill?" I knew from when I was thin once before that the treadmill was key in losing weight.

"You don't have to do the treadmill every day. You could do crunches or weights or something. Remember when you did *Body for Life*?"

I didn't turn my face from the mirror this time. The treadmill was my time—mine. Plus I knew it worked. Why was she trying to take that from me? "No, I pretty much have to stick to the treadmill."

"You know that this is about health—lowering your blood pressure. It's not about weight loss, remember?"

"It's all the same," I said, sitting on the edge of the bed and pulling on some boxers for the night. The doctor's colorful BMI chart flashed across my mind's eye. I had to get into the white.

Once a month at work, they had a birthday cake for all of the people that had a birthday that month. We all met in that same conference room where my high blood pressure knocked me unconscious at meetings. Since the lifestyle change, I'd been able to stay awake in most meetings as long as they were before lunch.

The people of honor took a seat nearest the cake, which just said Happy Birthday and the month.

"Where did you get the cake this time, Heather?" Katie asked.

"Just over at Safeway. They make pretty good cakes for a grocery store."

"Yeah, they do," John said.

"There's a little bakery over...I think it's somewhere near J street. Have you guys ever..."

I stopped listening to Rod's contribution to the cake talk. It amazed me that cake could be such a conversation piece. Who cared? It was just cake. You could almost see the fat oozing from it if you looked hard enough. I leaned up against the wall near the back end of the table and marveled at their interest in food.

*No wonder the whole world sees Americans as fat.*

Heather broke into the small package of birthday candles. "Six enough you think?"

"We don't want to set off the smoke alarms."

There was laughter. Heather jabbed the ends of the candles into the cake and lit them. We all sang, and the three birthday people blew out the candles. Heather sliced into the cake and Sandie helped her scoop squares of it onto small party plates.

"Just a really small one for me," Karen said, looking thinner with her Atkins diet in full swing.

"I'm going to want a small one too," John said.

"Are you on Atkins now?" Karen asked.

"Yeah. I've been doing it for a couple weeks."

"With everyone on Atkins around here, maybe we should have birthday steak next month," someone said.

There was laughter again. "I could go for that," Rod said.

"Hey, the boss just approved. Get on that Heather."

"I'll write it down," she said.

The small plates and plastic forks were making the rounds. I didn't like the idea of having cake. It wasn't a weekend. I could be like the Atkins people and ask for a small piece.

*What kind of dedication would that be?*

Heather held out a small plate for me. "No thanks," I said. I returned to my office feeling the best I had felt in years.

*Good job! Way to be!*

# Chapter 10

I had a follow-up appointment with Dr. Moraga since the high blood pressure numbers worried her so much. It was a morning appointment, and Brighid and I went in there before we went to Livermore.

Going in, I had no idea what the numbers would show, but I did know that the numbers on the scale showed 205. I was down 25 pounds. Even if the blood pressure numbers were still high, at least the scale number was lowered.

At the check in desk, they told me that Dr. Moraga was working on the second floor, so Brighid and I climbed the stairs. There was an elevator, but that was for the lazy.

"Can we read books?" Brighid asked after I paid my co-pay at the upstairs reception area.

"Sure," I said, "Will you keep me safe?"

She nodded.

We found two seats in the large, empty waiting room and Brighid searched through the magazines on the tables for anything that looked like a children's book or at least a kid-friendly magazine. She struck out but brought me a thick *Woman's Day* magazine with a big fat slice of cake on the cover.

"What is this, Brighid?" I said, pointing to a picture of a boy swinging on a swingset.

"Boy," she said.

We went through and named all the things we could while other patients arrived and were called through the doors of mystery.

It was a great day, as far as I was concerned. Being down 25 pounds, I was confident that my blood pressure would have improved. The clock on the wall said I should have seen the doctor a half hour ago. "I better go ask the nurse what is going on," I said.

"Ask the nurse?"

"Yeah. Daddy should have been called in by now."

"By now?"

"Yeah, baby. Come on."

We went to the nurse's desk again where we waited in line behind an older man that had a hard time hearing what the reception nurse was saying. I laughed to myself about the footprint pad on the floor that told me to wait here to allow for privacy for the people in front of you. This guy would need the privacy pad to be somewhere outside.

The nurse finally got that guy situated, and Brighid and I moved to the counter. "I was supposed to see Dr. Moraga at 8:10," I said, "Just wanted to make sure I didn't get skipped or something." I smiled to myself. The loss of the 25 pounds gave me a new confidence. There was a time when if I were sitting there this long, I would continue to wait. At most, I would call Kristin and complain. With my thinner body, I knew I could ask the nurse a simple question like that without imposing.

She asked for my name again and clacked around some computer keys. "With Dr. Moraga, right?"

"Yes."

"What's your name?" Brighid asked. I loved that my child had no shyness about her. Mine, especially with extra pounds on me, was crippling at times.

"Araceli. What's your name?"

"Brighid. And this is Daddy." She tapped my arm so the nurse would be clear whom she was talking about.

The nurse smiled and told Brighid she was cute. Her eyes went back to the computer screen, and her face scrunched up a bit. "Mr. Kohl, I'm really sorry."

Nothing good ever started like that, but I waited for the punch anyway.

"Dr. Moraga is off today. They didn't call you?"

"Not that I know of."

"Yeah. Well, she's not here today. I'm really sorry."

"That's not your fault. Listen, I'm supposed to get my blood pressure checked because it was high, and I'm hoping it is lower. Is there any way I can just have that done?"

"Sure. That won't be a problem at all. It'll just be a few minutes."

Brighid and I took seats that were closer to the door this time. In a matter of seconds, a nurse in maroon scrubs called my name and we went back. She apologized for the inconvenience again.

"It's no big deal, really," I said, "I've just been working really hard to lose weight and try and lower this blood pressure. I'm hoping not to be on the pills forever."

"What are you doing to lose weight?"

I beamed. "Treadmill for 30 minutes a day and just eating low fat stuff. I splurge a little on the weekends."

*You should really cut that down to just Saturday.*

"That all sounds good," she said, "Can I get you to roll up your sleeve."

Brighid stood quiet and watched the scene unfold.

My nerves jangled a little as she wrapped the band around my arm and pulled it tight against the Velcro. What if all my work had been for nothing and the blood pressure was still high? What more could I possibly do?

The band tightened, and the three of us stood in silence while the machine did its work. It exhaled, and she read the numbers. "125 over 80. Pretty normal."

"All right," I said, "Could you do me a favor and write it down on my card?" Dr. Moraga had given me a blue card for my wallet where the date and blood pressure readings were recorded.

"Sure." The nurse made the notation and handed me back the card. "Again, I apologize for the mix up," she said, "You can make a new appointment today before you leave."

"This makes it all worth it," I said, "Thank you."

Brighid and I took the stairs back down. I couldn't wait to tell Kristin. Her voicemail picked up, but I saved the news for when we really talked and just told her to call me. The sun was brighter and the colors of the world truer as I drove to Livermore for work.

Kristin and I sat in our normal positions on the couch and the TV played whatever celebrity gossip the evening had in store for us. Brighid was up in bed, and the other kids were off listening to music or playing video games, depending on if you were talking about Dominique or Lorenzo.

I normally zoned in and out when it came to this kind of TV. I really didn't care to hear who was seen with whom, and I hated the tabloid TV reporters who were just as excited to tell you about new celebrity love with its dance music sound bed as they were the latest break up with its slow piano dirge.

"Coming up next," the announcer said, "are they eating to live, or should the last rights we give." Okay, it wasn't that bad, but it was some stupid rhyme and it got my attention because it had to do with healthy eating.

The story turned out to be about a movement of people that believed in surviving on the minimal amount of calories each day. The people that lived this way were gaunt, but according to the report, they showed no signs of health problems.

They showed that they ate very little, but the food they ate was quality when it came to nutrition. A man with a skinny frame showed us around his kitchen and opened his refrigerator to the nation. He and his wife prepared a meal for the camera, which consisted of a bunch of vegetables, some nuts, and some other things whipped to a frenzy in a food processor.

The camera cut to the couple walking in the park together and playing tennis.

"They look like shit," Kristin said.

Being so light and being able to move your body with such little effort sounded perfect. "But their doctors said they are healthy," I said.

"But look at them," she said, pointing at the TV, "Their faces are all sucked in and their clothes hang off them. It can't be good for you."

The report ended with a website where the diet was listed along with the way they prepared their food. A doctor also appeared saying that he didn't think it was a healthy choice.

*But they were active.*

I thought about that report the next morning on the treadmill, and increased my speed.

# *Chapter 11*

A few Fridays had passed since I last met Emmeline, Gabrielle, and Caroline for lunch. They often were too busy to sneak away for an hour and worked through their lunches. For me, there was always time to get away from work for an hour. It made me question my work ethic sometimes, but it also made me think maybe I was just more efficient.

The orange bike beneath me cruised down the Lab's walking paths. The ride to lunch was always easier than the ride back to the office. This had something to with what was at the end of each ride, but in this case it also had to do with the fact that the Lab slanted toward the cafeteria.

I cut through some parking lots pedaling as hard as I could. The breeze against me felt great, and it felt even better knowing that I was pedaling harder than I had a few weeks ago. The scale that morning had me in the 190s. I started thinking of weight in decades. My goal was always to get to the next decade. The 190s would give way to the 180s if I kept up the treadmill and smart eating.

I saw Emmeline and Gabrielle walking to the cafeteria, so I pulled the bike to the side of the path to join them. My bike path had cut off their walking path, so we were walking toward each other.

"Jim!" Gabrielle said, "I didn't even recognize you."

"You have lost a lot of weight!" Emmeline said, "How much weight have you lost?"

"Thirty something pounds," I said, hoping it didn't come off as elated as I was. The happiness the weight loss brought me was mine. It was secret.

The three of us walked the path along the man-made lake that shimmered in the noon sun.

"Are you still trying to lose some?" Gabrielle asked.

"Yeah. My blood pressure was normal, but that is with the meds. I need to get where the blood pressure is normal without any help."

"Did your doctor say that?"

"It's always been my goal to get off the meds," I said.

We reached the cafeteria and went inside. I saw some guy with a cheeseburger and fries and thought how gross it was and what a lack of self control he had. I'd be getting my salad with fat free Italian again.

"What do you want to weigh?" Emmeline said, as we got back to the table.

"I don't know."

"You don't have a goal weight?"

"Not really, no. I just want my blood pressure normal."

"How will you decide you've lost enough?" Gabrielle said.

I shrugged and forked some lettuce and a cucumber slice into my mouth. "It's not like I'm not eating." The two of them looked at me with concern, and I was completely confused. I guessed they were used to me being fat, so the weight loss was a shock. I couldn't have been happier.

"Well, you look good right now," Gabrielle said. "I really don't think you should try to lose too much more. Maybe 10 pounds, but that would be pushing it."

*Ah! Ten more pounds. She was just being nice. You're at least 15 pounds overweight.*

"Thanks." I knew how to take a compliment.

"But seriously, Jim, I don't think you need to lose any more." Emmeline said. "What does Kristin say?"

"She's happy for me. She's trying to lose weight too, so she can get that gastric bypass thing." I finished my salad and sat with them while they ate. I could talk about this all day. Weight loss, diet, and exercise were the coolest things I knew. In a weird way, I delighted in their obvious jealousy. Why else would they think I was going overboard.

"How much has she lost?"

"I have no idea, but she's supposed to lose something like 32 before they'll do the surgery."

"With you as a teacher, she shouldn't have a hard time doing that." Gabrielle wiped her mouth with her napkin and set it on her empty lunch plate.

"She doesn't really listen to me," I said, "She gets on the treadmill now and then, and if she would just get on it every day, she probably wouldn't need the surgery."

Emmeline smirked and nodded. "You don't want her to get the surgery, do you?"

"No."

"Why not?"

"Because people have died on the operating table getting this done—or shortly thereafter."

"That's true of any surgery," Gabrielle said.

"True, yeah. But to me, you shouldn't just go get surgery. It would be one thing if she needed the surgery to save her life or something. But this is just…"

"Cause she doesn't want to diet?" Emmeline said.

"More or less, yeah. My opinion of course."

"Kristin doesn't care about your opinion?" Emmeline had a psychology degree from Stanford, which she didn't use professionally.

"She just really wants this, and so I have to support her in it. If I really want something, she'll support it. It's just the way it is. I don't like it though."

Emmeline nodded, looked like she was going to say something, and then didn't.

"Anyway," I said. This was my way of ending any conversation. Though I could have talked about my weight loss all day, I let it drop. I had tomorrow morning to think about. I was ready to move the treadmill up to a new speed.

# *Chapter 12*

I arrived at Storyland Preschool at 3:30, and found Brighid in the play yard bouncing a ball. She loved to bounce a ball, and she did it really well. The rest of her large motor skills left something to be desired, but she had always been great at that.

I signed her out when Ms. Annette approached me. "Has Ms. Carolyn talked to you?"

Ms. Carolyn was the associate director of the daycare, and I liked her quite a bit. Still, I dreaded the question because that normally meant that there was yet another issue with Brighid's behavior. "No, she hasn't." I stood my ground expecting to hear how Brighid was disrespectful to the staff or picked on another kid.

"She's probably shy about asking you. She wants to know about your weight loss."

"Oh!" I smiled.

"Are you doing the Atkins thing?"

"No. I had to go on a low fat, low salt diet for high blood pressure. That, and I'm doing the treadmill every day."

"She is trying to lose some weight because her wedding is coming up. She saw you for the first time in a while the other day, and she was like, 'Have you seen him? He looks great.'" Ms. Annette put her arm around a kid that pressed against her side.

"Oh my gosh, that is so nice of her to say."

"You really do."

"Thanks!" My smile wouldn't stop. This was such a nice way to pick up Brighid as opposed to picking her up and being hooked up to an EKG machine an hour later.

"She wanted to know how you were doing it," Ms. Annette said.

"I'd be glad to talk to her, but basically, any dish where you would have red meat, I switch it out for chicken or turkey. So like for spaghetti, I use ground turkey and I even make my own sauce with roma tomatoes. I did see that some of the jarred spaghetti sauce comes in a low fat variety, but I don't know that I 100% trust that."

*Good point.*

"Oh I see, wow, so you do most of your own cooking then?"

"Pretty much," I said, "Kristin doesn't get home till sometimes after 8 pm, so I do most of it. She taught me though. She's trying to lose weight too because she's gonna have that gastric bypass thing."

Ms Annette's eyes were blank.

"The stomach-stapling operation."

"Oh! Really? I've heard some good and some bad things about that."

"I know."

Ms. Annette shook her head. "I could never do that."

"It's not for me either."

"Well, you're doing fine with diet and exercise."

"Thanks!" If I could, I would've stretched my smile all the way around my head. I pinched my gut to see how much more I had to lose. There was plenty, so I took solace in the fact that I was going to be on the treadmill in 12 hours.

"So you'd be okay if Carolyn asked you about it?"

"Absolutely."

My mood skyrocketed for the entire ride home.


Kristin went for her psychological evaluation that was supposed to determine whether she was a good candidate for the surgery. The questions they asked really seemed to be aimed more as to whether or not she was a serial killer.

"'I often hear voices,' it asked me Bubba." She laughed into the phone. "And it asked me if I ever fantasize about hurting people."

"What's all that have to do with weight loss and whether you could control your eating once you've had the procedure?" I said.

"I have no idea. It was just one of those fill in the bubble tests," she said. "Whatever. As long as I can get the surgery, who cares, right?"

"I guess." It sounded to me like the test was probably to meet some law requirement that wasn't specific as to the type of psychological evaluation that would be used to screen gastric bypass candidates. The goal seemed to be to herd as many people as they could through the process to make a quick buck. That mentality scared me in relation to life-altering medical procedures, but I kept my smile on and acted happy. I had to be supportive.

"So anyway," she said, "Now I need to go to a couple of meetings a week after work for a while."

"Right on," I said, "What are they about?"

"One is just on healthy eating to help me change the way I view food before and after the surgery, and the other is a group meeting with the psychologist to discuss issues that we have and whatever."

"Sounds good. That's probably a good idea," I said.

The class that dealt with the eating was probably more beneficial to her than the rest. It taught her things like "The first bite of cake is just as good as the last one, so there really is no reason to go beyond the initial taste." This helped the gastric bypass candidate get used to the idea that a mere few bites of food was going to fill them, and it helped to prevent the dumping syndrome they experience when too much sugar enters their blood at once. Dumping syndrome includes dizziness, headache, lethargy, and it can also come with a side order of vomiting. In a gastric bypass patient, this can come on from eating a half a donut.

I liked the "one taste" philosophy a lot. It targeted people with a stomach the size of a walnut, but I thought it was a good way of looking at food in general.

The group psychology class was a different story.

They met on Tuesdays. Kristin would come home and talk about what they said there while we were in our normal positions at opposite ends of the couch. "It's really good because we get to talk about a lot of things that normal weight people don't realize."

"Like what?" I said.

"There is a basic discrimination against fat people. When someone sees a fat person, they assume that person is out of control. Or lots of people assume that fat people are stupid."

I thought of the guy in the cafeteria with the cheeseburger and fries. I saw her point to an extent. "So you guys just sit in that meeting and talk about how the world has been unfair to you?"

"Like one guy was talking about how he could tell in a job interview that they were being tougher on him because he was over weight."

"How could he tell?"

"You can just tell. Can't you tell when someone is being unfair to you?"

I guess she had a point there. "What about getting you guys ready for the psychological change that is coming your way when you get the surgery? Is the class addressing that at all?"

"Not really. Not yet."

"I don't know. It seems to me that if you guys are psychologically bruised from being over weight, that some people might take it to the ultimate extreme when they are not."

"Maybe," she said, "But you know me. I already have confidence. I don't care what size I am. I don't feel bad about going to the grocery store and stuff."

"I don't get what you're saying," I said.

"Lots of these people think that the grocery store clerk is judging them based on what they buy and stuff like that. It's true too; some people do. You don't get it because you're not one of those people. It's the same reason you don't get when people are racist to me." Kristin, being Mexican, was mistaken for a maid one time right in front of my face when we were staying at a hotel in Monterey.

"I don't know," I said, "It seems to me that since you guys are all heading for a thinner body, that the class should really concentrate less on the 'poor fat me' stuff and get you ready for what it will feel like when you're not over weight."

"They'll probably get to that eventually," Kristin said.

They never did.

# Chapter 13

Caroline got another job and left the Lab, in essence saving my life there. The project I worked on with Ron lost funding and as a result, there was no need for documentation for it anymore. It was a stressful couple of weeks as I scrambled for a position at the Lab, but with Caroline leaving, I found myself in the part of the Lab specializing in electronic security. I would miss Caroline, but I was thankful to be employed.

About this time, I started applying rules to my food. I remembered when I had done the Body for Life program that the six small meals recommended by that program happened at certain times in the day.

For breakfast, I had a bowl of Special K with berries, still my favorite cereal to this day. About 9 am, I'd have an apple. At lunch, I would have a Lean Cusine—usually one of the Mexican ones. About 3 pm, I'd have a protein bar of some kind or maybe a bag of raw vegetables. Then at home, I'd have dinner—one of the four things I knew how to cook.

Weekends were a little more open. At first, I'd eat whatever I wanted from Friday evening until Sunday night. It got to be less though.

"I think I'm only going to eat junk and stuff on Saturday." I told Kristin one morning as we were getting ready for work.

"Why?" she said.

"I'm tired of the feeling that I'm undoing all the hard work I did during the week when the weekend comes around." I sprayed cologne on my bare chest and flinched at its icy burn.

"I really think you're doing okay as it is right now. You have to let yourself have some fun."

*Food is not fun.*

Kristin slipped into two different pumps. "Which one?" she said, pointing down to her feet while holding the most likely outfit for the day against her body.

"That one," I said, going with my gut more than any kind of fashion sense. "In that Body for Life book, they said you should only have one day a week of eating off the program. As it is, I'm having 3 like that."

"I guess you can do whatever. But I really think you're doing okay as you are. What are you weighing now, anyway?"

"185," I said. I had made it to yet another decade, and I was thrilled about it.

"You're getting thin enough," she said.

"But I'm still on the blood pressure medication."

"When is your next appointment?"

"I don't have one," I said.

"You should probably make one. I bet you're about ready to get off the medicine by now."

It was tough getting in at Kaiser, especially if you were being picky about who saw you. I wanted to stick with Dr. Moraga. I had it in my head that since she diagnosed the problem and started the treatment that she was the only one that could legitimately tell me to get off the pills.

I first noticed it one day in the cafeteria when I met Emmeline and Gabrielle for lunch. They already had a table, and I bought my salad and met them there. The talk was about work.

"What they don't understand," Gabrielle was saying, "is that I'm really working toward the same goal they are. They act like I'm trying to sabotage the report instead of making it better. I don't even know why they asked for an editor in the first place if they felt they put it together perfect the first time. Hi Jim."

"Hey," I said.

Gabrielle sat across from Emmeline and I sat in the third chair of the square table, facing the window. With Caroline gone, the table was off balance. Out of charity, they tolerated my presence, though I wasn't any more necessary than the napkin a long-gone luncher left on another table. The air thickened around me until I thought I would drown in it. These two hated my guts.

Their conversation chirped and cackled on while I mutely forked through my salad. The words they said reduced to foreign sounds in my ears as my heart raced and sweat poured down my face. I ate with strangers every Friday, and I never spoke a word. We sat in the middle of the cafeteria that day, but I was boxed in.

Though I knew in my head and heart that they didn't want me there, leaving was too hard. Humility had me paralyzed in my chair. I checked the clock and only 5 minutes had passed. Time was paralyzed too.

Proving there was a merciful God in heaven, lunch ended with the usual confession that they had to get back to their desks because of all the work they had to do. They were really important you know. People were counting on them to get their words in the nicest, cleanest order imaginable. Not like me—I was having a slow Friday. Emmeline and Gabrielle were the most needed comma placers in all of modern science. That a plebian, such as I, could share their table spoke volumes of their tolerance. We should all be like Emmeline and Gabriele. They are the bar for which we reach.

"Gosh, you were quiet today, Jim," Emmeline said on our way out the door, "Everything okay?"

"Yeah. Fine."

It didn't stop there. I noticed that my family really just tolerated me as well. They were better off when I wasn't around. I lay awake at night while Kristin lay asleep facing the opposite wall. There was a time when she would have faced me. We would have spent the night wrapped in each other's arms. Now we barely even acknowledged that the other was in the bed.

I was in the way of other shoppers at the grocery store. Traffic was my fault. If I were not alive, there would be that much more water and a drought could be avoided. A far more worthy editor could take my job if I did the world the decency of quitting already.

There was a glimmer of hope. My eyes popped open most mornings before my 2:30 alarm sounded. Treadmill time had come again. Before that though, it was bathroom and then the scale. If I could just see a lower number on the scale, I could feel okay. I could have worth. Hope would reign.

I flexed my stomach muscles while standing in front of the toilet to force out as much pee as possible. Then I sat on the toilet and put my bowels through a work out to eliminate even the tiniest bit of waste. The less in me, the less I weighed.

The scale waited for me on the hardwood floor of the dining room at the bottom of the stairs. As I took each step, my stomach somersaulted and twisted around itself, knowing that there was a possibility that the scale would show failure today. The scale showed weight to the nearest tenth of a pound. I couldn't possibly weigh more. I'd been good. I'd worked hard.

I ground the coffee beans and filled the maker with water. Once the brewing started, there was no other way to postpone judgment. I dropped my shorts and T-shirt on the kitchen floor and peered around the corner out the front window of the house to make sure no one was passing by to see me standing naked at this ungodly hour. I breathed deep and let it out slow.

I stepped onto the scale.

The digital number settled itself and I sighed with a smile—184. I was down another number. Success was mine. Today might be an all right day after all.

"What's the matter with you anyway?" Kristin said. It was Saturday and the weather was warm, so we decided to have people over for a barbecue. Kristin was always about entertaining, and it seemed like every weekend we would empty our bank account and host a bunch of her family.

"I'm not sure. I'm not feeling good. I feel weird. Like the other day at lunch, I was paranoid that all my friends hated me."

"They do," she said, laughing.

"Seriously, baby. It's like I can't relax." I didn't want her family to come over, but they were. We had a pool, and the late spring heat was enough for swimming, so her family would be over all the time from now until August. Complaining would just make her tell me I had to go with the flow again.

"Have some wine."

"It's only 10 in the morning." I was drying off from the shower. I was still 184 that morning—before and after the treadmill.

"It won't kill you." She sat on the bed.

"What am I supposed to do though? Always have a wine buzz so I can deal with life?"

"It's not going to be every day," she said. "It's just to get you through today. My family is coming over, and I don't want you in a crappy mood. You won't become an alcoholic. I won't let you."

"Okay," I said.

"Get me a pad of paper and a pen so we can make a grocery list."

At about 11, I popped open a merlot bottle and poured my first glass. I used a wine glass, which made me feel like less of a lush. Someone that just wanted the alcohol wouldn't have made such a festive choice. They would have just poured into a water glass or drank from the bottle.

I used to prefer beer, but there was no colloquialism about a wine belly, so I switched. The taste had grown on me too.

The shopping list was on the back of an envelope and in the back pocket of my shorts. I had poured my third glass of wine when Kristin came down the stairs, ready to leave for the store. "Let's go," she said.

"Let me just finish this glass."

She rolled her eyes. "Sissy?" she called to Dominique, who had not yet been from her room. "Dominique?" Kristin huffed and opened the downstairs bedroom door. "We're going to the store. Your sister is staying here, so I need you to get up and watch her...Yes, she's had breakfast. Get up."

Kristin let the door shut and I drank down the wine as quickly as I could. The biting liquid soothed my mind, and I felt like I wasn't such a bad guy. Emmeline and Gabrielle were my friends, and they liked me. My lips were stuck in a knowing grin.

The wine made everything an event. The ride to the store, even though we were listening to Kristin's dance music, widened my perma-grin and the grocery store was an adventure.

"I see why people become alcoholics," I said.

"You're not going to be one," she said, glancing at me from the driver's seat.

"I know." I couldn't wait to explore the aisles. The warm buzz made it all new. I looked forward to her family coming over. I did like her family, but the buzz was enough to make me want people around me so I could share the glow. "Why do you think I feel so weird lately?"

"Lately?"

I laughed.

"You've lost some weight. The high blood pressure meds are probably affecting your body different. You need to make an appointment to see her and see about changing the dose or getting off them or something."

I nodded with a smile. "Yeah."

We criss crossed up and down the aisles of the store. Normally, Brighid and I did the shopping alone. It was a rare treat to have Kristin with me, and I was in love. A couple times, as the cart filled, I thought about how we were spending too much money and

I worried we'd be overdrawn, but with ease I shoved those thoughts into the sea of wine that sloshed in my stomach and coated my nerves.

The buzz lessened a bit by the time we were stacking the groceries in the back of Kristin's SUV. The new bottle I picked up and the half bottle I had at home would be good for the party.

"Randy will be here today," Kristin said. He was one of my brothers-in-law. "That dude is crazy. He'll understand what you are going through."

The doorbell started ringing and the house filled up. Raquel's kids and mine went straight to the backyard, and the splashing and laughing started. I had a couple more glasses of wine and the crowded day turned into a true event.

"Don't pass out," Kristin warned.

"I'm not gonna pass out," I said.

"I'm just saying."

She could have the last word, but I just needed to keep the perfect buzz so I could know that no one hated me.

Kristin sent Randy and me to the store to get more ice. I had him drive my car. "I don't know, man. I'm on this blood pressure medicine and it's kinda freaking me out."

"Yeah?" Randy said as he made the right turn toward the store down the street, "Like how?"

"It makes me really paranoid. Like I was at lunch with my friends at work, and I suddenly thought that they all hated me and were just tolerating me being around." I laughed. The wine made it all sound so stupid.

"I've had that before, man," Randy said.

"Kristin said you'd understand crazy."

"That I do," he said. "Yep. If I don't take my meds, things get all crazy like that for me too. Even with Gina." Gina was Kristin's sister and Randy's wife. "It sucks."

"Yeah…That's why I'm keeping myself lubed up on wine today. For some reason, it's keeping away the nuttiness."

"Whatever works, man."

"It's right up here on the left," I said, and Randy signaled and turned into the parking lot.

Back at the house, Kristin's brother Danny was working the grill in the backyard with his usual Budweiser perched on an outdoor end table. "What's up, Jim?" he said, as I made my way through the sliding glass door.

"Hey, how you doing?" I said.

"Good. Hey these steaks are almost done," he said, turning the meat again with the barbecue tongs.

"Right on. I don't eat red meat anymore though," I said. "Doctor says I have high blood pressure so I had to cut that shit out. I've lost a lot of weight though."

Danny peered down over the top of his sunglasses. "You have, man, you have. You look good."

"Thanks, man. I just stick to white meats now. It's cool though, you know. I'm still on these fuckin' pills though. I want to get rid of those."

"That's cool."

"Doing the treadmill too, so that's really helping."

"Cool. I need to get a treadmill."

"They're great. Yeah, I'm down to eating about 5 grams of fat a day. Maybe 8 at the most."

Danny nodded and poked at the meat some more. He didn't seem as into talking about diet as I was. I wrote this off as jealousy and circulated through the party.

Kristin's Aunt Mary and Uncle Art sat in the shade near the pool. Uncle Art had his Budweiser too. Cooky, my mother-in-law, sat with them. I stood near the pool and smiled at my family glowing in the red wine aura and worried about what I would do when it was time to eat.

# Chapter 14

Jeanette sat across the hall from me in the office building at work. Her idea of friendship was giving people food. I used to overhear her on the phone talking about how she kept the people happy in this building by feeding them. She had a huge stash of Hagen Dazs ice cream in the freezer in the break room. She had frozen chocolate chip cookie dough, and when she made a batch, she'd call a bunch of people and they'd come have a few.

It sickened me.

One morning, she came into my office with an oversized pink box filled with donuts. "Breakfast of champions?" she said.

"No thanks," I said, "I can't" The donuts were thick grease sponges. Had I poked one with a fork, yellowed fat would ooze from them like puss from a zit.

"You can't," she said as she turned from me with the box on her arm and headed back to her own office.

I went back to the document I was editing and thought that maybe I should have elaborated on my high blood pressure, but I didn't. She sounded hurt when she repeated what I said. What a lousy guy I was. I could have taken a donut and said thank you. No one said I had to eat it. There would be plenty of opportunities throughout the day to get rid of it.

Emmeline and I met for lunch alone the following Friday. There was a place in Downtown Livermore that had just opened and we went to try it.

"How are you doing?" She asked as the host set our menus down on the table and we took our seats.

"Great, how are you?"

"Been good."

"Right on."

The place seemed to specialize in burgers and steak, so I had to really look to find something safe to eat. I found it just in time for the waitress to take our order.

"Can I get you guys started off with a margarita?" the waitress said.

"No, thanks. I'll take a Sprite."

"Sierra Mist okay?"

"Sure."

"And for you?" The waitress made a slight turn toward Emmeline with her pen ready.

"Just water is fine," Emmeline said.

"Were you guys ready to order now or did you need more time?"

Emmeline and I looked at each other and nodded.

*Such a predictable ritual with food at its center. This country worships food.*

Emmeline ordered first. The waitress shifted her body back to me when it was my turn. "I'll take the grilled chicken sandwich with no cheese and no mayonnaise."

"Fries or baked potato?"

"Fries I guess."

"All right, I'll put that right in for you." And she was gone.

"Wow you are really doing well with your diet," Emmeline said.

"Thanks. It scared me pretty good when I had that near stroke thing so I just don't take any chances."

"So why the Sierra Mist?"

"No caffeine."

"Oh!" Emmeline said letting the vowel sound hang in the air. "So you're still not drinking coffee?"

I shook my head. "Decaf, but I'm even starting to wonder why I bother with that."

She laughed. "And the pills?"

"I'm still taking them." I sighed. "They're making me feel kind of weird. It's hard to explain."

The bright sun glowed off of Emmeline's black hair, and she looked at me, waiting.

"I mean like…You know last week when we had lunch in the cafeteria?"

She nodded.

"You probably don't even remember this, but I joined you guys late." I checked her expression, but it remained unchanged. "So anyway…This is just really weird and horrible. Anyway, I had myself convinced that day at the table that you both hated me and tolerated me, but that you would really rather not have me around."

"Jim!"

"I know," I said.

"First of all, you know that's just not true, right?" she said.

I blushed and nodded, looking down at the table.

"Are you sure it's the pills that are making you feel that way?"

"Pretty sure. I don't know what else it could be."

"When is your next appointment?"

"I don't have one."

"You really need to make one. That's horrible."

"I know. I will. It takes a while to get in to see a specific doctor at Kaiser, and the last time I had an appointment, she wasn't there that day and they forgot to call and cancel with me." I told her how the blood pressure was close to normal, but that was with the pills.

The waitress came to the table with her arms filled with plates. "Chicken sandwich?" she said.

"Me." She set the plate down and gave Emmeline her food and was gone again. I picked up half my sandwich and examined it to make sure there was no mayonnaise or cheese or any other kinds of fat-based sauce that the menu didn't warn about. It was clean, so I took a bite.

*The bread is filled with carbs though. Carbs are sugar, and sugar turns to fat, remember what Karen said?*

"I don't know, I just really think you should make an appointment as soon as possible. What does Kristin say?"

"She told me to drink wine."

Emmeline laughed. "Seriously? Did it work?"

"It did actually, but I don't want to have to drink wine just to feel normal."

"Definitely not."

*That bread is turning to fat on you.*

I looked at my sandwich again. I could probably squeeze it just right and get the chicken breast to come forward and then leave the empty bread on the plate without it seeming weird. Emmeline was busy with her own lunch and wouldn't see my magic trick.

"You're not going to eat your french fries, are you?" Emmeline said.

"Nah."

"You have some really strong will power."

"I have to."

At the Lab, most of us were contractors with a company called Johnson Controls. Johnson Controls had a separate summer picnic for their employees, and Gabrielle, Emmeline, and I went to it. It was near the Lab's pool in a picnic area with a stage and a concrete patio area. Johnson Controls employees were also allowed to go to the Lab personnel parties, so the Johnson Controls parties were a bonus.

We carpooled from our offices to the picnic area as there were limited spots there. After finding a table, Gabrielle and Emmeline marked it taken with their handbags and we got in the food line.

I got my plate and napkin.

*There is nothing here that is safe.*

The line moved up and there was a choice between potato salad and macaroni salad, each with a mayonnaise base. My hand quaked a little as I reached for the macaroni salad serving spoon.

*That is all fat.*

I brought my hand back and skipped both of the salads.

The next station gave us a choice of individual chip bags. I scanned the names, hoping for Baked Lays or light anything, but there was none to be found. My empty plate would draw attention, so I grabbed the bag that was closest to my hand and moved on.

*But you won't eat them.*

No I wouldn't. I work too hard on my body and my blood pressure to wreck all my hard work in a single afternoon.

The grill sizzled at the end of the line. "Hamburger or hot dog," the grill man offered to each person as they approached him. I bit at the inner lining of my cheek. Three people stood between me and my turn. Sweat formed on my forehead. I had no choice.

*You could leave the line and just meet the girls at the table.*

No, I couldn't do that. People would know I hadn't taken anything and there would be too many questions.

"Hamburger or hot dog?"

The chip bag sat stupid on my paper plate that shook in my hand.

*You shouldn't have come to this. You should have checked to see what the menu was.*

Hindsight is 20/20, as the cliché goes.

"Hamburger or hot dog?"

Emmeline made her choice without a thought.

"Hamburger or hot dog?"

Gabrielle made her choice, and they gave her the appropriate bun and slapped the meat down on it.

"Hamburger or hot dog?"

"Hot dog, please." I heard my voice say.

I was given a prepared hot dog wrapped in thin aluminum foil with red stripes going around it like you'd get at a ball park. I grabbed a drink from the basin of ice to the right of the grill. They had water, which was a miracle, considering the rest of the choices. People in general must not give two shits about their health as was proven by the tables I passed where people shoved the fatty animal flesh and goop coated macaroni into their mouths and laughed as if it were the best day ever.

I found Emmeline and Gabrielle at the table we staked out earlier. They looked just like everyone else. The world was out of control with eating.

Emmeline smiled at me as I sat down, and Gabrielle was going on about how the author of the document she was editing didn't understand the value of editors. They shoveled potato salad into their mouths and licked the plastic forks clean of thousands of grams of fat. I took the cap off my water and tilted the bottle back.

"You're not eating?" Gabrielle said.

"There is nothing here that I can eat," I said, taking another sip from my bottle.

"I'm sure just one time won't make that much difference," Gabrielle said.

Anger built in me like air in an over-inflated tire. "I can't eat this stuff," I said, avoiding eye contact and motioning to my plate.

"Jim, I really think that one time is not going to be that big of a deal."

"I can't."

*Tell them something. Make something up.*

"It's cool though," I said, "I brought a lean cuisine just in case something like this happened. It's no biggie." The women watched as I crushed my hot dog in its wrapper into a tiny foil ball that looked very much like a balled up, empty wrapper. "I'll eat when I get back to my office."

*Good one!*

The thrill of throwing away the hot dog energized me as we all got rid of our plates at the end of lunch. Once again, I had had a successful meal and didn't put anything in my body that would cause a problem.

On another Friday Gabrielle, Emmeline, and I went out for lunch at the gas station in Livermore that has a Mexican place attached to it. Emmeline picked me up in front of my office building and told me that Gabrielle would meet us over there later because she was in a meeting.

"There's something I want to tell you anyway, and I don't want Gabrielle to know right away," Emmeline said as we drove past the security gate and out onto the public roads.

"Right on," I said, waiting for her to talk.

She positioned the car in the left hand turn lane and turned on the signal. I checked her face, but she seemed in a fine mood, so whatever it was, it couldn't have been too bad. My curiosity was up though. "So, what's going on?" I said.

"I think I might be pregnant."

"No way!" I gasped. Her smile met mine. I knew that she and her husband were trying for a child. This was awesome news. "Wait...You think, or you are?"

"I pretty much am. I have an appointment to find out for sure, but I came up positive on a couple of home tests."

"Oh, Emmeline, congratulations! That is so great. You'll be a great mom. How is your husband taking the news?"

"Oh we're both really excited."

"That is awesome. I never really knew what love was until I had my daughter. I mean, sure, I loved my parents, and Kristin and steps kids and whatever, but it's different when you have a child. You feel how precious that kid is to you from the first second and then you realize that all people are like that to their parents. It helps you see the value in everyone—at least it did me."

"But don't talk about it at lunch, okay?" She turned her head from the road for a second in emphasis.

"No problem."

We waited for Gabrielle for a few minutes before taking a table and telling the host that we were waiting for one more person. Gabrielle had a way of getting herself caught in meetings for quite a while. This time though, she joined us just after the waiter delivered my Sprite and Emmeline's water with lemon.

"Hi, sorry I'm late," she said taking the empty chair next to Emmeline. "The Biochemistry Newsletter has a deadline this week, and they keep putting articles in and taking them out—and all of this is at the last minute. I keep telling them that at some point it has to be the final version so that I can edit it, but they don't want to listen."

Emmeline said something encouraging and I just nodded my head.

"How are you guys?"

"Fine," Emmeline said, smiling at me.

"I'm doing all right. Down another couple pounds."

"Don't you think you have lost enough?" Gabrielle said.

*Jealous.*

"My blood pressure was still a little high last time even with the meds."

"When is your next appointment to go back?" Emmeline said.

"I still gotta make one." My face flushed in shame because she knew about the paranoia that the pills were bringing on. I had told her I would make an appointment, and I hadn't. I let her down.

"How much do you weigh?" Gabrielle asked.

"179." That morning I had broken into a new decade. I pictured the 179 as it shined up to me in digital glory that morning. Before and after the treadmill, the weight had been the same. I even confirmed it by stepping off the scale and stepping on again a second later as my body dripped in sweat. I had taken a paper towel and dried off the sweat to see if it would make a difference for a third weighing, but it hadn't. That was failure, and I had to concentrate really hard on the 179 to kill the fact that drying the sweat off didn't make me lighter.

"How much are you supposed to weigh?"

"I don't know," I said. "I did my BMI at the computer at work, and it said that 179 is still in the overweight range."

"I don't think you should go by that," Gabrielle said.

*Oh, she's a doctor now?*

Emmeline shook her head in agreement. "Your face is starting to look really thin."

"Really?" That was the coolest news I had heard all day.

"Yes. It's starting to look a little sunken in."

*I told you she was jealous.*

The waiter came to take our order. The women ordered first. On my turn, I said, "I'll take the chicken tacos. No guacamole, sour cream, or cheese."

"What's left?" Gabrielle said.

This I found ironically annoying. Another time, when I didn't care about my health, the three of us had eaten in this very restaurant. I had ordered a chicken burrito with the works. During that lunch, Gabrielle said, "Man that is a huge burrito" when my food came.

Why was it that people were always so interested in my food to the point where they had to comment? Before, I had a reputation for always ordering a hamburger, and people always made a comment about that as well. Why was my food always a conversation piece? I hate food. People had lost their priorities. Going to lunch should be about visiting with the people you are there with, not about the food. And there was no way I was going to let some fatty cheese and sour cream pass these lips and mess up all my hard work.

I sat in silent anger and finally let Gabrielle's comment go as jealousy.

I sipped at my Sprite and didn't touch the chips while we waited for our food. Salsa was fat free but the chips were filled with it. They dripped oil on the way to Gabrielle and Emmeline's mouth. How could they put that in their body?

The food came. I took a couple bites of the taco.

"So how is your book selling?"

I finished chewing. "It's not really. I have a book signing coming up at GoodEnough Books though. With luck, that will help." It was the last promotional push for *One Truth at a Time.*

"Oh did you get in there?" Emmeline said, "That's great!"

"Thanks!" It had been her suggestion that I contact the manager.

I finished the first taco and reached for the second one. My refried beans sat on the plate untouched, and it was my plan to leave them that way. At home, I made them with fat free cream cheese, but who knew what they put in them here.

*Haven't you had enough?*

I stared into the back wall of the restaurant and tried to relax. I wouldn't eat the beans, that was a given, but three tacos? I was overdoing it, wasn't I? I worked my teeth against my lips and stared off with half a taco in my hand and another full one on the plate.

*Sure those are corn tortillas, but how do you know they didn't fry them up—just a little?*

I stared at the back corner until it was out of focus. With my left hand, I pinched my gut to measure the fat. I set the taco down on my plate and brought my focus back to the table. Emmeline's eyes met mine. She had been watching the whole time.

# Chapter 15

The Dead came to town. Jerry Garcia was gone, but the rest of the band still got together to tour now and then, and it was a must see for me. I'd seen them 30 times with Jerry between 1987 and 1995, and hearing the old songs live was good for my soul, even with the missing magic.

Kristin and I decided we were too old for lawn seats, so we paid the extra money and got reserved seats down front at the Shoreline Amphitheater in Mountain View—the arena Bill Graham designed to look like the Dead's Steal Your Face logo when viewed from above. I was home.

My sister Diane, and her boyfriend, Mark, were at the show too. They got lawn seats, so before the show, I made the hike up to visit them. I knew where to find them—centered at the video screen that would have been on Jerry's side of the stage. We always sat there.

There they were sharing a blanket.

"Hey!"

"Hey!" My sister said. She stood up and gave me a hug.

"Holy shit, dude!" Mark said, "I didn't even recognize you. There's like half of you here!"

"Thanks, man!" I said. He stood and we shook hands.

"No fuckin' way! You look great! How much are you weighing?"

"167." I said, smiling.

"That's awesome man!"

"Thanks! See, the doctor said I had high blood pressure."

"Diane told me, yeah."

"So I went at it. I still have to get off the pills though." I told about the low-fat diet and the treadmill.

"Well, that is fuckin' great, man. I need to do that." Mark grabbed the sides of his stomach. "Is Kristin doing it with you?"

"She is a bit, yeah. She's gonna have that surgery."

"How is Kristin?" My sister asked.

"She's good. She's down there." I pointed to the general area where our seats were.

We talked for a bit more, told each other to have a good show, and I returned to Kristin at the seats.

They played great, and I danced the full time for both sets. Kristin and I had a hotel room for the night, and there would be no treadmill the next morning. I made sure I danced up a sweat to compensate.

We had to pick up Brighid from my mom's house and meet Martin at Chili's for lunch before the tattoo appointment.

"I meant to tell you yesterday," my mom said as I got Brighid's things together, "You are really looking great."

"Thanks! I'm kinda freaking out because I'm not going to be doing the treadmill today."

*You could do it tonight when you get home.*

"Skipping a day won't make that much difference," my mom said.

"Really?"

"Honestly, dear."

*One skipped day will lead to another…*

"I guess," I said.

"Chili's!" Brighid said as we pulled into the parking lot. This was her favorite restaurant long before she could even read the name.

Martin waited for us on a bench in the lobby. "Hey, man!" I said as we came through the door.

"Martin!" Kristin hugged him and Brighid followed her.

"How was the show?" Martin said.

"Great, man. I had a great time."

The Dead's magic lasted on me through the lunch, and I ate the chips and queso we shared as an appetizer.

*Stupid!*

I stared out the window and blurred my eyes to the cars that rushed by on Lawrence Expressway.

"What's wrong?" Kristin said.

"Nothing. I'm cool." I pinched my gut under the table, disgusted with the amount of flabby skin I could hold between my fingers. Sweat formed at my hairline. Could they see it?

Kristin looked at me like she doubted that, but the waitress brought our food. "It is the weekend," Kristin said.

"I know. I said, I'm fine."

Martin started eating as if he didn't hear the conversation at all.

I looked at the fat-soaked sponges they called chicken crispers in front of me. How could I have been so stupid? I checked the others, and they were busy eating their lunches. I had no choice but to eat this.

*One weekend a month of junk food is really more than enough.*

That was true.

"So you're getting a tattoo?" Martin said.

"Yep." I patted my left shoulder that would be art before the end of the day. "Getting a Celtic clover. I got the idea when I was buzzing pretty good on Guinness at the bar in Fitzgeralds." I said.

"That's cool. I'd get one, but I'm not sure what I'd want."

My lunch still sat there, and there was no other choice but to eat it. The meal ended, and we drove down the street to Kenny's House of Pain, where I would get my tattoo.

I brought my own artwork, and I already knew where I was putting it, so it didn't take long to get started. The heavy lunch sat in my stomach like a rock, and I regretted not going with the low fat chicken tacos that Chili's has. That would be okay though. I could do better in the future, and tomorrow, I could crank the treadmill up. These thoughts kept me sane.

"This is not an infection unless you make it one," the tattoo artist said as he scratched the design into my shoulder. "A lot of guys will tell you to use A and D ointment, but I recommend Lubriderm. That's all I ever used. Don't get it wet in the shower for 2 weeks. Oh…and do you work out?"

"I just do the treadmill."

"You're gonna wanna stay away from that for a few days."

"A few days?" I pinched my fat gut with my free hand. "How many days is a few?"

"Like three."

*Three days! I told you not to order fatty foods.*

That would make a total of four days I didn't do the treadmill. I wanted this tattoo though.

*But at what cost?*

My stomach blubbered over the rim of my waistband. "How much…how much damage could I do if I use the treadmill?"

"You don't want to get it too wet for a while. That includes sweating." He continued his work, wiping away the blood as needed while he added the green and black color to the outline he made.

*Wait till you see your weight shoot up over the next few days. You're trapped. You surrendered control for a tattoo.*

The artist wrapped a bandage around my arm and taped it. "Leave that on for two hours. Wash it a few times a day, pat it dry right away, and put the lotion on it."

"Thanks man."

We left the shop and piled in the car for the 2 hour drive back to Modesto. My arm stung like a sunburn, but that was nothing compared to the no treadmill rule. "I'm not supposed to use the treadmill for three days."

"So?" Kristin said, "You can get back on it after that. It's not that big of a deal."

*What does she know?*

"Do you love your tattoo? I think it looks great. I wish I had gone there instead of the place I ended up when I got my Mickey Mouse."

"Yeah, I'm really happy with it."

*Three solid days of weight gain, fat boy. Your clothes won't fit and you'll never get off the pills.*

"After my surgery, I want to go back there and get the Evil Queen on my back," she said, "Kim rushed me on my birthday and I ended up with that old dude that didn't know what he was doing. That's why my Mickey Mouse looks so ghetto."

"It really doesn't look that bad, baby."

*Not as bad as your fat self will look after three days, mister.*

Through careful eating, I kept myself in the 160s for the three-day period. On day four, I was back on the treadmill again. Green sweat poured from the thick scab that formed on my tattoo. I was back in business.

# Chapter 16

I had never felt better in my life. My belts loop holes had progressed tighter by three. I could fit in jeans that were a 32 waist, and I could pull them off without undoing the button. My treadmill speed, which started at about 3.5 mph was now somewhere near the mid to high 4s.

The pills were still the problem, and one Saturday, Dr. Moraga finally called me back. I had left a couple of phone messages for her to talk about the paranoia.

"Paranoia?" she said.

"Yeah, like I'll be sitting with a group of my friends at lunch or something, and I'll suddenly be pretty sure they all hate me." I laughed to mask the pain.

"I have never heard of anyone feeling paranoid on those pills."

"I've lost a lot of weight—like over 60 pounds." My smile was real now. "Do you think they are just affecting me weird because of my weight loss?" I paced the backyard with the red cordless phone to my ear in the weekend sun. The pool pump hummed and rippled the water.

"I've still never heard of those pills causing paranoia, Mr. Kohl. I'm not saying it's impossible, but it has never been reported by another patient. But what you can do is cut the pills in half and see if that makes any difference for you. Also, I'll put you on hold and you can make an appointment to come in and we'll see about getting you off them."

"Awesome. Thanks." My goal would soon be met, and even chopping the pills in half made me feel accomplished. The nurse came on the line, and I scheduled an appointment. I turned off the phone and joined my family in the house.

"She said I could chop the pills in half."

"I told you to do that mejo." Cooky said. She and Kristin sat on the pink couch in the living room.

"I know I should have listened to you." Cooky was great, but I wouldn't go to her for health tips.

"You should always listen to your mother in law," she said, laughing.

"No kidding, huh?" I went to the chair across from them.

"Bubba, can you get me a drink?"

My butt had not yet touched the chair's cushion. "Okay. Water?"

"A Propel," she said.

"Okay." I headed for the kitchen. "Cooky, can I get you anything?"

"Just some water, mejo."

I delivered the women's drinks and took my seat across from them. "I have an appointment on Tuesday to see about getting rid of the pills. I'm pretty stoked that I get to cut them in half."

"Do you need a pill cutter?" Cooky said.

"Nah. They're small. I'll just use a knife."

"What time is your appointment on Tuesday, Honey?" Kristin said, sipping from her plastic bottle.

"2:30. I'll leave work early that day."

"You'll take Brighid with you?"

"Of course." My forehead wrinkled at the obvious answer.

"Okay."


The feeling of waiting for the doctor when you know you are going to hear some good news is much better than waiting for the right pain pills for your headache. The same kids' magazines Brighid and I looked at the last time were fun instead of annoying. The desk staff was cheerful. The other patients seemed friendly.

They called my name on time, and I jumped from my chair and grabbed Brighid's hand.

"Step on the scale for me please, Mr. Kohl."

*Take your jacket off first.*

"Sure."

She pushed the balance weights around in front of my face, and I was delighted to see them sliding more to the left. "Wow," the nurse said, "You've lost a lot of weight."

"Thanks," I said. The giddiness in my stomach was hard to contain.

"How did you do it?"

"Low fat diet and I do the treadmill a half hour each day."

"That is fantastic."

"Thanks."

In the examination room, Brighid and I read the kids books. She didn't need to use the bathroom, and even if she had, I would have been fine with it. Weight had been my only problem, and the weight was gone.

*You have lots more to lose.*

I pinched my gut and Brighid turned the page in the book about the duck and the typewriter. The BMI chart on the wall showed that I still had a few pounds to go before I would be in the healthy column. I would just keep doing what I had been doing, and that wouldn't be a problem.

"Hello, Mr. Kohl," Dr. Moraga said after tapping the door as she opened it, "Wow, you are looking great. Look at all the weight you lost."

"Thanks." I couldn't contain my smile. "I've just been eating low fat and walking on the treadmill a half hour a day."

*You never get tired of saying it, do you? You could do more. You could do better.*

"Well, it shows. You are like the poster child for recovery. I wish all my patients were as easy as you." She checked the chart. "And I see that your blood pressure is in the normal range today. Even a little on the low side."

I nodded.

Brighid looked at the pictures on the wall of the room that showed the muscle tissues and bones. Adult talk is boring.

"I think it's safe to say that you can stop taking the altelenol."

"All right!"

"Just keep living healthy like you are and there shouldn't be a problem."

"Thank you so much," I said.

"You are welcome. It's always a pleasure to have success with a patient."

When Brighid and I got to the parking lot, I turned my cell phone back on and called Kristin. I got her voicemail, so I called my mom. "Hey! I just got out of the doctor's, and I don't have to take the high blood pressure meds anymore."

"All right Jim! That is fantastic."

"Thanks."

"So what did the doctor say?"

"That I should keep doing what I've been doing and that she wishes all her patients were like me."

*Keep doing what you are doing. Is that really enough?*

71

"Well, that's just great Honey. I'm really happy for you."

"Me too."

I drove through Modesto, and the DJs couldn't find a bad song to play that day. Brighid wanted me to turn it down so we could play the make-believe games we always played with her animals, and I was glad to do that as well. Things were perfect.

I looked in the rearview mirror at a stoplight and pinched the fatty skin under my chin. I could work that off.

*You have a long way to go. Perfect is a long way from here.*

Kristin was almost done with her classes and counseling sessions, and she and I went to a pre-operation appointment with her surgeon, Dr. Nguyen. She worked out on the treadmill a couple times a week, watched what she ate, and walked at lunch when the weather was good. They had her step on the scale before we went in to see the doctor, and she was close to the 32 pounds she had to lose before they would operate.

"Why don't you just keep doing what you are doing and lose the weight that way?" I tried one last time as we waited in the examination room.

"I can't lose enough weight doing it that way," she said. "I'm not you. I don't have that kind of discipline."

I could never change her mind, so I gave up.

Dr. Nguyen joined us within a few minutes and got right to the business of Kristin's weight loss so far. "It looks good. We can probably schedule you for late October," he said.

That was the following month. I crossed my arms tight across my chest.

"He doesn't really like the idea of surgery," Kristin said, motioning to me.

"Why not?" Dr. Nguyen said.

"I'm afraid she will die."

"Have you considered that she might die if she stays overweight as well? Lots of complications can come from being overweight…high blood pressure, other heart problems, diabetes, back problems…and so far she has none of these, but she could develop them over the next few years if nothing is done." He looked at me across the examination bed with that thin paper I laid on when I was diagnosed with high blood pressure.

I nodded and pulled my arms tighter against myself so I could reach down and pinch my gut. A sigh escaped without my calling for it.

"He doesn't believe in surgery if there is nothing wrong," Kristin said. That was my thought, more or less.

"Like I said, this is a preventative measure. If we waited until there was a problem, there could be more to correct than this surgery could take care of."

With a smirk, I nodded again and caught my inner cheek between my teeth. "I see what you are saying," I said, "And I understand on an intellectual level. How many of these patients have you had die?"

"Jim!" Kristin said.

"It happened once to me, and she didn't die on the table," Dr. Nguyen said. "There was a complication a couple weeks after the procedure, and she didn't call me. She was misdiagnosed in an emergency room somewhere. They didn't know she'd had the procedure, and the point where the stomach pouch met the intestines ruptured. If she had called me, I could have saved her." Dr. Nguyen looked down at the floor.

"Show him how it works," Kristin said. To me she said, "I don't have to be cut wide open. They can do the whole thing laproscopically now."

"What's that mean?" I said.

Dr. Nguyen took a pen from the pocket of his white coat and went to work on the examination table paper. He drew a wide oval that was supposed to represent Kristin's torso. "Instead of making a large incision down the entire abdomen like we used to, in most cases, we can make 4 small incisions here, here, here, and here." He drew 4 short lines that would have been the 4 corners of a square had they been connected. The rest of the explanation got rather technical, but the main idea was they lift the skin and perform the operation through these 4 slats with the use of small cameras and TV monitors so they could see what they were doing.

"Wow," I said, unconvinced that this was safe.

"He just doesn't like surgery, Dr. Nguyen," Kristin said.

"What if you get in there to do it, and the 4 slats aren't gonna be good enough?" I said.

"Then we would have to do it the other way. But I'm 90 percent confident that we won't have to."

"Ninety percent." I repeated.

The doctor nodded.

I looked at the drawing he had made. It showed the 4 slices and the Frankensteined digestive tract that she would have with the large section of her stomach permanently sealed off and useless and the small intestine rerouted to meet the thumb-sized stomach pouch. It got really hot in the room, and I pinched at the fat of my gut some more.

"Why don't you show her how to lose weight?" Dr. Nguyen said.

"She won't do it my way," I said. And my way was mine.

*That's right!*

Kristin said something about not having my kind of will power. Dr. Nguyen gave her a paper reminding her of a couple things she had to do before the surgery, and he left.

"Do you feel any better about this whole thing now that you've talked to him?" Kristin said as she started up the car.

"I'll feel better when the operation is done and I see that you are fine," I said. Her silence told me that wasn't the answer she had wanted, and I felt worse.

*Nothing a pound less on the scale can't fix.*

True enough.

In the early morning, I woke before the alarm. The scale had to be less today. I had really done well yesterday, taking in less than 10 grams of fat, which was my new daily goal. The treadmill had gone well. I didn't eat or drink anything past 7 the night before, and I had used the bathroom once in the middle of the night. I crawled from bed and used it again. It would be a good morning.

The butterflies of early Christmas morning twirled in my stomach on the way down the stairs to the scale. Each step brought me closer to it, and I couldn't wait. In the kitchen, I dropped my shorts and boxers and turned on the light so I could see the dark gray on gray digital read out. Yesterday I was 164, so I had to be 164 or less today.

The scale waited for me in the pale light from the kitchen. The white oasis against the tan hardwood floor was the most important square foot of the house. The time had come. I put one foot on the scale, and then the other. 164.

No progress. I stepped off the scale and gave the readout a second to clear itself. I stepped on again.

164.

Tears welled in my eyes. What had I done wrong yesterday? I went through everything I ate. It had to have been dinner. I had had a second plate of turkey spaghetti. The sauce was just fresh roma tomatoes and seasoning, but two plates were too much.

*You did this to you. You're no better than you were the day before. I told you not to have the second plate.*

There was a chance I could move my bowels. I pulled on my boxers and went to the downstairs bathroom next to Dominique's room. The seat was cold, but that was the least of my worries as I pushed in vain to get more out of my body. A tiny bulb fell into the water below me, and I cleaned up and raced to the scale again.

164.

Nothing more could be done, so I headed to the garage and stepped onto the treadmill. The red numbers glowed to life as I inserted the power key and increased the speed until it was 4.5 mph.

*Not fast enough.*

Right, yes. I hit the speed up arrow twice more until the readout said 4.7 mph and kept in stride. A towel covered the time so I would concentrate on my book on tape that played through my headphones, but the calories burned number was visible as was the pedometer so I could see how far I had walked.

I checked my lower back every so often to feel how much sweat had built up there and I let the droplets of sweat pour down my face as a badge of honor—wiping them away only when they had reached my chin.

The treadmill hummed beneath me as Stephen King read me part of his book, *On Writing.* I had read it before when it came out, but I found it inspiring and worth going through again. It helped my own writing—the second most important thing in my life.

Sweat started to stain through the chest of my T-shirt, another sign of victory. I took the towel off the time clock and found I still had 20 minutes to go. The higher setting was doing its job. At 4.5 mph, the sweat wouldn't show through my shirt until at least 15 minutes had gone by, depending in part on how cold the morning was.

I reached behind me with my left hand and found a wonderful puddle in the small of my back. Sweat cried down my face and dribbled off my chin before I had a chance to sop it up with the towel. My hands were lubed enough to slide around on the hand grips. I was only halfway done for the morning.

A small sip from the bottle of water I had in the treadmill's cup holder cooled my drying mouth.

*Careful how much you take in. Water weighs a lot.*

With ten minutes left, I hit the speed up arrow one more time and finished the day at 4.8 mph. My legs ached, but the pain was good. I struggled to keep up with the belt as it hummed around beneath me. Sweat poured and I smiled as Stephen King went over the essential arts of revision in his calm voice.

I let the minutes part of the time clock show and kept the intensity up as the 20s slowly climbed toward thirty. This was the time to give your all. It was the 4th quarter in the playoffs. The men separated from the boys in the last 10 minutes, or any other macho cliché you prefer.

My thigh muscles burned and begged for the end, but the clock had 2 more minutes. I concentrated on my breathing, and felt the pulse in my neck as it thumped along to Stephen King telling me that my editor is right even when I know he's wrong.

One minute left, and I stared out the side window of my garage and watched the neighbor turn on the porch light, get the newspaper, and go back inside the house. Thirst nagged at me, but I didn't want anything in my stomach right now. I moved the speed up to 5 mph to really go all out in the final minute. My power walk tuned into a light jog.

The clock said thirty. I cut the power and the treadmill eased to a stop.

*Maybe you should do this twice a day.*

I took the water bottle and the sweat towel with me and went inside. In the kitchen, I set the water on the counter and peeled my shirt off. Sweat coated me, extra weight, and I rubbed my chest, arms, and back the best I could until I was dry. I let my shorts and boxers fall to the kitchen floor too, and dried the sweat from the rest of my body. The scale waited.

It had to be less now. The fat had run off my body and fallen onto the treadmill belt, which carried it away forever. The dim light of the kitchen shone just bright enough to see the numbers on the scale. I stepped on and waited till the number settled.

164.

*Loser.*

# Chapter 17

The most important thing I could do was keep my fat intake below 10 grams a day, but lower than 5 was ideal. Every day was a new day and the battle would either be lost or won.

Jeanette dropped by my office a few weeks after the donut incident. "I brought something for you," she said.

I looked up from the document I was editing to see what she had.

"I know you don't want to eat a lot of junk food," she said.

*None at all.*

"So, I picked you up this." She handed me an orange.

"Thanks," I said, setting it on my desk.

"You're welcome. I got it at Whole Foods. It's organic" She took a step back.

"Right on," I said, "That's awesome. Thanks a lot."

She nodded and left my office.

*Why does she feel the need to give people food?*

I had no idea. I didn't know what the deal was with her and food. From the look of her, it was clear that she loved food. She had a real problem. What must her blood pressure be, let alone her BMI?

*I'll bet she doesn't even know what a BMI is.*

I bet that's right. She's going to eat herself right into her grave and probably have herself buried with extra-fatty chocolate chip cookies.

*Disgusting.*

Yes.

The orange sat on my desk.

*Karen said Oranges were filled with carbs that turned to fat.*

She said orange juice.

*What's the difference really? An orange isn't too much more than juice anyway. An orange is not part of the regimen.*

What I ate on a daily basis was a calculated thing. I had the Special K with skim milk in the morning, a lean cuisine for lunch, a low fat energy bar in the afternoon around 3, and a small plate of dinner.

*You should really find something to eat besides that energy bar in the afternoon. It's got some fat even though it's low fat. It's more than you need, and it's slowing the progress.*

That afternoon bar was keeping me fat. No wonder I could still see my guts hanging over the rim of my jeans in the mirror. I pinched my gut and looked at the orange again. Jeanette's voice carried across the hall as she argued with her husband on the phone and the orange sat like a zit on my desk.

"It's an orange, for Christ's sake," I said to myself, "What's the big fucking deal?"

*Not part of the plan.*

I picked up the orange and rolled it around in my hand. There was no way I would eat it. What if Jeanette had found a special sort of orange that did have fat in it? Misery loves company— that's what my Dad used to say about peer pressure—and Jeanette was interested in fattening people up like a witch in a fairy tale. I unzipped the soft leather briefcase I carried to work each day and slipped the orange in to be tossed out later. No one had hurt feelings. I didn't have to eat it. Everybody wins.

October came and passed quickly with Kristin's surgery on the way. She would be in the hospital for 4 days, including Halloween. We shopped early for the kids' costumes and such. Brighid would be a witch again, as would Dominique. Lorenzo was a Dementor from Harry Potter.

Each step toward the surgery made me more nervous, but I had my treadmill to keep me sane. If she were to die on the operating table, I'd be all alone, Dominique and Lorenzo would have to live with their dad, and Brighid and I would have to move.

Two days before the surgery, she drank something that evacuated her entire system. She started her medical leave that day so she could stay near the bathroom while that medicine did its thing.

"That stuff was so fuckin' nasty," she told me on the phone.

"Really?" My face squished.

"I gagged it down. And oh…my…God. Like ten minutes later I had to run to the bathroom and I was in there for like an hour. By the end, my poop was clear."

"No way!"

"Yes," she said, sounding like she enjoyed the telling much more than the actual experience. I wondered if all this was worth it to her when all she needed to do was diet and exercise, but I kept quiet about. The surgery was 2 days away, and there was no time left to do anything but be supportive and pray that for some reason it was cancelled.

The day before the surgery, she could eat no food and was only allowed to drink clear liquids. We stocked up the house on Sprite and Propel.

"I'll do this with you," I offered. I didn't want her to feel hungry alone.

*Plus, a day of nothing but clear liquids could really help with the progress, don't you think?*

"No. You need to eat. I'll be fine doing it alone," she said. I was getting ready for work, and she was lying on the bed with the TV on.

*You should do it anyway. How long are you going to let her make your choices for you?*

"But I want to support you in this," I said.

"You are, Honey."

We discussed it a couple more times before I finally gave in to her.

The morning of the surgery, I woke Brighid up and got her ready for preschool. She and I did the 50 mile commute, and then I returned home to be with Kristin.

I took the week off of work that she would be in the hospital and a few days to be with her at home after the procedure. She posed for one last snapshot that would be her "before" picture and we went to the hospital.

We checked her in, and I stayed with her as long as I could in the intake room. They started the anesthesia process while I was still there, and Kristin got bleary eyed—a feeling that she enjoyed. I kissed her, and they took her down the hall into the operating room. I watched until the last tuft of her dark hair disappeared around the corner, convinced that I would never see her alive again but hoping I was wrong.

Cooky showed up at some point to be with me. "Do you want something to eat, mejo?" she said.

"No," I said, "but if you are hungry, I'll go with you to the cafeteria here."

"Do you know where it is?"

I nodded and stood from the lobby chair where we sat. Cooky followed me out of the automatic doors and around the corner into the hospital's café. Sneezeguards protected the food from germs all around the perimeter of the room and tables filled the center. Dr. Nguyen was in there wearing operating room scrubs.

"You sure you don't want anything to eat?"

"I really don't thanks. Maybe I'll have a coffee."

I sat across from Cooky at a long table and watched her eat. I held the coffee in my hand and swirled it lightly. The Formica table had a pink hue to it, though it looked gray from a distance. I stared the tabletop down.

"She's going to be fine, mejo." Cooky said.

"Yeah, I know." I didn't believe it at all. Dr. Nguyen sat across the room from us eating as if this were just another day at the office and not the day when my wife's life was in his hands. I watched him take a bite of a sandwich and stare across the room as he chewed. The institutional woman's voice from the PA system called him to surgery, and he wrapped up the rest of his sandwich and was gone.

This was it. She would live or die, based on the actions of some guy that saved half a sandwich.

"That was her surgeon," I said.

"Who?" Cooky looked around the café.

"They just called him to surgery." Tears welled at the bottom of my eyes, but I crushed them away before they could fall. "She'll be fine."

"I know," Cooky said, and she drank from her soda.

We left the cafeteria and went back into the main lobby of the hospital. There was a circle of brown vinyl cushioned chairs in the center of the lobby, and we took two of them. Cooky tried to keep me talking, but I didn't have much to say.

Aunt Mary, Uncle Art, Raquel, and her sister Juanita showed up. Seeing Uncle Art calmed me. "Hey," I said, rising from my chair to meet Uncle Art with a hug, "I didn't know you guys were coming."

"I didn't know either," Uncle Art said, "How are you doing, mejo?"

"I'm all right." We turned and walked together.

"Damn, look how skinny you're looking boy. You eating anything?"

"Yeah," I said, rolling my eyes. This shirt made me look thin.

"Well, don't lose any more weight, okay?"

They filled in the rest of the chairs, and it became just another family gathering. The only thing missing was a cooler of beer, and part of me wondered if Uncle Art had one out in his trunk. My stomach twisted less with the normal talk and the profanity in Uncle Art's Mexican accent. "How long is she gonna be in there?"

"They said it could take about 2 hours or something," I said.

"God damn," Uncle Art said. "We should go to dinner."

I laughed, but nothing was moving me from my chair. Visions of widow's walks came to mind. If she were to die, this gathering would be a morbid dress rehearsal for the three days of funeral activities that her family favored. It would be a forever feeling that she may walk up at any moment, and a stinging reminder that she wouldn't.

"Are you pregnant, mejita?" Cooky said to Raquel who sat opposite her in our circle of chairs.

"No, auntie," Raquel said, crossing her arms over her stomach, "I'm just fat."

Oof!

*At least no one will ever mistake that gut of yours for a baby.*

As loud and boisterous as Kristin's family could sometimes be, that set the awkward silence over us...for almost 20 seconds until everyone but Raquel and I started laughing. Even Raquel gave way and smiled a bit. Could there be something worse than someone pointing out your fat?

The time was over faster than I thought it would have been thanks to the company I had. A nurse approached our group and asked which one of us was Jim.

I stood before she had the question out of her mouth. "The procedure is over, and she's doing fine. She will be in the recovery room for an hour."

I exhaled hard and long. "Thank you."

The nurse nodded. "In about 45 minutes, we'll be able to tell you what room she will be in and then you can see her after they get her there."

"Thank you."

"You see, mejo," Cooky said, "She's gonna be fine."

81

"Thank you guys all for being here for me."

"Sure, yeah," Uncle Art said. He turned to his wife. "Ma, we gonna go get some dinner now?"

Aunt Mary agreed in her silent way, and they asked me if I would join them.

"I have to go get Brighid," I said, "But thanks, though."

I had a list of phone numbers in my wallet that I was supposed to call as soon as the surgery was over. I made the first call to Kristin's friend, Jason, as soon as I was out in the parking lot. His voicemail picked up, and I left details about how she was and my number if he cared to call back. Traffic was tight on 580 that afternoon, so I was able to dial a few more numbers on the drive to Brighid's preschool.

Joyce was the only one that was home. She and her husband Frank had hit it off with us years ago when both of our kids were in the same play. "Hey Joyce, it's Jim."

"Hey! How are things going?"

"I'm all right. You?"

"Doing great."

"Cool," I said, "Kristin's surgery is over and, and she's doing fine. They have her in the recovery room for an hour or so, and then she can have visitors."

"Awesome!" she said, "And you're all right?"

"I'm better now that the surgery is over. It was cool though cause her mom and uncle were there, so I had someone to talk to while she was in."

"Right on."

"Yeah," I said, "Right now, I'm going to pick up Brighid from daycare, and then we'll both swing back to the hospital to see her."

"That's cool. So is Brighid excited for Halloween?"

My God, that was right. Tomorrow was Halloween. "Yeah, I guess she is. She's going to be a witch."

"Wasn't she a witch last year?"

I nodded into the phone as I veered the car to the right for my exit. "And the year before."

Joyce laughed. "But Kris won't be out of the hospital by then?"

"Oh no. She'll be in there for three or four days or something like that." Of all Kristin's friends, I was closest with Joyce. The other calls would last seconds. It was nice to have someone on the phone.

"So what all else is going on?" Joyce said.

"I've lost 70 pounds."

*Now you're saying something.*

"Shut up!" she said.

I laughed and shifted myself in my seat at a stoplight. "Seriously."

"No way! How did you do that?"

"Just treadmill a half hour a day and low fat foods." I never got sick of saying it.

"Wow, so, my gosh, you must be really skinny."

I beamed, the light turned green, and I continued down First Street towards Storyland Preschool. "I'm feelin' really good."

"I'll bet you are. So did you have to buy all new clothes?"

"Nah. I just wear 'em baggy. And I use a belt."

"And I use a belt," Joyce laughed, "Fuckin' Jim." Joyce went on to say how she and Frank were trying to eat better too. I smiled and nodded along with the conversation.

I had reached Storyland now, and Brighid was waiting for me inside, but the conversation was too good to go in right then. I cut the engine and explained the recipes Kristin and I had worked out.

Joyce was interested, so I went on to explain more about the treadmill regimen. The conversation went on for 5 and then 10 minutes. Parents arrived after me, went in, and came out with their kids while mine waited inside for me to finish discussing how white meat is much leaner.

Guilt pushed me from my car, but I kept Joyce on the phone as I signed Brighid out and helped her into her car seat with the phone still pressed to my ear. It was wonderful to have someone on the phone as interested in weight loss—I mean healthy eating—as I was.

"So when can I come up and see Kris?"

"In the hospital?" I said.

"Yeah."

"Whenever you'd like. Like I said, she'll probably be there another 4 days or so. She'll be stoked to see you." I gave Joyce a rough idea of where the hospital was and we hung up.

When Kristin first came home from the hospital, she could only eat 4 tablespoons of broth at a time. She rested in the blue recliner we had against the wall in the family room. Her mom,

Uncle Art, and Aunt Mary were with her while I heated up broth on the kitchen stove. When it was ready, I filled two of the plastic shot glasses that the doctor gave us with the warm broth, set them on a tray, and carried them down the three steps to the family room where everyone was sitting. Conversation and laughter died.

"Here's your lunch, baby," I said.

"That's it!" Uncle Art said. "Jesus Christ, I'd starve."

"That's what she's supposed to have, man," I said.

Kristin thanked me, her voice rough and weak from exhaustion. She sipped at the first shot glass as the silent room watched. Halfway through the second shot glass, she said, "I'm full," and waved the tray away.

She was the luckiest person on the planet.

# Chapter 18

My sister, Diane, had a dinner party for our mother's birthday in November. Kristin couldn't eat regular food yet. She was still in the stage where all she could have was pureed beef about the consistency of baby food. I made the drive alone to San Jose for the evening.

"Hey," my sister said, opening the door. "How was the drive?"

"It was fine." I came into her one bedroom condo and said hi to my parents and grandmother. Mark was out on the back porch smoking. All I wanted was for one of them to tell me how good I looked, seeing as I had dropped 10 more pounds since I had seen them. The fun of going to San Jose was the reaction I got for all my hard work on my body. No one noticed until Mark came in.

"Jesus, Jim! You've lost even more weight haven't you?"

"Yeah," I smiled.

"Good for you, man, you're looking great."

I stood to shake his hand.

He looked me up and down. "Man, so what are you weighing now?"

"160."

"Shit, I haven't seen 160 since my college days. That is awesome. So still the treadmill every day?"

"Yeah. I'm starting to jog on it more than walk now," I said. This was the coolest conversation I had in a long time. "Plus, I'm just really careful about what I eat."

"It shows. Good job, man."

"Thanks!" The topic changed, and I lost interest. The voice coming from my mouth told me that I was talking to them, but the conversation didn't include me. I answered questions about Brighid while wondering what food Diane was planning to serve. I explained Kristin's surgery and recovery while worrying about the etiquette of refusing cake at your mother's birthday party. What was expected of me and how much of that could I pull off?

Taking a small portion and squashing it down onto the plate so it looked like more was a specialty of mine.

*It's all appearance.*

If the safety of the food seemed questionable, that was an option. The hot dog squashed in the foil that looked eaten came to mind, but my sister didn't serve things that came in a wrapper.

My voice talked about mundane things.

I could smell the food from the kitchen, and I knew that Diane wouldn't serve something that high in fat. My dad was there, and everyone was cautious of his high cholesterol.

*But this is a special occasion. How much fat have you had today so far?*

Eight grams in my Lean Cuisine.

My audible voice went on, reacting to the talk of the room.

*The truth is, you can't be positive it's low fat.*

I know.

Someone else carried the conversation in the room, and I knew that the right thing to do was look towards the person that was talking and occasionally look away so that it wasn't a stare down. This I could pull off. Insert a laugh at the appropriate time, and I'd be functional as any of them. Appearance is everything.

*Yes it is.*

My grandmother talked about some of her friends at her apartment complex.

Mark talked about selling cars.

Politics came up and went down.

Religion got its time.

I had the corner seat of Diane's couch and gripped the Heineken that rested on my knee. Beer didn't have any fat.

Diane called us all to the table. I sat at one of the ends. She made some sort of pasta dish with a romaine lettuce salad. The salad had apple bits, Italian dressing, and feta cheese crumbled throughout it. I scooped some onto my plate with the tongs that stuck out the top of the large bowl on the table.

"This is wonderful, Diane," my mom said.

"Yes it is," my dad agreed.

I looked down at my plate and wondered what kind of cheese was in the pasta. "I put a low fat cheese in the pasta," Diane said to the room as if reading my mind.

I picked at my salad and ate around the croutons. Low fat— what did that mean? How many grams was I putting in myself? Sweat formed on my forehead, and the room spun a little.

People didn't care about people anymore. Food always had to be at the center of things. It should be enough that we were all together in the same house, but it wasn't. We had to prove our love by sharing a meal together and then cutting a cake.

Someone asked me how work was going, and I heard myself say, "Not bad. Same old junk every day—you know how it is."

"Has there been any more talk about your clearance?"

My application for my Q-level clearance had been under investigation for almost a year and a half. As soon as that came through, I would be able to work on classified government documents. My paperwork had been the responsibility of three separate investigators so far and each one had handed it off to the next, who would start the process over. "No," my voice said, "I don't know what the deal is."

*The cheese in the pasta looks too creamy to be low fat.*

I took a modest serving of pasta to begin with and crushed it down on my plate as normal. No one else at the table seemed to be watching what I was eating. They were all busy with their own plates and going on about what a fabulous job Diane had done. It was my turn. "This is great, kiddo!"

"Thank you. It's mom's recipe."

"Mom's recipe from *Woman's Day*," my mom joked.

A bite of salad was grinding between my teeth. The rest of the salad sat on my plate, green and shiny with dots of white cheese throughout.

*You may have put some of that cheese in your mouth.*

No I didn't. I've been watching. I've been careful. The salad seemed innocent enough as I looked down on it. The cheese and the croutons were the only unsafe ingredients, and it was easy enough to avoid the croutons. The feta cheese was a little more challenging in that you had to scrape it off the lettuce leaves with your fork. Diane had left the salad dressing bottle on the kitchen counter, and from my seat at the table, I could see that is said fat free. At least the dressing wasn't a worry.

*Unless she didn't really use that dressing.*

That's ridiculous. Why would it be out if she didn't use it?

*Maybe she used it for something else.*

No.

The conversation prattled on at the table. I looked from one person to the next, but I had lost the content. I nodded and smiled and laughed when others did.

*The fat from the cheese is oozing into the lettuce. The lettuce is not safe.*

I checked my salad again. It sat on the plate and in the flickering light of the candle on the table. I could see that this was true. Just above a subatomic level, the lipids were meshing with the innocent lettuce. I could scrape the cheese off my lettuce all day; it wouldn't matter. The fat was already in me.

*There were walnuts in the salad too. They aren't exactly fat free.*

Good point. I set my fork down on the side of the plate.

The meal ended and the plates were cleared. Diane put candles in a cheesecake. We all sang the birthday song to my mother, and she blew out the candles—yet another human tradition with food as the focal point. We are disgusting in our food worship.

Between Diane and my mom, we each had a slice of cheesecake on a plate in front of us in a matter of moments. Coffee rounded out the dessert—good old, safe coffee.

The cheesecake festered in front of me. Diane's kitchen trash can was two steps away in the cabinet beneath the sink. The trick would be to get this cake to the trash without anyone noticing and asking questions. We all sat at a pretty small table. They could see my every move. I wiped sweat from my forehead.

They all talked and laughed. Forks stabbed into the wretched consistency and shoveled it into waiting mouths. I checked the table for eye contact, but no one was looking at me. The distance to the trash can stretched.

Diane gave us cloth napkins, so wrapping the cake in paper to make it look like I ate it was not an option. I was trapped.

My cheesecake was untouched, and my fork was dishwasher clean. I caught myself gnawing on my inner lip and stopped. This would be worse than the corrupted lettuce if I took some into my body.

*All your hard work for nothing. You will fail.*

There was no way out. The fork shook in my hand as I gripped it and moved it toward the pointy end of the cheesecake slice. Fat lived and multiplied on my plate and now my fork was stabbing through and tearing away part of the colony. With my elbow resting on the table, I held the yellowed piece of food in front of my mouth and thought of an easier escape.

If I took it with me to the bathroom, they'd know.

If I acted like I was too full, they'd know.

They would see me if I tried to throw it in the garbage under the sink.

To refuse cake on my mother's birthday would have been spitting in the face of tradition. The rest of them took down their cheesecake slices and coffee while they laughed and talked as if all was fine.

I moved the cold glob of fat into me and scraped it from the fork with my lips. My tongue crushed it against the roof of my mouth. I shivered as the rich flavor and goop spread throughout my nasal cavities. My teeth mashed it until I could swallow and then I did. A tear came to my eye.

*I don't have to tell you what you'll need to do with the treadmill tomorrow, do I?*

There—I had been social. Etiquette was met. Finishing the slice was out of the question, but no one could say I didn't participate in the ritual. Visions of digital scale numbers in the high 160s and low 170s haunted me. As others finished and plates were cleared, I waited for a clear path between me and the garbage can and put the rest of the cheesecake slice where it belonged.

My car needed gas to make the 100-mile drive back to Modesto. I called Kristin while the tank filled.

"How did it go?" she said.

"It was all right. I had a nice time."

"What did you guys eat?"

"Some sort of pasta, a salad, and cheesecake."

"Cheesecake for a birthday?" Kristin said.

The lumpy fat still oozed in my throat and a coating was left behind in my mouth that added fat to me every time I swallowed my own saliva. "Yeah."

"That's weird."

"It's what my mom likes," I said. I wondered how much fat I took in through that fucking lettuce.

*Much more than you could imagine.*

"Jim?"

"Yeah?"

"I just asked you if you were on your way home?"

"Oh. Sorry. Yeah, I'm getting gas, and then I'm on my way."

"Okay. Did anyone say anything about me?"

"No. I mean, they asked how you were, and we talked a little about the surgery. Not much else."

"Not *much* else?" she said.

The pump clunked itself off and I put the nozzle back in its holster. "Nothing more that I remember, honey. Diane made a salad and there was cheese in it."

"That sounds good."

"Sure. Yeah," I said.

"I might not be able to wait up for you, but give me a call when you are close, okay?"

"Okay, yeah. I will. It was hard to eat around the cheese in the salad," I said.

*Especially with the fat oozing the way it did. You should eat a smaller bowl of cereal tomorrow than normal. Maybe skip part of your Lean Cuisine too.*

"It was a birthday party," she said. "You are fine. Did you eat the cheesecake?"

"Only a bite, okay?"

"Don't get all defensive. I was just wondering."

"Sorry. It's just that…"

*Don't tell her.*

"What? It's just that what?"

"Nothing." I steered the car onto the 680 North onramp in the dark night and followed my headlight beams into the traffic.

*This is yours to know. Keep what's yours.*

We hung up. The feel of the cheesecake smooshing around my mouth and coating my digestive system played in my head over and over like a past humiliation. No matter how loud I played the radio, I knew I added a bunch of fat to my system and ruined my body in a single night. The scale in the morning terrified me from 10 hours in the future. What if it showed 161?

*What if it's even worse?*

And in all likelihood it would be, wouldn't it? Trapped in my fat body, I haunted myself all the way home and well into the night.

The Lab closed the central cafeteria where we would always meet for lunch, so we changed to the one near East Avenue. It was a close walk from my office, and Emmeline wanted to walk as much as possible for as long as she could with the baby on the way. She picked me up so we could walk over and meet Gabrielle. I waited in the lobby of my building until I saw her, and then went out to meet her with my heated Lean Cuisine in its box under my arm.

"How you doing?" I said, smiling for her.

"Doing well. How are you?" She looked me up and down, and the inspection made me smile. "You are really looking skinny, Jim."

No words had more beauty. "Do you think so?"

"Yes," she nodded. "I think, as a matter of fact, that you are too skinny."

*She's jealous because of the pregnancy weight. You can't be too rich or too thin.*

"What do you mean?" I looked down my own body and pinched my gut to show that I still had a lot to lose.

"You're face is starting to look gaunt."

Gaunt was a word Anne Rice used to describe some of her vampires, and they were beautiful and perfect. "Seriously?"

"Yes. In the face especially, you are looking kind of skeletal." We started the walk to the cafeteria, taking the short cut through the next building's parking lot. "What are you weighing now?"

*Lie to her.*

"162." What's a four pound exaggeration between friends?

"Really?" She stopped mid-step and shot me a look with those innocent eyes.

*Stick to it, man.*

"Yeah."

"And you are still doing the treadmill every day?"

I felt my eyes sparkle at the mention of it and knew she probably saw that happen. Her psychology degree was not for nothing. "Yes."

"So you are still trying to lose weight?"

"Yes." She had me in an eye lock and I had too much respect for her to lie.

"Jim," she said, "I really don't think you need to lose any more weight."

"Really?"

*Jealousy!*

"Really. And I think you may have a problem."

"What're you…what're you talking about?"

"I think you know. How could you not?" She broke the eye contact and we started our walk to the cafeteria again.

"What do you think, that I have anorexia or something?" That couldn't be. I was just really good at dieting. I thought of the cheese's fat and the lettuce. That whole thing seemed ridiculous on a walk far from any food. Maybe…

*She has a psychology degree. You know how those people are. She'll find and diagnose a problem in anyone. It's as natural for her as putting the commas in the right place is for you.*

"Or something. Are you making yourself throw up?" she said.

"No! Oh my God no." That was so beneath me.

"Do you know how thin you are?"

"I still have some more to lose."

"What is your goal weight? How do you know when to stop losing?"

*Never. But don't tell her that. Throw a number out there. The BMI chart says you can be as low as 150 and be in the healthy range.*

"I don't know…Like a 150 or something."

"So what's that, ten more pounds?"

I nodded. The overcast day chilled me, and I pulled my jacket closer. Emmeline wore a short sleeved shirt.

"Okay, so when you lose these ten pounds, what is your plan then?"

I bit at my inner cheek and searched the parking lot as if my plan would jump out from behind a car somewhere. "But see, it's like insurance. The lower I get, the further I am from fat. Then I have more to gain before I have to worry about high blood pressure again."

"You need to be able to find a good weight and maintain it. The choices aren't just fat and thin, Jim."

*Bullshit!*

We arrived at the cafeteria. Emmeline wouldn't talk this way in front of Gabrielle, and with luck, Gabrielle would make a rare on-time appearance. As we approached the front door of the cafeteria and I reached to open it for Emmeline, she said, "Just think about what I said, okay Jim. Maybe you need to go and talk to someone before this thing gets too far."

"I'll think about it," I said.

*You'll think about it when you are on the treadmill tomorrow morning.*

# Chapter 19

The scale still said 160 the next few days. Failure. There had to be something I could do to progress. Accomplishment meant a lower number—a new weight decade—the 150s. That's what self-esteem is built on after all—accomplishment. That's the only true self worth.

The kitchen floor was cold beneath my bare feet. I had toweled down before weighing after the treadmill as usual, and it occurred to me that maybe I wasn't vigilant enough at that. I found a roll of paper towels beneath the kitchen sink, ripped off a fist full, and rubbed them all over my body once more.

The front blinds were open, but no one was on the street. It was safe to drop my shorts again. The scale waited. I checked the sidewalk through the window one last time and ripped my shorts off. I put one foot and then the other on the scale.

160.

The paper towel wad was on the counter. My head and hair had to be the problem; I hadn't rubbed the paper towels through my hair. I scrubbed my head down with the enthusiasm of a well-tipped shoe-shine boy and stepped back on the scale.

160.

With a sigh, I pulled my shorts back up and reached the Special K box down from the top of the fridge. We had a small, clear-glass bowl that I liked to use, so I hunted it out of the dishwasher and set it on the counter. I shook the box a few times over the bowl, and then I went for the milk.

*That is too much cereal.*

The bowl wasn't even half filled. With the milk jug in my hand, I looked at the bowl and thought of the 160 on the scale that wouldn't lessen.

*You already know what you should do. You already know what you have to do.*

I pinched the top of the cereal between my finger and thumb and put it back in the box. The mound was still too big, so I did it again until the flakes just hid the counter through the bottom of the glass bowl.

*That is a safe amount.*

I added the milk and ate the entire breakfast in 2 spoonfuls.

"You have got to try this new energy bar I found," Kristin said on the phone on her way home from work. "They taste like those sugar wafer cookies, you know the ones I mean?"

"Like the vanilla, chocolate, and strawberry ones?"

"Yeah, except these come in peanut butter and some other flavors. I had the peanut butter one though. It's great. I brought one home for you to try."

"Right on. Thanks." I sat on the pink couch in the living room and pressed my cell phone against my ear. Sometimes I felt like I was married to my cell phone. Kristin and I talked mainly during her long commute. By the time she got home, she was too tired and just wanted to watch TV.

"How are the kids?"

"Fine. Brighid is watching cartoons, Lorenzo is somewhere, and Dominique is listening to music in her room."

"What did you make for dinner?"

"Turkey burritos."

"The kids were probably thrilled," she said. The kids were sick of the 4 things I knew how to make since we had them every week. I really didn't care because…

*The food you make is safe.*

Exactly.

Kristin came home, changed, ate, watched TV, and we went to bed.

On my way out the door the next morning after still weighing 160, Kristin said, "Wait a second, honey." She went into the bag she carried to work and pulled out the energy bar she had talked about. "You can have this for your 3:00 snack." She smiled.

"Thanks!" I took the bar and corralled Brighid out into the car. The bar rode in the shotgun seat. It stayed within my peripheral vision all the way to Livermore.

"C'mon baby, let's go," I said, unbuckling Brighid's car seat buckles and taking her by the hand. The cold morning bit at us, and the overcast sky made it look like it would be awhile before we'd get relief.

"I'm not a baby," Brighid said as she stepped from the car, using my hand to support her entire weight.

"Of course not, Schmooger." We looked for schmoogers on the way home every day. They were round creatures with one piece of hair that could be any color and that lived in the almond orchards we passed on our ride.

We walked hand in hand to the daycare door while the energy bar sat, with seemed innocence, on the passenger seat of my car. Ms. Annette met us. "Good morning, Brighid."

"Hi."

"How are you doing, Jim?"

"Great thanks, you?"

Ms. Annette nodded and looked me over. "So is there going to be a time when you stop losing weight?"

The question stunned me as it did with Emmeline. I stared at the far wall of the daycare as if waiting would change the subject. "I dunno," I said.

"Cause you know, pretty soon, you'll be nothing."

"I don't have to take the high blood pressure medication anymore."

*Good deflection!*

"That's good. I just don't want you to waste away to nothing."

I laughed and looked down at my gut. "Oh I don't think that will happen anytime soon."

"You're really thin." She stirred her coffee and Brighid joined her at the child-sized table.

"I don't know." This conversation had to end.

*Don't let it bug you. It's just another jealous person without your kind of dedication.*

"You're still doing the treadmill every day?"

"Yes." I smiled. "I'm going the usual half hour and I'm almost at 5 miles per hour now."

Ms. Annette just looked at me. "Okay, well, I hope you have it under control."

"Of course."

I left the daycare and started the car. The energy bar sat on my passenger seat. I picked it up after parking and headed into my office. The back of it said that it had 8 grams of fat. That was more than I wanted in a whole day. Why would Kristin give me something like this? Did she not understand what I was doing?

*People will try and sabotage you. Misery loves company—like Jeanette from across the hall.*

The whole day, the bar sat on my desk like a fat brick. Kristin would ask me if I tried it, and I knew I better be ready with a review. Around lunch time, I tore the corner of the wrapper off and sniffed the bar. The peanut butter and the powdery smell of the wafer cookie made me sneeze.

I held the bar in my hand for a long time and read the nutrition label again. I could eat the bar if it was the only thing I ate in a day. It was too late for that though, I had already eaten breakfast.

What if I just bit off the corner? The document I was editing changed to a screen saver on my PC. The dancing triangle resized, reshaped, and changed colors in the corner of my eye while the bar in my hand commanded attention. Kristin couldn't make me eat it. I was inside a government laboratory, and she'd never even be able to see the inside of my office. There was not a chance she would find out I didn't eat it.

I walked to the far side of my office and dropped the bar in the bottom drawer of my desk. With a little shove, it shut with the finality of a cadaver drawer in the morgue.

*You did good.*

I did well.

*Whatever. You didn't mess yourself up, and you should be proud. You should be seeing the 150s pretty soon.*

My desk phone rang later in the afternoon, and Kristin's number showed on the caller ID. The bar was great. The bar was great. The bar was great. "This is Jim."

"Hey Bubbah!"

"Hey honey, how's it going?"

"Pretty good. Busy as always. How are you?"

"Ah, you know." I laughed.

"Getting ready to go home?"

"Yep. Just a few more minutes here."

"Do you think you could go by Martinizing and pick up the dry cleaning on your way home?"

Martinizing wasn't on my way home. Once I got to Modesto, I just wanted to go home. My commute was half of hers, but it tired me out just the same. It wasn't easy to drive in that traffic, interact with Brighid and her stuffed animals, and hunt for Schmoogers in the forests. "Sure, baby."

"Thanks Bubbah. I'm really running low on work clothes."

"No problem." If I told her there was a problem, then there would really be a problem.

"I love you."

"I love you too. I'll see you tonight."

"Okay. Kiss my baby for me."

"Right on."

She didn't even ask. She might later though, so I had to remember that the bar was great. I would tell her that it was light in my mouth. I would tell her anything as long as she didn't mess up my progress.

# Chapter 20

Chris was going to marry his longtime girlfriend, Julie. The wedding was in San Jose, and I was looking forward to going. I was well into the 150s by the time the wedding came around. I craved people to notice how much better I looked. The validation was almost as important as the treadmill itself...almost.

Kristin and I shopped for a new pair of pants and a new jacket. "You are starting to look like a scarecrow in your clothes," she said.

Dressed in the new clothes, we made the drive to San Jose and dropped Brighid off with my mom.

Kristin struggled to clip her necklace the entire time we drove down. When the traffic stopped us, I would reach over and try to clip it as well, but the angle while driving made it hard.

We parked at the church a few minutes before the ceremony would begin. I wanted to be in the church before it started. The embarrassment of walking into a wedding in progress was more than I could take.

"Bubbah, can you clip this now?"

I turned to her and grabbed the necklace's ends in my fingers. The fastening side was so small, I had a hard time getting it open long enough to slide the loop in. People walked past us and into the church as I opened the clip just to watch it close again before I could get the loop through. "I don't think I can do it."

She sighed a long slow breath. "Fine." She balled the necklace up and slipped it into her purse. We walked toward the church without holding hands.

The church was set up in the round with the service in the middle of stadium-style seats on three sides. The fourth side had a giant cross. The flowers in the church were fantastic, adding color to the off-white walls and dulled orange seat cushions. I remembered that Chris's mother did flowers for weddings. She was a sweet woman, and I'm sure she was very proud and happy for Chris.

My friends Mike, Martin, and Jeff were all in the wedding. Nick, another of our group, and his wife were seated one section over from us.

The ceremony started. The groom's side of the altar felt like a who's who of my life. I couldn't wait for them to see that I wasn't as fat anymore. The ceremony ended, and Kristin and I walked down the stairs to where the wedding party was waiting for the photographer to set up.

"Jimmy James!" Mike said, walking over to me and shaking my hand. He leaned in close to my ear. "Jesus Christ, man, you're looking great. You're looking like a movie star."

"Thanks man." There were no better words he could have said.

*Careful what you eat today, or you'll mess it all up.*

I made the rounds and shook hands with the other guys. Chris was beaming and I congratulated him and met his new wife, Julie. Jeff, who knew a lot about exercising and fitness, gave me a grave look while he told me it was good to see me.

"Jim Kohl!" Nick said, "I saw you up there, but I wasn't sure that was you. You have lost a lot of weight."

"Thanks, man. Hey, do you guys know where the reception is? We couldn't find the invitation." I said. "You remember Kristin, my wife?"

She and Nick hugged. "This is my wife, Heather," he said. "The reception is somewhere over near Great America. Find Chuck. He should know." Nick looked around to see if he could see Chris's brother anywhere. The hall hummed with simultaneous conversation. Chuck had blended in with the rest of the tuxes waiting for the photo opportunity.

"Dude, I see him," I said. I headed that direction with Nick not far behind. "Chuck, how's it going? Congratulations."

"Jim Kohl," Chuck said, "Man, you look great. What have you been doing?"

"Treadmill, man. Thanks. Just thirty minutes a day." We shook hands.

"You're not on Atkins?" Chuck said.

"No, just low fat and the treadmill. The old fashioned way."

"Well, it's working. You look great."

"Chuck. Do you know where the reception is?" Nick spoke up from over my right shoulder.

"It's uh…It's over near Great America. It's hard to explain."

We ended up following someone over there. It was in a hall in a parking lot that was surrounded by different halls people could rent for whatever occasion. There were a couple weddings and a quinceañera that day. The people we followed knew which hall it was, so we followed them inside and took a table with a white tablecloth and a beautiful floral centerpiece. Nick and his wife joined us.

The bar was open. "I'm going to get a drink," I said and left Kristin sitting with Heather and Nick. The bartender handed me a beer in a sturdy glass with a long stem.

*Beer makes you fat.*

After this beer, I would switch to wine.

"You didn't get me a drink?" Kristin said just as my butt hit the seat cushion.

Gastric bypass patients weren't supposed to drink alcohol or soda, and there was water on the table, but I hadn't even asked her. I was a bad husband. "I…uh…Sorry. You're not supposed to have alcohol."

"This is a wedding. I can have one drink," she said.

The left side of my face, where her eyes bore into me, burned. "Sorry. What can I get you?"

"Can you believe he didn't get me anything?" She said to Rick who had joined our table when I was at the bar. Turning back to me she said, "See if they have tequila sunrise?"

The Eagles song popped into my head as I crossed what would soon be the dance floor. "Tequila sunrise?" I said to the bartender.

"Beer, wine, and soft drinks are all we have here," she said, "Sorry."

"Okay, wine then please."

"Red or white?"

"White. I guess."

She poured the glass and I slipped a dollar in the glass jar on the bar for her trouble.

"They only have beer and wine," I said, setting the glass in front of Kristin.

"Thanks, Bubbah."

"Have you had a drink yet?" Heather asked. She had had the gastric bypass operation about a year before Kristin, and didn't look that much thinner to me.

"This is my first one," Kristin said.

"Wait till you see how it affects you." Heather laughed a long cackle. "Right to your head." She pointed to her stomach and made a sweep with her finger that ended at her temple.

After my beer was drained, I switched to red wine and stayed with that the rest of the reception. Heather got louder and drunker, but my wine buzz just made her seem fun. Kristin stayed true to her one drink. "Holy crap," she said when she was halfway through her glass, "It does go straight to your head."

I laughed. That was the last time I ever laughed when it came to Kristin and alcohol.

The hall filled in and the married couple was announced, walking through the door like a knight and his lady, hand in hand, all smiles and flashing cameras. This was horrific. Soon, it would be time to eat, and then what would I do?

Rick sat on the other side of me, and I asked where his wife, Deena, was.

"The baby is sick," he said, "So she had to stay home with him."

"Oh, that sucks," I heard myself say.

*Not as much as trying to get through this wedding with only safe food. What are they even serving? You best not have any cake.*

"Thanks yeah," he said. "It's been shitty. My dog got out and was run over." Rick had a great German Shepherd that reminded me of a dog I had as a kid.

"Oh Jesus, I'm really sorry to hear that, man," I said.

"Thanks, man." His eyes got a little watery, and I knew we needed a subject change.

"All that's up with me is I've lost 70 something pounds."

"Fuck," he said, looking down to my mid section, "yeah, you do look thinner. Good for you, man."

"I've been doing the treadmill 30-minutes a day..." I went on to give him the rap about the low-fat diet, just as I went on to give the same rap to anyone that was tolerant enough to listen. There was no cooler subject. I had a new book in the works called *Through the Fog,* but that didn't matter. Everyone could see, appreciate, and aspire to weight loss.

The time came to get in line for food. We were all here. We had music. What was with the human need for food to celebrate? Not one social gathering of any consequence is food free. At weddings, the cake is the central decoration and often elicits as much praise as the bride herself. "Oh, and the cake was beautiful." People say it all the time. We are a revolting species.

Sweat trickled down the inside of my shirt as Kristin and I stood in line for the long table with silver trays perched above blue flames. People got a plate, opened the silver coffins to check was what is in there, and scooped part of a dead animal onto their plate.

"Oh there was pasta," someone said, "Dammit—I shouldn't have filled my plate up. Oh well, I'll get some on the next round."

Buffets are heaven for fat people. Even the phrase "all you can eat" sounds like a challenge to gluttons, implying that the purpose is to over eat to get your money's worth, or in this case, the father of the bride's money's worth. To not gorge yourself is the equivalent of being financially irresponsible. Buffets manufacture fat people out of thin ones.

*Use extreme caution.*

We were about two people away from the plates and silverware, and I was praying that they had some sort of chicken breast, preferably skinless and boneless with no goop on it. That was not to be. The chicken was smeared in a creamy, semen-like sauce. Green oregano particles rounded it off. Just the oregano would have been fine.

*The fat in that sauce is infinite.*

Tell me about it.

The other choice was some sort of beef, which even without the extra sauce they drowned it in, was pure fat.

"I can't eat any of this," I said to Kristin.

"You're at a wedding."

*Don't listen to her.*

"Look at that crap all over the chicken. If that even is chicken."

"It's chicken," she said, "Take some."

"But it's…"

"Take some." She dug a fingernail into my arm and glared at me, demanding I take food. The line came to a dead stop behind us, and it was clear she wouldn't move until she got her way.

With a sigh, I scooped the smallest piece of chicken from the white muck and onto my plate. I would have used the serving spoon to cut it in half, but Kristin watched me. I took some of the vegetables too even though they were coated in oil. She didn't push the issue with the potatoes because I didn't eat them much even before my diet, and I got away without taking a dinner roll as well.

There was no way to scrape all that slime off the chicken. There were microscopic nooks in the chicken that the sauce flooded—little poultry caves that I couldn't see much less clean out.

*She made you take it, but she can't make you eat it.*

True enough. A couple of the oily green beans made it into my mouth. I found the corner of the chicken that looked the driest and cut my bite from there. The rest of the people at the table ate and talked. No one paid attention to what I was doing. A crumpled cloth napkin on my plate hid the rest of that gunk-logged chicken. The morning treadmill would take care of the oily green beans and whatever amount of that fatty sauce made it into me by mistake.

*But you would have been better off without having taken either of those in. It's undone the work you have already done. You are a failure.*

I'm so fucking stupid. Around me at the table forks clinked against plates and piles of the fat moved from the table to everyone's mouths. I sat back and sipped at my red wine. Heather laughed like Janis Joplin, and Nick talked about politics. Rick went to get more food.

*You have no control. Do you want to be a fat loser forever? Look at your gut.*

I kept my eyes on the people at my table and laughed at the appropriate times.

*Look at your gut.*

Under the table, I pinched the repulsive roll of fat that lumped under my shirt. I checked the eyes at the table and, certain that none of them were on me; I looked down to see my gut flapping over the top of my Dockers. My tie lay on my chest like an arrow pointing down to my fat. I pulled my jacket tighter around me, but all that did was show my bulges beneath a tighter jacket. There was no escape.

The wine helped though. I kept a steady pace on the wine all day long. It made me feel good enough to relax. I avoided the wedding cake though. The wine made me relax—not insane.

# Chapter 21

I did all the grocery shopping for our family, so I was in control of what food came into the house. Kristin had what she wanted me to buy, and if I forgot to or even if the store was out of what she asked for, I beat myself up for hours. The look of disappointment on her face was too much for me. It was failure, and it was mine.

My diet and treadmill seldom disappointed.

*The energy bars that you eat in the afternoon have 2 grams of fat.*

I held one of those bars now in the health food aisle of the grocery store. Each day, I would eat one of these bars at 3 pm. I bought 7 of them every Saturday, so I would always have a week's worth. If I didn't have the bar, it was better not to eat anything at all. My regimen was precise, perfect, and improving all the time.

*You know what has less fat than those energy bars?*

There were only 4 of the kind of bar I ate at the store that day. That meant there would be three days with no bar. If either of those days were not work days, Kristin might see and she might butt in and try and make me eat something else.

*Raw spinach leaves.*

I set the 4 bars back on the shelf and pushed my cart to the produce section.

"Why are we going back here, Daddy?"

"I forgot something, honey."

Near the lettuce and pre-bagged salads was a bag of spinach leaves. Kristin had me buy them before and she used them in a pasta dish, but there was no law against eating them plain and out of the bag. From that day forward, there was a rule about raw spinach. I ate 5 leaves of it a day at 3 pm.

In the frozen entrée aisles, I examined all the Lean Cuisine boxes until I found the one with the least fat: Chicken Marsala. I bought one to try it and enough of my regular Mexican food ones for the rest of the week. I loved grocery shopping. No one was watching.

"Hey baby, we're home."

"Did you remember creamer?"

"Shit!" I said.

"I'll take that as a no," she said, walking down the stairs to the kitchen where I set the blue plastic bags on the ground.

"I am so sorry baby."

"It's all right," she said, but she didn't really mean it.

My throat dried in failure. How selfish could I be? Just because I don't use creamer, I didn't think to get her some. She even said it to me on the way out the door. I pressed my hand against my face and then I felt the fat building up under my chin.

*You can't remember to get your wife a simple item that most people use in coffee and you have a double chin.*

The reflection in the glass door of the oven showed that to be the truth. I pinched that fat again.

"What are you doing?" Kristin said.

"Nothing."

She walked from the kitchen, and I put away the groceries.

On the weekends, I didn't get up early to do the treadmill, and I rarely was up early enough to write. When the groceries were put away, I went upstairs to change into my workout clothes.

"Bubbah, can you get a load of laundry going?" She was somewhere downstairs.

"Sure."

The mirror caught my attention as I was getting ready to put on my shirt. It was the bathroom mirror, and it cut my body off right below the stomach. I grabbed my stomach and wrapped my fat up in my fist. The scale said 154. I had four more pounds before this decade would be behind me, and still the fat sat on me. I turned around to see how fat I looked from behind. "I never look better."

*You didn't pinch off as much cereal this morning as you normally do.*

It was the weekend.

*And if you followed the plan closer on the weekends, you'd have much more success. You wouldn't be hovering in the mid-150s seeing if you'd ever succeed. You'd have the 150s beaten by now.*

"True enough."

"Did you say something honey?" Kristin called from downstairs.

"Just talking to myself...Like a lunatic."

The pile of laundry mountained to the left of the television in our room. I started separating out a dark load until the laundry basket was full. I picked it up by the rim and pushed open my bedroom door with the hulking weight of the basket. About three steps from the bottom, I lost my footing somehow and fell the remaining way down. Laundry littered the bottom of the stair case and my ankle throbbed.

My ankle had slammed to the floor and bent my foot in as it hit. Pain brought nausea, and I breathed heavy trying to stop the flow from my stomach. The room spun, and Kristin's voice sounded far from me. "Are you okay?"

My senses returned. "Shit!" I said.

"Are you okay? What happened?"

That seemed like the stupidest question ever, but I answered it anyway. "I guess I lost my footing coming down the stairs." Another wave of nausea pushed me against the floor. "Fuck." Every morning I worked hard to make my characters say just the right thing in a given situation, and when I am actually in trauma, profanity is pretty much the best I can do.

"Can you stand up?" Kristin said.

*You have to stand up. You have to get on the treadmill.*

"I think so," I said, rolling from a seated position to being on all fours. My stomach tried to pump its contents to the floor, but I willed them to stay down. "Yeah, I'm fine."

I stood and my ankle throbbed.

*She won't let you on the treadmill if she thinks you're hurt.*

I grit my teeth and took a step. It hurt, but I could walk. If I could walk, I could do the treadmill. The room spun a little slower as I gathered the clothes that fell from the basket and piled them back in. The extra weight from the basket made walking harder, but I couldn't miss a day of treadmill—not at this stage. High blood pressure wasn't a threat right now, but it could easily be a problem again. One missed day on the treadmill would lead to another, just as one fast food meal would lead to more. Next thing you know, your weight is back up, your health is gone, and you can't fit in your clothes.

*Right. Now you're thinking straight.*

I started the washer and piled the clothes into it, drew a circle around them with a lid full of liquid Tide, and set the basket on top of the dryer on my way to the garage. The treadmill made me smile. I fired up the fan that kept me cool during my walk, and fit the headphones over my ears to see what was going on in my book on tape.

The motor geared up and started moving the belt that I straddled until it got to the right speed. The first ten minutes were hard and I found I had to slow down my normal pace a little because of this damn ankle, but doing the treadmill a little slower was better than not doing it at all. Right?

*It's going to slow your progress. Let yourself warm up, and then push the speed again. You could always go longer than the half hour.*

My ankle hurt less the more I walked on it. I was able to get the treadmill up to my normal speed, but not for the full half hour. The seconds counted up to the 30-minute mark in red numbers on the upper right hand side of the treadmill's control panel.

*You feel good. Go an extra 5 minutes.*

The sweat on my lower back was pouring down, and a pretty good flow also glazed my face. The digital calorie counter was not to the number it would have been had I been able to keep up the full half hour at my normal speed.

*Now's the time to push it. You have nowhere to go; it's the weekend.*

I have things I have to do. I need to get Brighid lunch soon and finish the laundry.

*This is the only thing you do just for you. You don't see Kristin worrying about whether her nail appointment is taking too much time.*

But when the red 29 turned to a 30, I pulled the ignition key and let the treadmill wind to a stop. Sweat dripped into my eye, and I blinked away the blinding burn. I took my water bottle, turned off the fan, and went back into the house in time to move the load of laundry from the washer to the dryer.

Kristin sat on the couch in front of the TV. "How was the treadmill?" she said.

"Great." My lungs pumped hard, trying to normalize my breathing. "But I had to take it a little slower at first cause of this ankle. I didn't get my full good 30 minutes."

"You'll be fine." She didn't look away from the TV.

"You really think so?" I got the laundry basket and let it dangle in my hand against my good leg. "It's really bugging me."

No answer.

"Babe, it's really bugging me that I couldn't do my normal treadmill stuff."

No answer.

"Honey?"

The glue gaze she had with the TV broke. "Huh? What? I'm sorry."

"I said it's really bugging me that I wasn't able to do my normal treadmill stuff. Do you think it's going to be okay?" My ankle throbbed again sending electric pain up my spine. I leaned a little harder on my other leg.

"Is what going to be okay?" she said.

That was a good question. 'Everything,' is what came to mind, but it sounded like a stupid thing to say. It felt like the right answer though. "You know," I said. The obviousness of what I meant made it feel like she was messing with me. What I really wondered was how fast I would gain weight having not done my normal treadmill. Could she already see the fat building back?

I pinched my stomach.

*There is more, isn't there. I told you to go longer. She is too busy with the TV to keep track of your time out there.*

"You'll be fine," she said. The TV had her attention again. I had an attentive wife during commercials breaks.

*She doesn't know what she's talking about.*

I used the banister more than usual on my way up the stairs. I filled the laundry basket again, so it would be ready for the washer after my shower. I kicked off my right shoe and went to do the same to my left when the dizzying pain punched me in the gut and I struggled not to vomit. The ceiling spun around the still ceiling fan as I lay on my back and tried to catch my breath.

When things settled, I sat up and sighed. I reached down to carefully untie my shoe and pull it off. There was no blood on the sock, which surprised me. As bad as it felt, I expected to see the bone jabbing through the skin. I peeled away the sock, revealing a large purple bruise that wrapped from my ankle over half the top of my foot.

"Fuck," I said, looking again as if the first time had been some sort of mirage. The purple skin ached to the touch. How could I have done the treadmill with my ankle looking like this?

*Because you have to.*

I limped to the shower and got the water hot as I could stand it. It hurt to stand. Walking wasn't so easy either, but I hadn't noticed this so much during the workout. There was laundry to do though. My ankle went back to its normal color eventually, but I never missed a day of treadmill.

# Chapter 22

Americans are unique in their celebration of Thanksgiving, a holiday that is literally about preparing and then eating more food than the group of people participating would need for a single meal. It's gluttony in the guise of thankfulness. Thanksgiving also kicked off the holiday season, where you were lucky if you started the new year at the same weight you were in early November. It sickened me.

Normally, we would go to my mom's house for this and stop by Kristin's sister Bunnie's house on the way home. Kristin came to me in early November with another plan.

"Has your mom asked you about Thanksgiving yet?" she said over the phone.

I sat at my desk at work and leaned back in my chair. "No. Why?"

"Good. I want to have Thanksgiving with my family this year."

"You mean at our house?" Kristin's mother didn't cook. Bunnie had her church friends over, but they were all gone by the time we, her "worldly" family, showed up. There were certain brothers and sisters that we didn't speak to, but who we spoke to changed depending on who was off drugs. Her brother Danny sometimes showed up when you invited him, but most of the time he didn't.

"No. Juanita invited us up."

"Oh! Right on." That meant Thanksgiving with Uncle Art. "That's cool."

"So tell your mom we can't make it this year," she said.

"Okay. When she asks, I will."

"No. Tell her now. Call her now, and then call me back and tell me what she says."

"I'm busy right now," I said, glancing at the document on my screen, which was partially hidden behind an e-mail I was writing to a friend.

"Jim."

"All right, fine. I'll call her."

"And then call me back."

"Okay." I folded shut my cell phone, set it on my desk, and went back to the e-mail I'd been writing. In ten minutes, I would

111

call her back and tell her that I got my mom's voicemail. The guilt of the lie would eat at me. Maybe I could skip lunch all together.

*That would be good.*

I had a chicken marsala Lean Cuisine. If I could just eat the chicken...

*Cutting the lunch in half is a good start. You don't need that much food to function.*

I know. Most people over eat and don't even realize it.

Maybe a week or two later, my mom brought up Thanksgiving, and I told her we were already invited somewhere else. She was disappointed, but she understood. "Diane's going to be disappointed too," she said, "She hardly ever gets to see you and Brighid."

"I know. I'm sorry. Kristin just really wants to spend it with her family this year."

The subject changed, but the tone of the conversation stayed the same. I had hurt her and probably my sister too. Uncle Art lived in Stockton—far enough from San Jose that there was no way we could split the holiday like we had in previous years with my family and Kristin's sister.

*Why do people even care anyway? See how important food is? Thanksgiving is just a Thursday, but since there is a traditional meal involved, people get their feelings hurt.*

Still though, I was a bad person. I had disappointed my mother and sister and lied about when I disappointed them to my wife. I pictured the scale, which we had moved to our bedroom when Uncle Art installed a tile floor for us. If that scale showed me a lower number tomorrow morning, most of this guilt would be washed away, and I could know I was a good person. Numbers don't lie.

If it was more though, my failure would be complete.

I'd been hovering around the mid 150s for a time now, and I had to do something about that.

Thanksgiving came and the 5 of us piled into Kristin's SUV. Kristin spent the entire night before in the kitchen making pumpkin pies from Halloween pumpkins and her trademark magnolia pecan pie that used white chocolate instead of brown sugar. That magnolia pecan pie was my favorite, and I had to get through the day without having any. The challenge was that Kristin would be very upset if I didn't have any. She loved to cook and bake, and for her the best part was to see other people enjoy what she made.

The pies rode in the back of the SUV, stacked in boxes as if they were coming from a factory. "Did you put a blanket on top of the boxes so that they don't move around in there?"

"Yes." I said.

"Did you push it down so it could act like padding?"

"Yes."

I got the feeling that she would leave the kids at home before she would leave the pies there. If it were legal, one of the kids might have had to ride in the box and the pies would have had a seatbelt.

"Dominique, can you make sure that box isn't sliding around back there."

We arrived safely in Stockton, and to Kristin's great relief, so did the pies. Juanita's house was always busy with three kids around Brighid's age. She let us in and we all hugged her. "I gotta get back to the kitchen," she said, and she scurried across the white tile floor and rounded the corner toward the stove.

Brighid found the kids and disappeared among a mountain of toys. Dominique and Lorenzo plopped down in front of the TV, and Kristin and I joined Juanita in the kitchen.

"So how have you guys been? I'm so glad you came!" Juanita said as she tended to the food on the stove and in the oven.

"We've been good."

"You look really good, Girl," Juanita said, "But the last time I saw you, you were in the hospital." She laughed as she mashed potatoes.

The talk went on about what we were up to and how we were doing and what the kids said and did. Then the gossip round started with tales of who was on drugs, who was off drugs, who said what messed up thing to whom, and who was no longer on good terms with anyone. Juanita had her back to us and glanced over her shoulder on occasion as she talked, padding around the kitchen barefoot.

She never once brought up how I looked, and it deflated me. I knew for a fact that I was noticeably thinner than the last time I had seen her. The scale proved it, and so did my clothes. Someday maybe the mirror would agree. The two women talked, but to me it had reduced itself to clucking.

*Kristin told everyone not to notice your weight loss.*

Would she have? Would she really bother with that? She told Juanita a story about someone at work, and I studied the side of her face and the flexing of her jawbone.

The doorbell rang and the door opened at the same time. Netty, Juanita's sister, walked through the door with her kids. "Hey, girl!" Netty said to Kristin, and the two hugged.

"Hey," Kristin said, "Where's Javier?"

"He'll be over later," Netty said. "How have you been, Jim?" Netty's eyes popped open, and she looked me up and down. "My God, you're so thin."

*Kristin didn't talk to her.*

"Thanks."

"What are you doing?" Her eyes jumped back and forth across my face as she reached to hug me.

"Treadmill and just not eating fatty foods and whatever."

"You don't need to lose anymore," she said, her hands still on my biceps.

"Can't be too rich or too thin," I said.

"Yeah..." she said, "I guess." Her eyes dropped down to my middle again.

*She can see your tremendous gut as well as you can. You better watch what you eat today.*

Soon, the house filled and the beer and talk flowed. Uncle Art held court in a chair in the backyard, and talked in Spanish with some people I didn't know. Carl, Juanita's husband, came home. Kids were everywhere and their laughing overpowered the constant prattle of the TV.

I took a chair near Uncle Art, who changed his talk to mostly English for my benefit. He told a story about getting caught stealing a car when he was young. After the punchline, he said, "How are you, mejo?"

"I'm doing great, Uncle Art, thanks. How are you?"

"Pretty good," he finished his Budweiser. He looked me over from head to stomach. "Are you eating?"

"Yeah, all the time."

"I hope so," he said. "I had a nephew stop eating before."

"I promise you I'm eating."

He looked me in the face with his beer-watery eyes. "Okay," he said.

Like any Thanksgiving, food was everywhere. There were snack trays of various types all throughout the house. The guilt of Uncle Art's concern sent me to one filled with vegetables encircling a tub of ranch dressing. There were cherry tomatoes.

*Fruits have carbs.*

The safest foods there were the carrots and the celery. I grabbed a piece of celery and bit the end off to be social.

*Are you sure no ranch dressing dripped on that stalk by mistake?*

I examined what was left of the stick in my hand. There was no sign of the white goop, but I had no idea about the part that I was getting ready to swallow. Once you swallow it's too late. There is no way I'd make myself throw up. That was unhealthy.

I took another stick of celery and then another. They were mostly water and probably one of the safest foods in the house. The partition of the tray that I had been attacking looked empty, so I started on the other partition that sat diagonal from the first one.

I heard a voice and looked over toward the kitchen. Raquel and Kristin were watching me. Even before I started this diet, people were always fascinated with what I ate and had to point out if I was having a huge burger or whatever it was.

"You liking that celery?" Raquel said.

"Yeah, it rocks," I said.

"I'm sure," she said to Kristin, "look at him going on that celery." She mimed a piece and pretended to systematically grind it to pieces in her mouth. "Mmm," she said, "This celery is delicious."

You don't eat food for the taste, I thought to myself, you eat it because you have to. All food is vile, but at least celery is safe.

*Now you get it.*

The turkey came out of the oven and Kristin and her cousin's started preparing things for the meal. My stomach tied itself in knots. "Bubbah, will you go make sure Brighid is cleaned up so she can eat?"

"Sure."

I found Brighid in the family room with a toy truck in her hand. "C'mon honey. Let's go wash your hands up for dinner."

She dropped the truck and took my hand so we could walk to the bathroom.

"Are you gonna make Brighid a plate?" Kristin said when we joined the others in the dining room where the table was set up like a buffet.

"Yeah." Brighid stood by me and I asked her what she wanted. She said yes or no as we made our way down the line of food on the table. When she had all she wanted, I sat her down with the other kids at the kitchen table and returned to the dining room to get my food.

This was hard. I took the thinnest piece of white breast meat I could find. The stuffing was way too fattening, but I took a small dollop anyway. Cranberry sauce seemed pretty safe.

*Your plate is already too full. Don't eat that much.*

Dare I put gravy on my meat?

*That would be stupid.*

The hum of talk and screams of laughter filled the room as I worked to make my plate look filled without filling it. I added a small amount of salad and found a place to eat alone.

As if that wasn't bad enough, dessert came next. "Bubbah, can you help me with the pies."

I got up off my isolated spot on the couch where I pretended to be engrossed in some movie I had seen before and hurried to her side in the kitchen. We lifted the pies from their transport box and pealed the foil back from the tops of them.

"Oooh! Those look good, girl!" Juanita said as she flew by on the way to help her youngest out of the high chair.

"I boiled the pumpkins myself. These are real pumpkin pies," Kristin said.

"Nuh-uh."

"Hell yeah."

"No way." Juanita came in for a closer look.

"Yeah," Kristin said, "Huh, Bubbah?"

"Yeah. It's a crazy process. I don't like to be in the house when she's doing it."

"I get a little crazy," Kristin said.

"I'm that way when I'm cooking too," Juanita said.

"And these are magnolia pecan pies. They're different than normal ones because instead of brown sugar..."

*You better think of a way not to have any dessert.*

I was working on it, but since she was probably going to have me help serve, that would be a challenge—it would just be me, her, the pies, and that look when I wouldn't take any.

She cut into the first circle of fat and the fleshy pumpkin reminded me of worms twisted around in an intestine-like array. She handed the plate to me and I shivered. Then, she sliced into the pecan one. "Just start passing them out."

The kids were gathered around the coffee table in the living room. Dominique was seated in the corner of the cream-colored couch, and I started with her.

"Thanks," she said, looking as bored as a teenager should.

Juanita and Raquel were also making runs between the pies and the people, so it wouldn't be just me and Kristin in the end if I timed it right. No. She would probably serve us last, and then it would be just me and her with me saying I didn't want any. It could only get worse from there.

*She shouldn't care what you eat.*

But she did. It would be nothing less than an insult if I didn't eat what she made. It would make for an evening where no one would talk to me once we left here. I thought of the thick silent air between us for the half-hour ride home from Stockton and shook the thought away.

*One bite is too much.*

Then we'd get home and I'd put Brighid to bed. The older kids would watch TV downstairs and Kristin and I would sit in bed. I'd beg her to talk to me, but she wouldn't. Then I'd lay awake all night a foot away from a woman that wouldn't talk to me. I'd wake her a couple times to beg to talk it out and she'd just get angrier.

"Wait...what?"

"I said, can you check in some of Juana's drawers to see if you can find more forks," Kristin said.

The third drawer I tried had the silverware in a neat divider. I took the remaining forks to Kristin.

"Do you want some of each?" Kristin said, with a blank paper plate ready for me.

"I...um..."

"What?" She said. Her voice sharpened.

I gnawed on the inside of my cheek.

"You don't want any, do you?" Her stare chilled and bore into my skull.

"I'll take a small piece of the pecan."

Her attention fell to what was left of the pecan pie in front of her. She cut me a sliver.

*That's too big. Tell her that's too big.*

"Thanks," I said, taking the plate and grabbing a fork.

The skinny triangle of pie was barely large enough to wedge a door open. I stood near the staircase and studied it. My breath became rapid; the gnawing on the inside of my cheek intensified. Dare I take a bite of this? I thought of Eliot's Prufrock questioning whether he should upset the universe by eating a peach.

It felt like the heat of a spotlight shone down on me. The heat of embarrassment pumped into my face. I checked the room though, and the family laughed, talked, and joked as if I weren't there at all. It would be easy to find a garbage can to dump this in.

*And that's exactly what you should do.*

Raquel appeared in the opening to the kitchen, which was my clearest shot to a garbage can with the least amount of questioning. Even to get to the bathroom, I would need to go through that opening. Going up the stairs was too chancy—everyone could see me from their spot in the dining room, and really I had no business going up the stairs.

My choices were gone. I had to eat it. I sighed at the prospects. You could only walk around the house balancing a pie slice on a paper plate for so long before people would start asking questions. When was the last time any dessert had made it past my lips? I couldn't remember.

I stabbed into the pie and brought the bite to my mouth. I chewed it. Taste wasn't important—I just had to get it over with. With the next forkful, the piece was half gone already. Maybe if I swallowed it whole, there would be less fat added to me? Maybe the more carefully I chewed, the more fat I'd burn off during the eating process.

There was no way around it. I was putting poison into my system and destroying the progress. I was undoing what I worked so hard for so long to do.

*You are one worthless piece of work. You had options to get rid of the pie without being caught. You are weak and undisciplined. You are not good enough. You never will be.*

The car ride home was silent anyway, except for the choice phrases I had for myself in my own private thoughts.

# Chapter 23

Emmeline met me in front of my office for our weekly walk over to the cafeteria. Her eyes widened when I came out of the door. "How's it going?" I said.

The shocked look on her face pleased me. It meant I was thinner than the last time I saw her. No matter how I looked in the mirror, these shocked looks proved that my progress was still good. Of course, 20 minutes after the shocked look and whatever conversation they brought on, I could see my flabby gut again. I'd pinch at it to see how bad it was. I'd do the same with my double chin.

"I'm fine," she said, "How are you?"

With a shrug, I said, "Oh, you know. Same old stuff."

"Yeah?" she said, with her tone sounding as pregnant as she was.

"Yeah. You know."

"You're really looking thin, Jim." The worry in her voice overtook the shock, and left me in an awkward situation. Causing worry wasn't the plan. Staying healthy and showing people that even someone as fat as me could get thin was the plan. That and the lower number on the scale were the most important things I knew.

"Thanks."

"No. It's not a good thin. With me gaining weight with this baby and the way you are losing, our weights will probably meet each other at some point."

"I'm 153."

"They've already met then," she said. She walked on my right side as we cut through parking lots on the way to the cafeteria. "You said a while back you might think about going to see a therapist."

"Yeah."

*You don't need that. You are doing fine. Since when is having great diet and exercise ideas insanity? You should write a diet book is what you should do. After you're thin, of course.*

"I really think it's about time you do that."

"Really?" I said.

"Yes," she said, "Like when you came over for my baby shower, I saw you there not eating anything."

"I ate before I got there."

"Uh-huh."

"No, really. I did. I had a Lean Cuisine." I needed to assure her that I was all right. "I really feel good. There's no problem or anything."

"If there's no problem, then seeing a therapist won't hurt. They'll just be able to tell you that there's no problem, and you'll be fine."

*A therapist will find a problem with you. That is how they make their money.*

"I wouldn't even know how to go about finding a therapist," I said.

"Do you have Kaiser?"

"Yeah."

"If you call the Advice Nurse, they can usually refer you to someone. Or if not, they can give you the number to call where you can talk to someone that can refer you."

"And you really think I need this?" Cars crawled by at the Lab's strictly enforced 25 mph speed limit.

"Yes."

"And you really think that seeing someone like that can help?"

"I think," she said, "That you have little control of your life. I think that is causing this whole not-eating thing."

"I eat."

Her look changed from concerned to annoyed. "You are too skinny, Jim."

"Seriously?" I said it like she had just brought the subject up for the first time.

"Yes. And you really need to get some help."

I opened the cafeteria door for her and found a table. I had eaten my Lean Cuisine at my desk—well half of it—before I met Emmeline. Gabrielle wasn't in the cafeteria yet, and maybe she wouldn't be. I didn't mind advice from Emmeline, but I didn't feel like I knew Gabrielle well enough to really get into how things were.

And how were things anyway? I tossed them all around my head while I waited for Emmeline to get her food. I was eating, and I had never felt better in my whole life. Jeans that used to be tight needed cinching with a belt now. What could be finer than all that?

*Yep. And she is trying to get you to ruin it. You heard her. She's jealous that your weight dropped below hers because of her pregnancy. That's what this is about.*

I spun the salt shaker on the table, testing its balance. Maybe I should see someone.

*You don't have a problem.*

Maybe I do.

Emmeline joined me at the table, with a bowl of soup and a small salad. "What did you mean when you said I have no control of my life?" I said.

"Just from everything you've told me over the time I've known you, it doesn't seem like you have much choice in what happens to you. Dominique is a problem, and you know what should be done, but Kristin undermines you."

"Not all the time," I said.

"That's just one example."

*She is feeding you crap right out of a textbook. Remember, she has a psych degree. Anyone who has ever watched a talk show can tell you that anorexia comes from a lack of control in your life. She doesn't know your life.*

I worked my upper lip against my lower teeth. "Maybe I will look into seeing someone."

*No!*

"Please do."

Kristin sat in a TV daze on the couch. During the next commercial break, I planned to bring up counseling.

My chance came when Entertainment Tonight gave way to an ad for credit counselors.

"Remember when we did that?" She said, breaking the bond with the TV and looking my way.

"Yep," I said, "We probably should have just filed for bankruptcy."

"I heard that."

"Hey, I was talking to Emmeline today at lunch."

"Yeah."

"You know, she was saying that maybe I ought to think about seeing a therapist or something about this whole weight thing." I waited for the reaction. Kristin didn't believe in therapists and thought that they were for the weak.

"Do you think you need that?"

"No."

"Well, there's your answer then," she said.

I had limited time. The first commercial was already over. "But Emmeline is convinced I do, and she has a psychology degree. So I don't know. Maybe I do need to see someone."

"Then find someone to see." Kristin's eyes were already back on the TV waiting to see whose secret celebrity wedding was crashed by paparazzi.

"Really? You think so?" I said, wishing for more commercials.

"I told you what I thought, but for some reason, you care what Emmeline says. So do what you want."

"So you really don't think I have any kind of a problem at all?"

She paused as if in thought. "You are getting really skinny. How much do you weigh now anyway?"

*Lie to her!*

"160."

"Still?" She broke her bond with the TV again to look at me. I couldn't tell whether she bought it or not, but she didn't question me further.

My voice stuck somewhere just above my lungs, so I nodded.

"Well, it's up to you. You know how I feel about it," she said, returning her attention to the Hollywood gossip.

She was right about that. The challenge was finding out how I felt about it. How many times a week would I need to go? Would it affect my exercise time at all? Would I still be able to get to bed early so I could get up to do the treadmill and write?

I wasn't crazy though, and that is what therapists were for, right? I mean, I was fine.

*Better than fine, and if you stick to the regimen, you'll be perfect someday. Emmeline is pregnant and hormonal. She's smart and all, but you can't trust what she says. Not right now. You have too much to lose.*

I let a couple days pass and thought about it. At work, it was Emmeline's pleading face and voice echoing in my mind. At home, I knew that I would be admitting a weakness if I got an appointment. I got to the end of a section in a thick document about Lab security, when I looked over at my phone. I pinched my gut and checked the thickness of my double chin.

*You would be wasting the therapist's time. There are people who really need a therapist, and you would be taking up their appointment time.*

But Emmeline's voice and face pushed through those thoughts for a moment. I looked up the number for Kaiser and reached for the phone.

# *Chapter 24*

Dr. Porter's office was in a converted house near the edge of downtown Modesto. It had no parking lot, and it was hard to find at night. There was no sign in front of it, and people lived in the houses on either side.

I parked my car by a tree and stepped up the uneven curb. Near the front door was the name of the office, and Dr. Porter's name was there, washing away my fear that I would walk in on some family in the middle of dinner.

There was a woman putting on her coat behind the receptionist window that had been carved out of what was once the foyer to the house. I stepped to the window.

"Oh," she said, turning to see me, "Can I help you?"

"I have a 7 o'clock appointment with Dr. Porter," I said.

"Is this your first time here?"

"Yes."

*They are never going to believe you have a fear of food the way you told the Kaiser advice nurse you did. You are way too fat for that. They will laugh about you when you are gone.*

The woman pointed around the small reception cage as if her eye were on the end of her finger. She found a couple forms and put them on a clipboard for me. "You'll need to fill these all out. Dr. Porter will need to review them to have some background on you before he sees you."

I took the clipboard and took a seat in the waiting room next to a small table covered in magazines. They wanted to know my name, address, and insurance information. There were about ten blank lines where I was to briefly describe the reason I was here. For that, I said possible anorexia and a fear of food.

"I'm off now," the receptionist said as she turned off the light and shut the sliding window between her office and the waiting room, "But if you'll just leave the forms on the counter ledge here…" She tapped the counter.

"Okay," I said.

Another man stepped from the restroom and took a seat in the waiting room. I wondered what kind of crazy he was. I was fine. I was here to verify once and for all that I didn't have anorexia.

But I did have a weight obsession. I definitely liked the treadmill more than your average person.

*You just have really good diet ideas.*

Yeah. That's true.

*This is just a huge waste of your time.*

That's probably true too, but it did get me out of the house and gave me a night off from getting Brighid ready for bed.

I completed the forms and took the clipboard and pen and set them on the counter. I moved as sanely as I could in case the other guy there was watching me for signs of craziness. This way, he would know that I was safe to share a waiting room with and that I was not on the verge of going on a psychotic rampage. "Don't worry, dude," I thought to myself, "I'm a safe kind of crazy."

The man didn't make eye contact or give me any other clue as to what sort of nutjob he was. I opened the book I brought to read and avoided looking at him.

A moment later, a door opened and a teenage girl came out followed by a man with glasses and a notepad. My waiting room partner stood. "Ready to go, honey?" he said.

"Yep," the teen said.

"Thanks a lot, doctor," the man said, "So we'll see you next week then?"

"Yes. You guys have a good one," the therapist said, and he retreated behind the door he came from.

I had been the only nutjob in the waiting room.

*There is a lot of fat in nuts.*

An older man with glasses and white hair walked down the stairs. The top of a pack of Marlboros poked out of his red shirt pocket. He picked up the clipboard with my forms on it. After studying the first page, he flipped to the second and looked up at me. "You Jim?"

"Yeah," I said.

"I'm Dr. Porter. I'll be with you in just a few minutes."

"Right on."

Dr. Porter headed out the front door and I saw him reach for his smokes just before he stepped out of my line of sight.

*You are not thin enough to be anorexic. He will never believe you have a problem. You are taking up an appointment that some other person could have really used.*

My throat felt dry.

*If you drink anything now, you can expect that extra water weight on you in the morning.*

The bells on the inside door handle jingled, and Dr. Porter stepped inside. "Pretty cold out there."

"Yeah," I said.

"Well, you ready to go up?" He motioned toward the winding stairway he had come down a few minutes before.

I followed him up the stairs thinking of the day I made the call to Kaiser to make this appointment. "Fear of eating," the nurse had said, "I wish I had a little of that myself."

After setting the appointment, I dialed Emmeline's extension. "I'm really glad to hear that, Jim, good for you."

"If that's what you think you need," Kristin had said.

I followed Dr. Porter into what was once a large bedroom and was now a large office. His framed diplomas and certifications decorated the walls. From the pictures on his desk, he either had a daughter in her 20s or a very young wife. I saw the long couch against one wall and thought of the many cartoons showing someone laying there and pouring their guts out while the psychiatrist scribbles manic notes. I chose the chair near the window.

"I was told I'd only be charged my regular Kaiser co pay. Is that right?"

"It should be," he said. He set the papers I filled out on his desk and took the chair nearest the desk. "So, what is it I can do for you?"

"I have a real aversion to food. I hate eating it, and I hate the way it feels in my mouth. I'm scared of gaining weight. I weigh myself at least three times a day—sometimes more." I paused and noticed that he wasn't writing anything down. "I hate you know, that feeling of being full. I do anything I can to avoid that. As a matter of fact, I get kind of a rush off of feeling hungry."

"And these are things you want to change?"

*No.*

"I guess so."

"You guess so?" Dr. Porter said.

"Well yeah, I mean. It wasn't really my idea to come here."

"Your wife's?"

"No. I have a friend at work that said she thinks I'm developing, if I don't already have an eating disorder."

"Do you think you have an eating disorder?"

I shrugged.

"But your friend does. How about your wife?"

"She thinks I'm too skinny. She's said she doesn't want me to lose any more weight."

"And you've lost weight since she told you that."

"Yes," I said. Is this how this was supposed to go? The guy didn't write down a single thing I had said so far.

"And how about you? Would you like to lose more weight?"

*Don't tell him. It's a trap.*

"Yes."

*Are you not listening?*

"Why?" Dr. Porter said.

I felt my face twist into a puzzled expression.

"I mean you seem thin enough to me. So why would you want to lose more weight?"

I thought and stared at the purples, blues, and reds of the abstract painting that hung above the couch against the wall to my right. How did people make money off that kind of thing and my books didn't sell?

*Cause you are a nobody.*

"Because I like to."

"Like to?"

"Yes. I like to lose weight. It makes me feel good about myself."

"Does it make you feel good because people compliment you?"

"Well there's that, yeah," I said, "But there's also just the sense of accomplishment I get from seeing the lower numbers on the scale."

"Tell me more about that," Dr. Porter said.

"There's not much more to say," I said, shaking my head. "I just feel really good when the numbers on the scale are lower."

"What's lower?"

"Like one pound lower."

"What if the scale is one pound higher?"

I shuddered. "It makes me a little nervous."

"Nervous?" he asked.

"Yeah. You know…It kind of freaks me out."

"Can you still go to work when you are one pound heavier?"

"Yes."

127

"So it doesn't get to the point where you can't function." He adjusted his glasses on his nose and shifted his weight in his chair.

"No. But I do think about it all day, and I usually do things to try and make myself lighter so I can feel success."

"Like vomiting?"

"God no. Like wiping down my body of the excess sweat—I always weigh before and after I am on the treadmill in the morning," I said. "Or by forcing myself to go to the bathroom. That kind of stuff."

"Do you use laxatives?"

"No."

*But what a great idea. Thanks, Doc.*

"How many calories are you eating each day?"

"I don't keep track of that. I count my fat grams, and I keep them below 10."

He paused and nodded. "You know, it's not fat grams that will make you gain weight so much as it is calories."

"Really?" I said.

*Another excellent tip! Thank you again, Dr. Porter. I wish we had found you sooner.*

"Yeah," he said. "Now what is it you'd like to accomplish here?"

That wasn't such an easy question. After all, I was fine. My discipline level was exemplary. Emmeline came to mind. "I want to fix this eating disorder before it gets out of control."

"You think you have an eating disorder."

"No, but my friend thinks I do," I said. Hadn't I already said that? Is this guy listening?

*This guy is perfect.*

"Your friends. Yeah."

"And I'd also like to take care of this problem without getting on any kinds of meds."

"Okay," he said. He appeared to be in thought, but maybe that was just a look you can master after so many years in his profession.

"So what do I do?" I said to remind him that I was in the room.

"Well, first of all, you don't have anorexia because men don't get anorexia."

*I love this doctor. Did I mention that? We can keep doing what we are doing because we can't possibly have anorexia.*

"Really?"

He nodded. "Typically, it's a young girl that gets anorexia."

"Ah," I said.

"What you have is some sort of an anxiety disorder."

"Really?"

"Mmm hmm." He nodded. "They come in a variety of forms. Yours is centered around food. I've got some other patients that have them regarding work, germs, leaving the house. It can be almost anything that can bring it on."

"So I am not an anorexic?"

"That's right."

*There it is. We just got ourselves a blank check.*

"So what do I do?" I said.

"Next week when you come, I'll get you started on some exercises that can help with the anxiety. But for now, I want you to not listen to the urges."

"Huh?"

He stood up and raised his voice. "You see that couch?"

I nodded.

"I want you to pretend that the voice telling you to weigh yourself all day is there." He yelled like I was a kid being schooled.

"Okay," I said, looking at the empty couch.

"Now what are you going to tell it?" He swung his arms around as if he were surrounded by bees.

Should I be laughing or feeling threatened? I sat at the ready in case he got too close.

He pointed to the empty couch again. "What are you going to tell it?"

"I don't know," I said.

"You tell it fuck you!"

I laughed.

"I'm serious. Let me hear you say it."

"Fuck you?" I said.

"Don't tell it to me, tell it to him," he pointed to the couch where my food panic disorder's imaginary body was.

Not only did I have to worry because Emmeline thought I was crazy enough to need a shrink in the first place, but if I yelled at my therapist's imaginary friend, then I better start worrying about being stupid too. He stormed back in forth in front of me saying

129

something about taking hold of my own life. "You have to do it. Tell it to fuck off."

"Fuck you!" I said to the poor empty couch that did nothing wrong except have the misfortune to be placed here in Dr. Porter's office.

"Good," he said. "So I'll see you in a week then."

Kristin was in her normal spot when I came in through the garage door. "How was it?" she said.

"I'm not sure," I said, flopping down into my spot on the couch.

"What do you mean?"

"Well, I don't know, you know. It was just the first session. I guess the good news is that I don't have anorexia."

"Is that what he said?" She looked away from the TV, and it wasn't a commercial.

"Yep. He said men don't get anorexia and that I just have a panic disorder regarding food." I yawned and stretched.

"So what are you supposed to do about that?"

I shrugged. "I don't know. He said he'd tell me more next week, and in the meantime, I'm supposed to..." It was too stupid to even say out loud. "...I'm supposed to ignore the impulse to weigh myself as much as I do."

"How many times a day do you weigh yourself?" I had her full attention now.

"Lots. Like five times or more."

"Jesus Christ, Jim."

"Just 'Jim' will do."

"Seriously," she said, "Weight fluctuates throughout the day. You need to weigh yourself when you first get up and have gone to the bathroom. That's your true weight."

My weight was not allowed to fluctuate, but that was our little secret.

*Yes. We're better than that.*

I know.

# Chapter 25

Even though Dr. Porter told me I didn't have anorexia, I looked it up on the Internet. I liked hearing about people's experiences, which sounded so familiar to me even though I wasn't at their level. I had a minor panic disorder.

*Let's show Dr. Porter how anorexic you can be.*

Any time things got slow at work, I'd do a web search about anorexia. In particular, I was interested in reading about male anorexia, and I wasn't surprised to find that there wasn't a whole lot out there on it. One man had it and talked about eating nothing all day but a head of lettuce with lemon juice on it for dressing.

*Have to keep that in mind.*

There was also a site dedicated to the anorexia prevalent in gothic teen boys. Their rail thin bodies dressed in black gave me role models. If I were younger, I would have gone gothic myself. Black is a slimming color. I looked into the eyes of the boys on that site and wished they could tell me their diet secrets. I'd be glad to trade for mine.

One day I did a book search on male anorexia, and one title came up. It was written by a man that had died shortly after he reached 75 pounds. The reviews of the book said that all he did in the book was talk about how therapists were worthless and that they didn't understand and couldn't help him. Dr. Porter came to mind.

*Don't be stupid. Dr. Porter is the perfect doctor for you. Who else is going to be better? You're an idiot if you look somewhere else. You saw how he reacted to you. No one believes you have anorexia. Do you really want to have to explain that to someone else?*

Not really, no.

*Okay then.*

I clicked off that page and went back to my search results. No one was at my door, and I didn't hear anyone in the halls outside my office, so I looked at a couple more sites. I had to settle for female anorexia because I had seen all the male anorexia sites.

Lots of message boards appeared in the search list. "They have those for everything now," I laughed to myself.

I clicked one open and saw the predictable picture of the thin girl at the upper left of the screen.

Below the title and the picture were the topics of discussion. They were things like:

"What do you eat?"

"What don't you eat?"

"Support"

"Friends and Family"

I clicked open the "What do you eat?" topic and learned within a few seconds that there were foods, such as apples and cabbage, that required more calories to digest than you actually got from them. Therefore, the net gain would be negative if you only ate apples.

Most people posting on this site seemed to really enjoy listing what they ate every day and writing about their diet rules. I couldn't blame them for that. I loved talking about that stuff too.

Looking in the "Support" category showed me a bunch of topics ranging from "Things to tell them" to "Why don't they understand?"

The pages all spoke true to me. I had found my people. I got ready to bookmark it and register as a poster there, when I finally noticed the description of the site. It said that this was a "pro-ana" site meant to help people get better results from their anorexia. It went on that the site's moderators were very aware of the arguments against anorexia, and asked that those kindly not be posted here. This site was a safe place for people with anorexia to learn from each other.

This was not the only website on the Internet that had this focus. I wasn't so far gone that I didn't know that a site like this was wrong. I couldn't imagine a site on the Internet that would be "Pro-cancer" but I didn't do a search for it just in case there was one. I closed my browser. That was enough Internet for today.

*Apples and cabbage. Got it. Don't forget.*

I wasn't pro-anorexia, was I? I just really loved my great diet ideas and exercise regimen. Nothing was wrong with that.

*No one has to know how much you love it.*

My desk phone rang. "This is Jim."

"Hey, Jim it's mom."

"Hey!" I said.

"How are you doing?"

"Doing all right," I said, "I was lighter today. Lost another pound."

"All right!" she said, "What are you down to now?"

"153."

There was a pause on her end of the line that lasted long enough for my smile to fade. "Oh my God, Jim. That's um…That's really light, isn't it?"

*Jealous.*

"Nah," I said, "You can't be too rich or too thin, right?" I laughed at the tired cliché.

"Oh Jim. Well, I don't know."

"It's not like I'm not eating." I rattled off my daily food, omitting little details like how I would pour a bowl of Special K and return all but about 5 flakes to the box. "I have a bowl of cereal, a Lean Cuisine for lunch," half of one really with the balance ending up in the garbage, "and just whatever for dinner."

Our family always ate off paper plates, and since I did the grocery shopping, I bought the smallest plates you could get—the size just bigger than party plates. That way, people would see me eating a plateful of food for dinner.

*Genius!*

I know. Oh wait…My mom was talking.

"That doesn't sound like you're getting all the nutrition you need, Jim."

"Oh, I forgot to say that I have spinach every day at 3 pm."

"Spinach?"

"Yeah. I just grab some of the raw leaves like you'd use in a salad."

"And you do the treadmill every day?"

I leaned back in my office chair. "Yeah. I'm up to about 5 miles per hour now."

"And you are walking at that rate?"

"It's more like a slow jog."

*You're not doing all you can. You have that thing set flat on the ground.*

"It's not at an incline or anything though, but it's still an all right workout, don't you think?" I said. God, I wanted her approval.

"I don't know, Jim," she said. "It sounds to me like you might be over doing it."

"Well, it just sounds like…"

*Don't listen to her. She doesn't know what she's talking about. Everyone, and I mean everyone wants what you have. Jealousy is everywhere. Your friend Mike said you looked like a Hollywood actor, and he knows the score.*

"I feel fine," I said, "Better than I ever have."

She sighed at me over the phone. "Well anyway…I have to get going because I'm meeting with Gale and going over to the gym today."

"See. You work out almost every day." Now the hypocrisy and jealousy was showing through.

*Told you.*

"There is a big difference in what I do and what you are describing," she said, her tone so defensive you could almost see the boxing gloves covering her face. She went on to detail the difference, but I had heard all I needed.

*No one is going to be happy for you anymore. You are too successful.*

The cafeteria rumbled and hummed as groups of people huddled over their food trays. The potential of the oncoming weekend made Friday start to feel like a holiday. Emmeline was getting very pregnant and Gabrielle was still working with impossible people.

"Did you start seeing a therapist?" Emmeline said before Gabrielle could make it back from the cashier.

"Yeah, I've seen him a couple times."

"And how is that going?"

*He's awesome.*

"He's kind of weird, but I guess that might come with the profession."

"Weird how?" She said.

I pictured the ending of both sessions I had had so far with him standing from his chair, raising his voice, and flailing his arms. If someone walked in on us, it may have been a challenge to pick which one was the therapist. The effort of getting into the whole explanation was too much. "He's kind of loud at times. He also says I don't have an eating disorder."

"Really?" she said, setting her fork on her plate. "What does he think it is then?"

"He says I have a panic disorder that is triggered by food."

*Don't tell her how he taught you that it's not fat to shy away from, it's calories. Don't mention how after a good ten minute inspection of the frozen entrees in the grocery store, you found that the chicken marsala Lean Cuisine had the fewest calories with 140.*

"And what does he say you should be doing about this?"

I glanced over Emmeline's shoulder and saw that Gabrielle was third in line at the register. "He gave me a CD with breathing exercises on it."

"Are they helping?"

"They are relaxing. You sit for 20 minutes and breathe in and out with your eyes closed. Every time you think of something besides your breathing, you make the conscious choice to return your attention to your breathing." I shrugged when Emmeline gave me an incredulous look.

"I don't see any lunch in front of you," she motioned to my part of the 4-seat table.

"I ate at my desk earlier."

"Uh-huh." Emmeline fidgeted in her chair and kept looking down at the table. "And you've told the doctor all the things you have told me about your eating."

"Yeah."

"And he says you don't have an eating disorder?" Her words sputtered from her mouth like rapid fire.

"Right. Like I said, he says I have some sort of panic disorder about food. He compared it to being scared to going outside and he compared my weighing myself to the thing some people have where they wash their hands a bunch of times."

"How is it not an eating disorder?"

"He says men don't get eating disorders."

"You need to find another therapist," she said.

*Don't listen to her. The guy has a PhD in psychology. He didn't get that just falling off a log. He knows what he is doing.*

"You think so?" I said. Emmeline had been so happy when I first made my appointment.

*Are you listening? She's just all pregnant and hormonal. She doesn't know what she is talking about.*

"I don't think he's addressing the real issue here." Her eyes were tearing up. I was upsetting my pregnant friend. I was a scum.

"But he says I don't have an eating disorder."

"And you think that is right?" Emmeline said. Her eyes locked on mine and pushed me back against my chair. My fingertips went numb.

"I guess," I said. I broke the eye contact with her and stared at the ridged salt and pepper shakers in the middle of the table.

"And what did you have for lunch today?" She showed no signs of letting up and Gabrielle was about to pay for her lunch.

"My usual…Lean Cuisine." I was a second grader caught stealing a pencil.

*No matter what she might ask next, don't tell her how it's become your regular practice to eat a couple bites of the meat and throw the rest of the meal away.*

"And you ate the whole thing?"

*Lie to her. Look right in those kind eyes and tell her yes.*

"Yeah."

Her face tightened and one corner of her lip bent down.

"Sorry I'm late," Gabrielle said as she set her tray on the table, gathered her change, and stuffed it into her purse. I had never been so glad to see her.

# Chapter 26

I poured five flakes of cereal a day and let them swim in a spit of skim milk.

*Careful with the milk. It adds calories and adds them quick.*

Guilt could paralyze me, but I'll get to that in a minute.

The chicken marsala meal Lean Cuisine came with a small breast of chicken and some string beans—140 calories. That and the Special K were foods I considered safe. However...

*Fruit have carbs and carbs turn to fat. Those string beans can't be that different than fruit.*

...Yeah. That's what I was thinking too. So if I gained a tenth of a pound or more, or if I had been the same weight for too long, then I would eat half of that piece of chicken breast and throw the rest of the meal away.

I was safe at dinner because I was cooking it. The calories at dinner were harder to keep track of because you never knew how mixing the foods together might affect the calorie count. Would heating the foods make their calories mix? Multiply? Increase exponentially? The safest bet was to concentrate on fat at dinner

When I made spaghetti, I used lean turkey and lean turkey sausage. Brown them both together while adding minced garlic, oregano, and whatever other spices. Then chop up roma tomatoes to let the whole thing stew together while the pasta boiled.

Ragu and some other companies made low fat and even nonfat spaghetti sauces, but those big companies also made regular fat-filled spaghetti sauce. People worked at those factories, and people made mistakes. How could I be sure that the jar of fat-free spaghetti sauce I bought in the store was really fat free? Who tested my jar for fat, and even if he was competent, did he get a phone call in the middle of the test that could have distracted him and messed up his accuracy? This wasn't a risk I was willing to take.

To eat out of the safe list brought on complete guilt at the first swallow. It was the ache of an unfixable disaster. The calories and the fat came into my body and wrecked all my work. A gained pound was something I could lose again in a rational mind, but for me it was a delay in progress, and it was unacceptable. The guilt helped keep me in line by reminding me what an out of control loser I was.

It was a cultural fallacy, the belief that we needed three meals a day and that they had to have certain elements in them. The less you ate, the less food you needed. It takes food to digest food. So the less food you take in, the less you have to digest, and by simple logic, the less food you really need.

I had safe people to eat with too.

Kim worked upstairs from me as an administrative assistant for a different project at the Lab than I was assigned to. She was newly divorced and sharp witted, and we became fast friends when drama broke out between her and Jeanette, the orange giver. Kim would stop by my office on the way to her own.

Kim would invite me to join her and her friends for lunch once or twice a week.

"No thanks," I'd say, "I already ate."

After being shot down time and again, Kim confronted me on it one morning in her direct way. "What the fuck, anyway?" She said, "We've asked you to go to lunch all the time and you always say the same thing…" she slouched down in her chair and deepened her voice to what I assume was a characterization of mine, "…No…No…No."

Kim had an extra sensitive lie detector, and although it went against all my inner thoughts…

*Don't even tell her the truth.*

…I figured I'd better tell her the truth.

*No!*

"It's because," I started, twisting my office chair from left to right.

*This is none of her business. It's no one's business but yours. Plus, you don't have anorexia, remember? Your doctor said so, and he should know.*

I exhaled hard through my nose.

"It's because I have anorexia, and it makes me uncomfortable to eat around people."

I had been looking at the floor while I was talking and I shied away from moving my gaze to her eyes.

"It's nothing personal against you," I said, "It's just everyone. I mean, I can eat in front of my family and certain friends that I have known since before I got like this. But..."

"Not new people?" She said.

I nodded. "Yeah. I'm sorry."

"What are you sorry for?" she said.

A better question would be, "What was I not sorry for?"

I shrugged. "I didn't mean to offend anyone. And I do really like you and hanging out with you and talking with you. But I just can't..." This was one of the hardest things to admit. No one on the planet could or should understand what I meant by this.

"That's cool, I understand," she said.

"You do?" I looked up at her. Maybe she had had an eating disorder before.

"I mean, I don't understand why, but I get how it would probably be hard to eat in front of people if you have that."

I nodded again and looked at the ground.

"Is it because you are afraid people will see how little you are eating?"

I thought of Gabrielle asking what was left of the food I ordered after I told the waitress all the things I wanted left off. "That's part of it, but it's just the whole eating in general. I don't really know the words."

Kim looked at me like she thought I probably did know the words and chose not to say them.

"I don't know," I said, "It's just the whole thing makes me feel uncomfortable."

"Okay, well then we won't be offended when you don't want to go from now on."

"And the thing is," I said, "I do want to go...I just..."

"Can't?" Kim said.

"Yeah."

Kim nodded and looked me up and down. "What are you doing about this?"

"What do you mean?"

"You know," she said, "to get better?" She sat in the visitor chair in my office and glanced up at the clock. She needed to make it upstairs before her boss came in.

*This chick is asking too many questions.*

"I'm seeing a therapist."

"Is that working for you?"

I pictured Dr. Porter ranting and raving at the end of each session. "I guess."

"You guess?"

"I've only been going a few weeks."

*He's the perfect therapist. Tell her.*

"I mean, he seems pretty good," I said. "He has me doing breathing and relaxation exercises."

"What the fuck?"

"Well, he says I don't have an eating disorder because men don't get them. He says I have an anxiety disorder brought on by food."

"What does your wife say?"

"Not a lot." I said. "She says I'm getting too thin. She doesn't really believe in therapy though."

"Hmm." Kim said.

*This bitch better mind her own business.*

As I got to know Kim better, I learned that for her, she was minding her own business and holding back during these early conversations.

# Chapter 27

"How are you doing on those breathing exercises?" Dr. Porter asked as he shut the door to his office behind us and I took my normal chair.

"They're pretty cool," I said, "After they're done, I always feel like I'm back in college smoking weed."

*Without the munchies.*

He nodded as if he'd heard that one before. "If you do them right, they do have the potential to bring on that kind of a feeling."

"Cool." At least I knew I was doing them right. Every day at lunch, I'd been popping that CD into my office computer and locking my door. I'd lean back my office chair and let the new age music that accompanied by Dr. Porter's voice have my full attention. Of course, his voice was telling me to give my breathing my full attention, and I was listening to his voice and doing what it said—thereby giving his voice my attention. Maybe I wasn't doing it right after all.

*You don't do the exercises well enough.*

"And how is everything else going?"

"Like what?" I said.

*Perfect answer.*

"With the eating and the weighing and your anxiety level." Dr. Porter shifted himself in his chair and fixed the position of his glasses.

"Oh, well...I don't know. That's about the same I guess." My gut bulged in front of me. I crossed my arms in front of it so he couldn't see.

"How many times a day do you weigh yourself?" His voice was so familiar from the CD yet a bit deeper now than whenever he recorded it.

"Four or five," I said.

"Why so much?"

"Because I have to."

"No you don't."

I huffed a laugh. "I don't?"

*This guy might be an idiot after all.*

"No," he said, shaking his head.

"Well how do I avoid doing that?" He may as well have suggested that I didn't need to pay taxes.

He tossed a carefree hand into the air and said, "You just don't do it." The condescending grimace on his face took over when his hand fell back to his lap.

"But I have to?"

He raised one of his legs in mock lack of control and had it step on an imaginary scale. "It's just like those guys with OCD. They don't really need to check the door 10 times or wash their hands until they bleed. Like them, you just have to ignore the urge."

*You can't do that.*

"I can't do that. I need to weigh myself."

"What's going to happen if you don't weigh yourself?" he said with a sigh as he leaned back in his plush leather office chair.

"I'll gain weight," I said, making sure my crossed arms were covering my gut.

"When you weigh yourself...how many times a day did you say?"

"Four or five."

"Right, mm hmm, yes. When you weigh yourself four or five times a day, are you ever heavier?"

The hot pain of failure flashed across my face. "Yes." I looked at the patterned throw rug on the office floor.

He shrugged with his palms toward the ceiling and raised his eyebrows as if he had just presented an unbreakable argument and I had no choice but to join him at his conclusion.

"But if I don't monitor my weight closely, it will go up even more."

"Weight fluctuates throughout the day. It's just how the body works. After you've been up for a while, you tend to weigh more than you did first thing in the morning because you've eaten and all of that." His tone made it clear that he viewed this as some sort of universal fact that was scientifically proven.

"I can stop that from happening."

"You can? How?"

"By monitoring my weight and making adjustments as necessary," I said.

"Making adjustments?"

"Speeding up the treadmill or taking in less food."

"You know you don't have anorexia," he told me again, "You may have some anorexic-like behavior, but you are not an anorexic. What you are doing is behaving like someone that is on a brand new diet."

*Huh?*

"How so?" I said.

"People on new diets weigh every day because they are trying to see progress. Once they reach the weight they want to be, they weigh themselves once a week or so...maybe less, but on average it's about once a week."

"I don't get what you are saying." It was my turn to shrug and face my palms toward the ceiling.

"This started as a diet for you, you said, right?"

I nodded.

"Well, you just haven't gotten into the next stage of the diet yet where you stop trying to lose and you start maintaining."

"Maintaining?"

"Keeping your weight at a reasonable range—knowing that it will fluctuate."

We spent about a minute looking at each other.

"Do you or did you have a goal weight in mind?" he said.

"No."

"Well then how will you know when you are finished losing weight?"

I shrugged.

*You're never finished.*

"If you don't have a goal weight in mind, then how will you switch to the maintaining behavior?"

"I won't."

*It's called anorexia, Dr. Chucklehead.*

"You know this will kill you, don't you?"

"I don't think it will," I said.

"Hmmm," he said, nodding. And then it was time for the usual Dr. Porter rant and rave session. He got up from his chair, but at least this time, I knew what he was doing. "What does your wife tell you?"

"That I should gain some weight."

"And your friends?" He was already pacing.

"Same thing."

He cut back in forth in front of me like a tiger at the zoo moments before feeding time. "And yet you still continue doing what you are doing?"

I had to commend him on his brilliant understanding of what I had been telling him for the past few weeks. You could almost smell the wood burning in that nearing retirement brain of his as it wrestled with the known fact that men don't get anorexia. "Yes," I said.

"I'm telling you right now, you are in for a rough road if you stay like this." He raised his voice, quickened his stride, but the arms weren't flailing yet, so I knew we hadn't reached the climax of the show. "Eventually, they'll stick you in a hospital, you know."

I nodded in agreement. I'm a firm believer in humoring the insane.

"You'll lose everything you care about. You won't be able to work anymore. No one will hire someone with this problem."

Now he was a bitter school teacher. What is it that I cared about that I would lose anyway? Ooops, wait a second, he's still going off…

"They'll be feeding you through a tube, and you won't even be able to stand long enough to read the number on the scale that you need to see so badly."

I had the scene in my head: me in a white hospital gown with nothing to worry about. It didn't sound all that bad. His right arm was starting to wave though, so I knew I better throw him a bone. "I guess I have my daughter to think about," I said.

"Oh yeah," he changed his voice to sound like a pitiful child, "I have my daughter to worry about, wah, wah, wah."

That was the last time I would respond.

"Cause what's your poor daughter going to do with a dead father?"

If he meant to irritate, he did, but I wasn't going to give him the satisfaction of a reaction. Belittling me or my situation wasn't going to stop anorexia. The fact that he wouldn't call it anorexia actually drove me to prove to him what a great anorexic I really was.

# Chapter 28

The pool in the backyard in Modesto was a necessity. In the summer, it was not uncommon to have a week or two of temperatures above 105. Brighid hadn't learned to swim yet, so she went into the pool with floaties on her arms and a floating ring around her chest for added protection.

Kristin never wanted to get in the pool. "Are you going to take the kids swimming today?" she said as I sat on the pink couch in the living room and read. Really that meant Brighid because the older two could take themselves in the pool whenever they wanted.

"I don't know," I said.

"It's going to be really hot."

"Yep." I said, holding my finger on the paragraph she stopped me on in the book.

"You haven't gone in with her in a while."

You haven't gone in with her ever. "I know, hon. Yeah, I'll probably take her in a little later in the afternoon," I said, putting my bookmark in place.

"I have a nail appointment in an hour. Do you think you could get some laundry started?"

"Sure," I said. I had already used the treadmill and showered and dressed. I had given Brighid her breakfast, helped her shower, and got her dressed. What's a little laundry and taking the kid in the pool on top of all that? Her nails were one of the only things she did for herself, after all.

I got off the couch and climbed the stairs to the bedroom where the dirty clothes piled all week. With a sigh, I sorted a dark load into a basket and headed down the stairs, fired up the washer, and put the load in. On Monday, I could go back to work and rest.

The pump made a current from the shallow end to the deep end of our pool. The patio was heated beyond the limit of barefoot walking, and Brighid stood by the pool in her Scooby Doo bathing suit with her floaties already in place.

I was waist deep in the water and freezing. "C'mon in baby, the water is fine."

She gave me a doubtful look but kicked off her flip flops and stepped onto the top step anyway. "It's cold, it's cold!" She pulled her foot back.

"Honey, it feels good after a while." That was a lie. My legs numbed beneath me. After a bit more coaxing, begging, and moving around in the water, she finally gave in and joined me.

We played Motorboat, Motorboat and had splash fights. I dragged her around the pool, but it wasn't long before I was tired. The pool never warmed up for me, and the shivers punched outward from deep within my chest.

"Baby, we have to get out of the pool now."

"No. We just got in," she said.

"Daddy's really cold."

"I'm not."

"Well, Daddy is, babe, and you can't stay in here yourself." Now my teeth were chattering and the cold crushed every part of my body.

"Can I stay in with Brother?"

Lorenzo had just stepped out into the backyard in his swimsuit. He draped his towel on one of the lounge chairs.

"I'll get out and dry off for a while and you can stay in for just a little while longer with Lorenzo. But when I say it's time to get out, then it's time to get out. Got it?"

She nodded and kicked herself in circles while I climbed the steps to my towel. "How's it going, man?" I said to Lorenzo.

"Pretty good."

I couldn't wrap my towel tight enough around myself. I was standing in the 108 degree afternoon sun and shivering. "The pool is colder than normal," I said to Lorenzo.

"Really," he said.

"To me it is anyway."

I tried laying in the sun but the cold wouldn't leave me. "Brighid, we have to go in now." I didn't see how the kids could take the cold water. When you are a kid, fun outweighs comfort.

I went upstairs, cursed the air conditioner for making things worse, and peeled off my trunks. The shower water ran on the hot setting until steam billowed over the top of the door. The steam as I entered felt almost as good as seeing a lower number on the scale. If the house and the world were the temperature of the hot water, all would be right.

The tile beneath my feet burned with cold as I dried off. The mirror showed my enormous gut and my skin pink from the shower. I looked away from it and felt a tear burn in my eye.

Once I had sweatpants and a T-shirt on, I took a thick blanket from the linen closet and wrapped myself in it on the rust-colored futon in the loft that served as my writing room. I shivered, even in the mummy wrap of the blanket, but the shivering lessened and the warmth made me sleepy. From the backyard, I could hear Dominique and Lorenzo splashing around the pool as my eyes closed and sleep took me.

"What are you doing?" Kristin's voice jolted me awake.

"I feel tired," I said.

"What's with the blanket?" She sounded mad. She always sounded mad lately.

"I'm cold."

"Jim Kohl…It's 108 degrees at least out there, and you're cold?"

"Yeah," I said. It felt stupid to say it to her, and my guess is she would be quick to agree.

"That is just fucking ridiculous," she said.

"I can't help it if I'm cold. Why are you mad that I'm cold?"

"I'm not mad cause you're cold. I'm mad about the reason you're cold."

I thought for a second. "Cause I went swimming?"

"Don't be a fuckin' smart ass. The reason you're cold is that you are not eating enough. You are too skinny."

*Tell her.*

"The doctor said I'm not an anorexic cause men don't get anorexia."

"That doctor is a fuckin' moron," she said.

"He has a PhD."

"I don't fuckin' care. You have yourself so fuckin' skinny that you can't stay in the pool with your kids more than ten minutes and then you have to wrap up in a fucking blanket for an hour." She walked away and left me to feel uncomfortable in my warm blanket.

Brighid and I would often have breakfast outside by the pool in nice weather. Even on the hottest days of summer, mornings were still cool enough to eat outside. I got the cereal ready while Brighid got the spoons.

*Your bowl is too full.*

I had poured a little more than I needed. I pinched off a bit with my thumb and forefinger and put it back in the box.

*There is still too much in the bowl.*

It didn't look like I had put any back in the box. Brighid laughed and talked and danced around the kitchen with our spoons in her hands. "When breakfast is over, do you want to watch cartoons?"

"For a little while, honey. But then Daddy has to go upstairs and work on his book."

*Are you gonna fix that bowl, or what?*

The bowl still had more cereal than I needed. The weight hadn't been doing quite what it should over the last few days and I needed some extra help. I could increase the slope on the treadmill and put some more of this cereal back in the box.

For the second time I gathered up a good chunk of my cereal and sent it back to the box. I did it one more time just to be safe.

"Can I have some orange juice?"

"Sure, Babe."

*Remember what I told you about orange juice.*

I could go without the juice, and one more small pinch back into the box would be a good idea. "Brighid are you going to get the milk?"

"I tried. It's too heavy."

"Okay."

The two bowls sat next to each other on the counter as I crossed the kitchen for the milk. I pulled the rip tab around the gallon jug's cap and popped the cap off. Brighid stood by with her fingers wrapped on the counter's edge like a perching bird. She cocked her head. "Is that enough?" she said, pointing to my bowl.

By the time I had finished putting cereal away, there were about 5 flakes left. This was the safest amount for breakfast. Any more than this was not only too much, but would drastically sabotage the progress. "That's enough for me. Yeah, Honey."

The two of us sat on the bottom edges of lounge chairs and ate from our bowls that sat on a couple of outdoor end tables with frosted glass surfaces. The sun rose pink and slow in front of us.

The pool pump kicked on and covered up the soft titter of the morning birds. It was colder out than I had expected.

Kristin would normally find out about my weight when we were around people. I stopped telling her what I weighed. It was making her mad, but what didn't?

"My God, Jim, you've lost a lot of weight," someone would say.

"Yeah..." I'd sing the praises of the low-fat diet and the treadmill. I'd say what my speed was on the treadmill, usually something like, "Yeah, a half hour a day. I'm going at 4.7 miles-per-hour at a 10 percent incline."

"Shit, no kidding? Every day?" They might say.

I'd nod or whatever, beaming a smile from my skeletal face.

"Wow, so how much do you weigh now?"

As soon as the question was out of the person's mouth, Kristin was right next to me. No matter what state of drinking she was in or how far away she seemed to be when the question came up, she was always within easy ear shot and coherent when it came time for me to give the answer.

The bitch of it was, there was no way I was going to lie. I loved telling people my weight. It was an accomplishment and it was the one thing in this world that was all mine. Even my books had her name on the dedication page, which was normally about as far as she read in them.

"I'm at 153 right now."

"Well, you're looking great," and whomever I had been talking to would shift away to mingle and I'd be left with Kristin at my arm.

"You weigh what?" She said.

"Um...153."

"One fifty three?" She took a step back and examined my face with darting eyes.

"Yeah."

"Jim Kohl, that is fucking ridiculous. If you get down into the 140s, I'm leaving you."

"My parents saw me. They said I looked fine."

"What?"

"Yeah...Last time I was down there...like a week ago, they said I looked fine," I said.

Her face twisted in disgust. "They didn't see you naked though."

"I took my shirt off," I said.

"What?"

"I took my shirt off right by their front door as I was leaving. They said I looked fine. They saw my tattoo though."

She laughed. "Woops."

"I know." I smiled.

"Jim…You need to only believe me when it comes to your body. You can't trust the mirror, and you can't listen to your parents. Do you understand?"

"Okay."

"You are too thin, Jim. I am starting to worry."

"Sorry," I said.

"I'm not looking for an apology here. You need to stop losing weight."

*Jealous. She can't stand that your diet works better than her big-bucks surgery.*

Whatever her motivations, I knew that when I got down to the 140s, I'd need to be more discrete about my progress.

# Chapter 29

I stopped needing an alarm clock in the morning. My eyes would open at just before 2 am, and I'd be ready to go. I'd sit up in bed and reach for the workout clothes that I left at bedside the previous night. The bathroom was divided into 2 rooms: one with a toilet and the other with the shower, Jacuzzi tub, and vanity area. I'd set the gym clothes on the counter on my way to the toilet.

After leaving the toilet, it was time to weigh. Kristin lay asleep in bed not ten feet from the scale, so I had to leave the vanity light off and read the numbers from the beam of light cracking from the toilet room's door. Since the previous night, I had faced the next day's weigh in with a mix of anxiety and anticipation. So much depended on the number on the scale.

If it was lower, I could relax because I had done well, but I'd still needed to push the limits on the treadmill to help ensure the next morning's weight would be a success too.

If the number was higher, my treadmill speed from the previous day would be increased by 2 tenths of a mile per hour. When I maxed the treadmill out at six miles per hour, I would increase the incline on the treadmill by a couple percentages. The idea that I would soon have the speed and the incline maxed petrified me, but I had it in the back of my head that I could buy another treadmill with higher speed settings. I had already approached Kristin with the idea, and she didn't seem opposed.

I'd step on the scale one foot at a time and wait for the dark gray digital numbers to settle. 152. Lower than yesterday, so I smiled and sighed. For today, I was safe. All I had to do was stick to the plan, and things would probably be all right. Weight affected my mood, my activities, and what would happen to me each day. It governed what I ate and how much of what I ate. It decided how intense my exercise would be.

In three more pounds I would be down to my next decade of weight, but I'd have to keep quiet about it because Kristin said she would leave me when I got below 150.

*She won't.*

She might, and I couldn't take the chance that she would. I loved her, after all, but I needed to get down below 150, so I would just have to do so and not talk about it. The mirror made it obvious that the weight loss was essential. Besides, the alternative was weight gain, and that was not acceptable.

I switched off the bathroom light and groped my way to the bedroom door, opened it as quietly as possible, and went down the stairs. The treadmill was in the garage, so I had to deactivate the house alarm in order to get to it. I punched in the code and watched the display light switch from red to green, filled my water bottle at the Alhambra cooler, and rushed to the treadmill with the excitement of a child for Christmas presents.

The games only started once I got on the treadmill. I designed them to help pass the 30 minutes, but they developed into something more subservient to the disease.

Like the numbers on the scale, the numbers on the treadmill were everything. At first, the pedometer was the most important. With the treadmill belt whirring away beneath me, I could watch the miles count up as I walked. Most people probably do that to some degree. The calorie counter was soon second only to the number on the scale in the list of important numbers in my life.

Since I knew that my breakfast was 110 calories, my lunch was 70, and I had a rough approximation of what my dinner was, I could keep track of burning away the previous day's food. When the calorie counter hit 70, my lunch was gone. When it got to 180, breakfast was taken care of as well. Whatever other calories I burned chipped away at the dinner.

Even more important than this, I could imitate the speed I walked on the treadmill in my every day walking to and from the bathroom, to and from the printer at work, and anywhere else I might walk. On the treadmill, I would count my steps and see how many steps burned a calorie. Based on the step count, I would have a good guess as to the calories burned during regular living.

I always held onto the handles on the treadmill. Even though I knew that swinging my arms the way I would in normal walking would burn more calories, it was just more comfortable for me to hang on. My sweat towel lay in front of me across the clock's numbers because these numbers were the least important to keep track. I had no fear of walking longer than a half hour.

Sweat also measured progress. I kept aware of my body as the calories clicked up and checked it for sweat every little while. The small of my back started first. I'd reach behind me without breaking stride and swipe my fingers across the small of my back to check for moisture. At the first sign of my fingers gliding across there with sweat's lubricant, I would smile, knowing I was on my way. I allowed myself to look at the time once my lower back was sweaty.

Each drop of sweat that poured the length of my face was a celebration. The first one of each treadmill session was the most exciting, but I smiled through them all and didn't towel them off until they had run the full path from my hairline to my jaw. Every ounce of sweat was food out of me, and I knew of no better feeling.

The Zen of it all was the books on tape that played in my Walkman as I exercised. My body and mind got a simultaneous workout, and the words pumping into my head prepared me for the writing session that would follow the treadmill.

I pictured wads of pulpy fat flopping from my body, splatting on the treadmill belt, and being carried away from me.

Sometimes my shins ached, but it was better to walk through the pain than it was to slow the speed and face a possible weight gain.

At 28 minutes, I would allow the towel to show the tens place of the second that counted up toward my 30-minute ending time. When 29 minutes came, I'd allow the whole clock to show the final minute. I'd watch the calorie counter and cheer it on. If it was at 200, I'd urge it to 205 before the final minute ended.

The 30 would show and I'd turn off the treadmill. On a few days, I had to stop it at 27 or 28 for one reason or another, and the fact that I hadn't completed my 30 minutes haunted me the rest of the day and made it harder to eat the food that I normally considered safe.

The euphoria of a good treadmill session lasted longer and felt better than the afterglow of sex. My body pulsed and ached in the small muscles of my legs, and I felt electric shocks of spasms throughout them. It was the feeling of a job well done, of victory, and of near perfection.

Writing was next on the schedule. I was working on my novel, *Through the Fog*. I'd climb the stairs as fast as I could to burn a few extra calories and boot up the computer. While it went through its various boot screens, I ran down to the kitchen to start the coffee. My reflection in the darkened kitchen window was fat. I stared at it in disgust. "I better weigh myself again after the writing and before the shower."

*Yes you better. Try and use the bathroom before that too.*
Good idea.

The coffee filled enough for me to take a cup, so I carried it back up the stairs, excited by the burning calories. The coolest thing was that as long as I was moving, I was burning calories. My fingers tapped along the computer keyboard, putting the story from my mind into the Word document, and every little move they made was helping to burn calories. When I was thinking of what to write next, my eyes scanned the text I had just written, and that too was a series of fine muscle contractions that burned calories.

After an hour, I'd save and close the work, take the coffee cup down to the dishwasher, climb the stairs again and sneak into our room so I wouldn't wake Kristin. I'd use the bathroom, strip out of my workout clothes, and wipe any excess sweat that might have been on my body. With the crack of light from the all but closed bathroom door beaming onto the scale, I went to weigh again.

The second weighing of the day didn't make me as nervous as the first, but a higher number would be devastating. I'd have to be really careful eating that day.

Then I would shower, force more urine or crap out in the bathroom, and weigh one more time unless Kristin was already up. She didn't like to see me weigh, and I didn't like her to see what she didn't like.

Back down the stairs to get another cup of coffee and to make a triple shot of espresso for Kristin. If I paced the floor while the espresso cooked, that would be more burned calories. Once the three shots had squeezed out of the nozzle, I'd walk the stairs again careful not to spill. My speed was slower, but it was still burning more calories than standing still. The last thing I needed was to hear about spilled coffee on the stairs.

In the dark of the room, I'd find my night stand and set the coffee down so I could grope around for the light.

"Hey Bubbah," Kristin said, her voice weak and scratchy from sleep.

"How's it going?"

"Pretty good." She'd stretch and yell out a yawn. I'd hold her espresso cup, feeling like an employee at some spa she was staying at, until she had positioned herself. When she was ready, I'd hand her the cup.

We had 30 minutes to talk before she would get up and take a shower. At that time, I would go get Brighid up and start corralling her through the morning ritual and into the car. Once the shower was had, the clothes were chosen and on, the hair was combed, and the backpack was packed, we got in the car for the commute to Livermore.

She would want to play with the stuffed animals she brought in the car, and she'd want me to be active in that play. "I'll play animals on the way home," I would say.

I had a sharp pain in my left kidney. I'd notice it while driving, and I still have visual memories of the pinkening sky in my rearview mirror, the dashboards lights becoming less necessary, and the sensation of a needle jabbing into my side.

"That can't be a good thing," I would think, but the breathing exercises that Dr. Porter taught me took care of any worry the pain might have brought with it. The exercises took care of the fact that when I stood, my vision would blacken too. Even though my vision stayed blacker longer now than it did a couple weeks back, as long as I had my breathing exercises, a higher speed on the treadmill, and a lower number on the scale, things were great.

Walking Brighid to and from daycare was calories burnt. I could walk faster on the way out because I wouldn't have to slow to her stride and faster was more and more was better unless you were talking about food, but that goes without saying.

Once I got inside the gates of the Lab, the further I parked from the entrance to my building the better. However, I was there first each morning, and what would people think if they came after me and saw my car at the far end of the parking lot? It's a possibility that they might think I was ultra concerned about my car's paint, but there was also a chance that one of them would have me figured out. I had no interest in discussing my motivations with these people. I'd share diet tips with them anytime though.

So I'd park in the closest available spot to avoid suspicion, but I'd walk like it was raining to my office building each day. No matter where I walked or what the distance, it was better to imitate treadmill speed. Of course, I couldn't do this if I was walking with someone from work and the lost opportunity would nag at me. I would try and rationalize that walking even at a slower pace with someone still burned more calories than not walking.

*But you still could have burned more.*

Some of the pro-anorexia sites said you should always be in motion. Fidgeting your fingers or shaking your leg up and down while seated at a desk were great ways of burning extra calories.

Lunch would come. I'd avoid eye contact on the off chance that someone would invite me to eat with them. In the freezer in my building's narrow break room I had my Lean Cuisine waiting among the 20-something pints of Ben and Jerry's and Hagen Dazs that Jeanette had squirreled away there. I wrinkled my face in disgust.

If it was a Friday and they were available, I would meet with Emmeline and Gabrielle after heating my food in the microwave. They were good judges of my progress because they had been there at the beginning. That's why it was both safe and satisfying to eat with them.

The microwave would beep and I'd grab the tray from the compartment, carry it back to my office at treadmill pace while holding the hot tray by its edges, and set it on my desk. I'd peel back the plastic and check the clock at the bottom right of my computer screen. It was best to let it sit for 2 minutes before starting to eat.

I always kept a 24 pack of Arrowhead water underneath my desk because the Lab didn't provide a water cooler in the particular area that I worked. Water was safe to a point. Water could also add weight, so I had to be careful how much I drank or how close to the next weight check I drank. The safe level of water was something you felt as the day wore on.

When the two minutes passed, I would eat part of the lean cuisine and spend the rest of the lunch period reading, doing breathing exercises, or napping. Sometimes I would daydream of Jeanette sitting across the hall shoving loads of chocolate into her mouth, and I would feel superior.

Slipping half the Lean Cuisine back into its box and throwing it in the garbage thrilled me. I truly had transcended the human need for food.

At the end of the day, Brighid and I commuted home. We played animals and sang songs to pass the 50 miles to the house, but my mind was on the scale for most of the ride. As soon as I got home, I would strip my clothes under the guise of changing into sweats and weigh a time or two before Kristin got home.

The weight determined how careful I would need to be at dinner and my treadmill strategy for the next morning. A bad number on the scale made me short on patience with the kids. Nothing was worse than a bad number on the scale.

I would head down to cook next and then eat dinner with the kids. Dominique would ask me how my day was and fill my head with the latest teenage drama from the middle school. Brighid would compete for attention any way she could think of. Lorenzo would take it all in and eat in silence.

No one knew that I bought the smallest paper plates, so no one knew that my plateful was really less than a plateful. In truth, the kids wouldn't even bother to notice and Kristin wouldn't be home until almost 8 when the kitchen would be cleaned and all evidence tossed.

I'd be tired by the time she got there. The phone would ring at about 7:45.

"Bubbah, can you put a couple of those frozen chicken wings in the microwave for me?"

They would be hot and ready by the time she got home. The two of us would sit on either end of the couch while she ate her wings and we watched TV with me falling asleep only to have her slap me on the leg to wake me.

"You can never stay awake for me," she would say.

"I'm sorry. I'm tired."

"That's because you don't eat enough."

*Don't listen to that crap.*

"Yes I do."

That's when her anger would escalate to silence, and I would spend the rest of the night asking what is wrong and being ignored.

# Chapter 30

I got more reading done in the waiting room to see Dr. Porter than anywhere else, so it was worth it to me to get there at least 20 minutes early. Kristin didn't know how long it would take me to get there on the rare evenings when she would have been home before I left, so I was free to leave when I wanted.

The waiting room was empty at 6:40. The receptionist had gone home. I pored over the book and hoped that Dr. Porter wasn't in and had forgotten to cancel so I could sit in private for an hour and read. No one could say Bubbah, or Daddy, or Jim. No one could ask for a thing. I even had an excuse not to answer my cell phone since I was supposed to be in therapy.

About five minutes after 7, Dr. Porter lumbered down the stairs from his office followed by a distraught looking woman. My guess was he had ended her session with the normal yelling and carrying on that he did mine—the fireworks finale—and she didn't take it well.

"I'll be with you in just a second," he said to me as he headed out the door for a smoke.

"Right on." He could take his time for all I cared.

*You'll be heading up those stairs soon. Bonus calories burned.*

I watched the leather rope of bells that hung from the doorknob swing to a gradual stop and waited for the door to open. My reading was ruined with the knowledge that I was one cigarette away from having to stop anyway.

He came back and I followed him up the stairs to the office, taking my usual seat near the window. "So how has your week been?" He asked as he shut the door. I got the sense that the meter was running the way it starts when a cab pulls away from the curb.

"It's going all right," I said.

"Are you still weighing every day?"

"Yes."

"More than one time a day?"

I nodded.

"Have you even tried to do it less?" He asked as a sigh escaped through his nose. He rested his ankle on his knee and swiveled in his brown leather chair.

"I can't."

"You can't," he said, switching the position of his legs, "What does that mean?"

*Get yourself a Webster's, buddy boy.*

"It means I can't." I smiled. "I have to weigh myself."

"Or else what?"

"Or else things could get out of control."

"Things?" he said.

"I have to monitor my weight to make sure I'm not gaining."

"But even if you do gain, wouldn't you agree that you know how to lose it again anyway?"

"Well, of course, yes," I said.

"Then what difference does it make if you gain weight?"

"Because if I don't gain any weight, then my progress remains the same."

"But what is your ultimate goal?" He started to stand and I thought we were going into rant mode early tonight, but then he settled back into his chair.

"What do you mean?" I said.

"You mentioned progress. Normally if we say progress, it means that there is an ultimate goal that the progress is leading to. So how will you determine when you have made enough progress?"

"I have no idea," I said.

"But you must, or you wouldn't have used the word progress. Progress towards what?"

I thought for a moment despite the semantic leaning of his questioning. "Weight loss."

"What?"

"Weight loss is the ultimate goal," I said, "Weight loss and not gaining weight are the ultimate goal, and the only way to make that happen is to monitor my weight throughout the day and take action based on what the weight is."

"Take action?"

This guy was just not getting it. "Eating less or speeding up the treadmill or both."

*Take it easy on him. This is the best therapist I've ever seen.*

"And you are perfectly happy doing this?"

"Yeah."

He set both feet on the floor. "Well, let me tell you a little bit about what will happen to you," he said, interlacing his fingers across his stomach. "Judging from your height and build, you'll probably be able to get down to the 120s or so. Maybe not quite that low."

*Did you hear that? He thinks you have weight to lose. You need to be in the 120s.*

Yes, I heard him.

"Once you get down about there," he said, "You'll probably have lapses in consciousness. They may have to take away your driver's license." He looked up at me to check my reaction. "Then, eventually after you lose maybe a few more pounds..."

*Lose a few more pounds. Is there any phrase in English as cool as that?*

"...they'll have to put you in the hospital." He paused again to release a dramatic sigh. "And in there, they will hook you up to a feeding tube, and you'll have absolutely no control over it. They'll drip food right into your veins, and there will be nothing you can do."

*Come on. He says the same crap all the time. We've heard this before.*

That was the most horrific notion that I had ever heard in my life. Was that really a possibility? Could they really force food into me?

*There are things we could do even then. Let's not worry about that until we have to.*

"So in the end, you'll either die, or you will change your ways. But right now, you don't want to change, am I correct?" Dr. Porter pushed his glasses up the bridge of his nose.

"Yes. That's right," I said.

"Okay...Well then I can't help you."

"What?"

He shook his head from side to side and scratched his chin. "If you don't want to change, I can't help you."

"So this is it then?"

"Unless you want to change," he said, "But you seem pretty happy just doing whatever it is that you are doing."

"I am."

"Yeah, well then I can't help you. You have to want to change in order for me to show you how to change. You're welcome to keep coming here, but I don't see how good it will be for you if you don't want to stop this behavior and get rid of your anxiety."

"Okay," I said, "Well...Thanks a lot."

He nodded. "I do wish you the best."

On the way home it occurred to me that a psychiatrist had just told me that I was beyond his help. That's how crazy I was.

"What do you mean he won't see you anymore?" Kristin said. It must have been important because the TV show hadn't gone to commercial yet. She sat in the blue easy chair against the wall in an oversized Mickey Mouse night shirt and sweats.

"Well, I mean he will see me. He'll take my copay and whatever, but he said he can't help me because I don't want to change." I shrugged and took a seat on the couch.

"So that's it then?" She said.

"Pretty much."

She looked like she wanted to say something, but she didn't. Her attention went back to the TV and stayed there the rest of the evening.

# Chapter 31

"I brought you this." Kristin handed me a Styrofoam cup filled with what looked like vanilla soft serve ice cream.

*You can't eat that.*

"What is this?" I said.

"It's sugar free and fat free frozen yogurt. It's peanut butter." She handed me a white plastic spoon from the yogurt shop bag.

"Fat free and sugar free?" I said, sitting at one end of our small kitchen table.

*She's probably lying. She says you are too thin, and she wants to sabotage the progress.*

"Yes," she said.

*You can't trust her.*

I looked down at the yogurt and then back over at Kristin, who was separated from me by the tiled kitchen counter. "What?" she said.

My glance moved between her and the yogurt a few more times.

*You don't need to eat that, and it's really a bad decision to do so.*

"What, Jim? What are you thinking?" She bellied up to the counter that was now a barricade keeping me safe.

I didn't say anything to her. There was nothing I could say that wouldn't be met with rage. "Fine then, don't fucking eat it." She slammed one of the plastic spoons against the counter top. The scoop part broke off and somersaulted through the air before coming to rest on the floor near the garbage can. Kristin disappeared up the stairs.

The cup sat on the table. If I ate the yogurt, that might make her happy again, but it would still be hours before she would talk to me. My guess was well into the morning. If I didn't eat the yogurt, it would be even longer.

I took the plastic cap off of the yogurt and set it upside down on the kitchen table. The plastic spoon and a napkin sat nearby on the table. It wasn't like she bought me a small either. This was easily the biggest frozen yogurt I had ever seen. I don't think both of my hands could have wrapped around it.

*She's not going to come back downstairs. Just toss this thing in the trash and be done with it. She's mad anyway. May as well be mad for a reason.*

She bought this with me in mind though. It has no fat and no sugar. She brought me this to be nice.

*If she really cared about you and your feelings, she wouldn't have brought you anything at all. Plus, how can you be so sure there is no fat and no sugar in that glob of crap?*

I can't be sure.

*Exactly. Better safe than sorry. Toss it in the garbage where it belongs.*

That night, I went ahead and ate it for the sake of my marriage. Each spoonful was a chore, and when the container was finally empty, the guilt and the fear of the next morning's weigh in kept me awake for hours.

My weight dropped. I was losing at least a pound a week if not more. My clothes hung off me like a scarecrow's—so I was told anyway.

In the mirror, there was more to lose. I could see it flabbing over my belt line and pushing at the seams of my shirts. When the mirror got me, I would stop and stare into it for minutes at a time taking inventory of all the parts of my body that needed trimming up. My gut was the worst.

I would pinch at it and see how much extra skin I could grab, and the red heat of failure would climb from my neckline until my face pinkened.

My jawline was bad too. I had the worst double chin. I would pinch it between my fingers praying there would be less to pinch, but there never was.

*You know how on the weekends, you sometimes eat extra stuff. Like last weekend, you had a pint of low fat Ben and Jerry's frozen yogurt? Yeah, that's why you're fat now. One weekend enough to eat whatever you want is one weekend too many. I mean look at you.*

I released the double chin from my death pinch and saw that it was bigger than before. I gasped in panic and pinched at my gut. It was worse too. The mirror confirmed my fear.

*You'll never get ahead in the game if you allow your fat self all these diversions from the path. You either want progress or you don't. You choose to be a success or you choose to fail. Sure the scale said 136 this morning, but keep it up and soon you'll be 250 again with your skin pushed to the breaking point like your shirt is now.*

Tears dripped from my eyes and rolled into my double chin.

*There is either being fat or getting thin. That's all there is.*

"Get out of the mirror."

I jumped at her voice. Kristin stood near the bed, and I could see her over my reflection's shoulder with her arms crossed.

"Get out of the mirror." This time was sterner than the last, and I wouldn't have described her tone the first time she said it as coddling.

"I was just…"

"Get out of the mirror. I don't want to hear what you were just doing. Just get away from the fucking mirror."

I bowed my head, looked at the floor, and turned from myself.

She let her arms drop to her sides and took a seat on the bed. "You need to get your daughter ready for bed," she said as she crawled to the head of the bed, adjusted her pillow for lounging, and turned on the Food Network.

"Brighid?" I called to her from the top of the stairs and fought against the blackness that tried to squeeze out my vision.

*That's a good thing. It's a sign of progress. And the fact that you are so tired and dizzy right now is a good thing too. It means you have worked hard enough on the treadmill. It means success— almost as much as the lower numbers on the scale.*

Nothing was better than the lower numbers on the scale.

*Well of course not.*

"Brighid?"

She rounded the corner from the family room. First one eye peeked up the stairs at me and then her huge smile.

"Come on, honey. Let's get ready for bed."

"Is it bed time?" She held the banister with both hands and guided herself up the stairway.

"Not quite yet, but we need to get ready for it." I took hold of the banister myself as another wave of black separated me from Brighid for a second. The trick was not to surrender to the faint.

I left Brighid in my bedroom while I went to hers to get her pajamas. By the time I got back, Brighid stood naked and waiting in the middle of the master bathroom. "Do you need to go potty?"

Kristin sat on the bed in the same room as us, hypnotized by the dorky guy on the Food Network that talked about the science of cooking.

"I already did." She pointed to the toilet.

"Are you sure?"

"I did." She nodded and raised her voice at my implication. "You don't believe me." That phrase always introduced a stream of tears, and tonight was no exception. Kristin's eyes never left the TV screen.

"Fine I believe you, baby, just put on your pajamas." Some nights you just have to take the clear path.

"I not baby."

I nodded. I knew the mirror was right behind me and I knew what it would show me if I looked.

*All the areas of your body where the fat won't leave?*

Yes.

*So most of your body.*

Yes.

"Daddy, I need help with this shirt." She had her pajama top all twisted in on itself and was in the process of trying to force her head through the sleeve.

"Just a second, honey." I kneeled to the rescue and tamed the wild shirt.

"Thank you," she sighed. Her eyes fixed on something near my neckline.

*She probably sees how fat you are.*

Her thumb and forefinger reached out as if she were going to pick a booger or lint ball off me. "What is this?" She wrapped her fingers around my collar bone as if it were a handlebar on a tricycle.

"That's my bone," I said, and I brushed her hand away from it.

Brighid looked at it again and ran her fingers along her own collar area.

Kristin's attention never left the TV.

# Chapter 32

It was nearing 3:00 on a workday, and all the pages in the document I was editing started to look the same. I rubbed my eyes and swiveled the chair back and forth a bit. With a nod, I got up from my chair and headed to the fridge down the hall and my spinach snack.

*You don't really need the spinach.*

The thought stopped me mid stride near the community printer. That was true. It's not like I felt hungry. No reason to eat just for the sake of eating, right? I turned around and headed back to my office.

With a sigh, I took my seat and turned away from the computer. I threw away half of my lunch, and really how much damage can 5 spinach leaves do? Plus, the treadmill was going really well and I was burning about 200 calories less than I was taking in each day. Spinach leaves barely had any calories. It should be okay.

I got out of my chair again and turned the corner out of my office door.

*You are weak minded. There is no reason in the world that you need to eat that spinach right now. First you'll eat this when you don't need it, and what's next? A dozen donuts? A large pizza? Fast food? Get back to that office.*

I turned around and headed back to my desk.

But seriously, it's only 5 spinach leaves. Surely that won't be that big of a deal. I turned around again in the middle of the hallway and headed for the fridge.

*But if you don't eat the spinach leaves, then you won't even have to speed up the treadmill. Why do something to slow the progress? Better yet, you could skip the spinach leaves and speed up the treadmill.*

Yes. That was the best plan. It would be one thing if I felt hungry, but I didn't. I never felt that anymore. I grabbed the spinach in its plastic baggy from the fridge and threw it in the garbage can. I walked back to my office feeling better than I had since the scale was a lower number that morning.

Lee came out from the backroom where all the engineers sat and where I would eventually go when my clearance came through. There was a document of his in my pile of work, and he wanted to know how it was coming along.

"Have you lost some weight?" He said when we were done talking about the document.

"Yeah," I said with a smile. "Thanks."

He paused and looked me over. "Is it healthy?"

*Yes. Tell him yes, you are fine.*

"No."


I came in from the treadmill happy that I had a successful run and still riding the buzz of being in the 130s. I rounded the corner from the family room and found Kristin sitting on the stairs. "What's the matter?"

Her eyes were tearing so I sat on the stairs in front of her and waited for her to talk. "What's wrong, Honey?" I moved closer and tried to hug her. She let me at first, but then she pushed me away. "What?" I said.

"Don't you see you are killing yourself?" she said.

*Oh for God's sake...*

"No," I said, "No I don't see that." I ran my hand across the blue carpet of the stairs and drew lines with my finger.

"This whole family will fall apart if you die," she said.

That seemed like a lot of pressure and it also seemed overdramatic. "I'm not going to die, Hon." I looked up from the design I was tracing in the carpet and saw the tears running down her face. "I'm not."

"You are so skinny."

"No I'm not."

"Yes you are." She raised her voice and we both scanned the area to see if any of the kids were around. An awkward silence stretched like the pause after a bad joke.

"Well, what do you want me to do?"

"You need to stop this," she said.

"How am I supposed to do that?" I rested my hand on my leg and stopped playing with the carpet. "I have these urges. It's like a whole other voice and it fills my head with what seems like really great diet ideas."

"Urges?" She said, straightening herself up on the stair, "I have some urges of my own. You know what my urges are? I have the urge to walk right out of this house and never come back."

"Honey, I am sick."

"You're not sick, you choose to be this way. You're just like any kind of drug addict. A crank addict has a choice to either be a crank addict or not. You have a choice too. And I'm telling you now I'm not going to stay around here and watch you kill yourself."

"I'm not killing myself."

She sighed hard, stood, and climbed the stairs to our room. I followed her, which is the worst thing to do when she is mad, but I had to take a shower anyway.

"You need to stop this shit."

"Should I try and find another therapist?"

"I don't give a shit how you fucking do it, but you need to stop this shit."

"Okay."

"Do you know that every morning when you get up to write I lay awake and listen for the tapping of the keyboard just to make sure you are still alive?"

A puff of breath was my reply.

"It's true. And sometimes I wake up with you next to me and make sure that you are breathing."

"Of course I'm breathing," I said.

"You can't see yourself. You don't know what you look like. Your parents say you look fine, and I'm telling you now the only person you should be listening to is me."

*Well, that's nothing new. She's just jealous that you've lost more weight the old fashioned way than she has with her surgery.*

"I'm not that thin." I knew she would say I was, and this was a chance to hear it. I loved to hear it.

"Yes you are that fucking thin."

I could have done without the F word part of it, but she said it. The next trick was not to smile while she was yelling at me, I conjured up my best concerned face.

"You have the body of a 12-year-old boy," she said. She pressed her palms together and touched her index fingers to her chin for a moment. "Your breath is always horrible because you are not getting enough protein."

I blew into my cupped hand to see if I could smell my breath.

"You're not going to be able to smell it, you have no sense of smell."

"What do you want me to do?" I said.

"I want you to stop doing this."

"Stop doing what? Exercising? Stop trying to eat healthy?" I spit the words out like they were high in fat.

"You're not eating healthy. You never have any energy except for that fucking treadmill. You fall asleep on me every night. You can't even stay awake for sex. You make me feel undesirable."

"You're desirable, Honey."

"You can't stay awake to prove it to me."

"Fine, I'll try and stay awake," I said.

"Oh don't do me any favors. I don't need a charity fuck." She sat on her side of the bed and reached for the remote control.

"I don't know what you want me to say."

"I don't want you to say anything. I want you to stop this bullshit. I want you to eat." She turned on the TV.

"Honey," I said, "Don't you understand. This is a disease. I am sick."

"You'd be smart to stop talking to me now, Jim."

"I can try and find a new therapist."

"Whatever."

Rachel Ray glided around her TV home's kitchen and showed us how to make a great meal in 30 minutes. She was so cute. Too bad she cared so much about food.

It was easy to get up in the morning. According to the Internet, anorexics awaken deep in their brain the primordial instinct to hunt and gather at night, which was the best time for hunting in ancient times. My eyes would pop open at 2 am without a problem, and my energy would be the best it was all day. I used that for the treadmill and to write.

Over the next week or so, Kristin accused me of having an affair with anorexia. I did love anorexia. Anorexia was easy to please and very satisfying as long as the number on the scale was right. With Kristin, I couldn't even fold the towels correctly after doing the laundry.

In my office at work, I shut the door and reached for the phone. The familiar voice of Kaiser's automated phone service came on the line and, I made the number selections to get me to an advice nurse.

"Hi," I said when the live person finally interrupted the recordings about why it was important to get a flu shot, "I need to get a therapist...Like a psychiatrist or something."

"Okay. Tell me a little bit about what's going on with you."

"I am..."

*It's none of her business. Hang up. Plus, you're not even anorexic. There are plenty of anorexics out there that are much thinner than you. They are going to see you and they are going to think you are joking calling yourself an anorexic. You'll take up a therapist's time and a real anorexic somewhere will die.*

"I have some sort of an eating disorder...I think. I mean, people say I do." Sweat formed at the base of my hairline and trickled down my face.

"Are you over eating?"

*Yes.*

"No. Pretty much the opposite," I said.

"Are you making yourself vomit?"

"No." That was the most offensive thing I had heard in a while.

"But you are underweight. Are you over exercising?"

*There is no such thing.*

"Not to me, no. But people in my life are telling me that I have lost too much weight."

"Okay, let me see who I might have for you..."

"I've been to Dr. Porter and he was no good for me. I lost 20 pounds and he insisted I had a panic disorder and that men don't get anor.."

*Don't use the word. You're not even, and stop putting down Dr. Porter.*

"...that men don't get eating disorders." I looked over my shoulder to make sure no one was opening my door. "I'd really prefer that I see a woman."

"Okay, let me take a look and see who we have...That is accepting new clients..." She tapped on a computer keyboard and I waited for what I guessed was a number of screens to display. "I have Peggy. She is supposed to be really good. She is at the office near Standiford and Tully."

That met my second requirement. I wanted to see a woman that was not in the same office as Dr. Porter. "Sounds great."

"You'll need to call that office directly to set up an appointment." She gave me the number, and I wrote it down on whatever piece of paper was handy on my desk. With sweet sorrow, I hung up the phone and looked at the number I had written. I wrote Peggy's name above it, and decided to wait an hour or two before I called it.

*You are nothing if not an anorexic.*

A tear ran the length of my cheek. I let it dry there and wondered if the amount of calories burned by forming a single tear would be on the Internet somewhere.

Kristin got a temporary job in Livermore, so for a short while, the three of us commuted to Livermore together. I would drive in the morning and drop Kristin and Brighid off, and in the afternoon I would pick them both up but Kristin would drive the commute part of the trip.

That was a perfect arrangement for me because I started getting tired around 4:00, and I could take a short nap in the car on the way home, just as Kristin would sleep on the ride in most days.

I liked the feel of the road twisting as I slept in the passenger seat and noticed how little of the seatbelt I had to pull out to fit around me. It was a good afternoon.

My eyes opened at one point and Kristin was crying.

"What's the matter?" I said.

She huffed a sigh like the problem should be the most obvious thing in the world. Evanescence came from the radio singing "My Immortal."

"What's the matter, baby?"

"Everything is the matter. This song makes me cry. Have you ever listened to the words of this song? This song is me and my life."

> I'm so tired of being here
> Suppressed by all my childish fears
> And if you have to leave
> I wish that you would just leave
> 'Cause your presence still lingers here
> And it won't leave me alone

"Honey, I am not going anywhere." I reached over and tried to hold her hand, but she dodged me.

"You are already gone."

"What the hell are you talking about?"

"You are not you anymore. You are killing yourself and making me watch you do it."

"Hon, I have a new therapist that I am starting with next week. I'm gonna be fine."

"Why am I not important enough to you for you to stop this?"

"Stop what, Daddy?"

"Nothing honey." I turned the radio up, faded the music to the backseat, and turned to Kristin. "You are important to me."

"Not as important as anorexia."

"That's not true, Honey. Anorexia is a disease…"

"You can tell me that a million times and it doesn't fucking matter. We all have choices. You are making this choice just like a crank addict. It's no different."

The road beneath us switched from Corral Hollow to 580 South and finally 132 East.

"I'm not choosing to be this way," I said.

Kristin stared out the windshield with both hands on the wheel.

"Hon, why won't you talk to me?"

"Leave me alone, Jim."

My ribs stabbed into my skin where the seatbelt strap crossed them. I pinched at my gut and checked my chin for fat.

We pulled into the driveway. Twenty miles and she hadn't even looked my way by accident. She was mad at me for being sick, as far as I could tell.

*She is jealous.*

That could be part of it.

*It's a lot of it. You've shown her that you can get really thin with just diet and exercise.*

She went to the loft where I write and played Bejeweled on the computer. I joined her there and sat on the rust colored futon behind her. She didn't talk. Once the silence went from awkward to normal, I left the room and sat on our bed to read. When it was time, I gathered Brighid from the TV room and got her ready for bed.

"Give mommy a kiss goodnight," I said as we walked by the loft on the way to her room.

"G'night, Pumkin," Kristin said turning from her game. Her voice tone was nice and I had a shadow of a hope that maybe the fight was over and she'd be my wife again. There was a better chance of that than there was of me understanding what the fight was about.

"What's your favorite part?" Brighid said to me as I lay her down in her bed.

"My favorite part was when I picked you up from school, what's your favorite part?"

"My favorite part was giving you a hug, what's your favorite part?"

"I already told you," I said, laughing.

"Oh yeah." She curled up on her side beneath her Disney Princess blanket as I stepped out of her room.

Kristin was playing Spider Solitaire now on the computer, and I watched her from the loft entrance. She didn't turn or show any sign that she knew I was there, so I went back to the bed and my book.

In a while, I heard the familiar tones of the Windows system shutting down, and Kristin joined me in the room.

"Hey, Hon," I said, looking from her to the mound that was my gut as I lay on my back on the bed. I tried to suck it in but it wouldn't go away. So gross.

*You really should get the treadmill going a bit faster in the morning. You've been coasting lately. And watch how much cereal you pour for yourself.*

A box of Special K would last me over a month.

*So see if you can stretch it out to 2 months.*

"Hi," Kristin said. She didn't look at me as she crossed the floor to the bathroom and shut the door.

I got a word out of her though, and that is pretty good compared to the rest of the evening. Maybe things were okay. I hated going to bed angry, but even worse was going to bed despised.

She joined me on the bed and reached for the remote control. The Food Channel was already on and she watched the show in silence. She didn't look my way.

"Babe, are we going to talk about this?" I said.

"There is nothing to say."

"But why are you still mad."

She shrugged and kept her eyes fixed on the TV.

"Are you still mad?" I said, "Because I don't want us to go to bed mad."

"Fine, I'm not mad then." The commercials interrupted that southern woman cook that makes all the innuendos as she bakes, but Kristin kept her eyes away from me.

"Honey. Yes you are. We should talk about it."

"There is nothing to say."

"What do you mean there is nothing to say? If you are mad about something, you should tell me what it is. That's the way we solve things."

She clicked the remote control and rolled over to face the wall. "Turn off the light."

"Kristin…"

"I am tired. Turn off the fucking light."

I got off the bed and flipped the switch on the wall. I stumbled over a pair of shoes on the way back to the bed. "Honey, I really think we should talk about this."

"I am praying," she said, her voice in a growl that made me question to whom she prayed.

"Sorry."

The darkness between me and the ceiling drew strange patterns that battled each other for my attention. The air thickened around my ears and increased the silence. I sucked my gut in so that the covers wouldn't bulge so much. I shouldn't take up so much room. I had no right.

I grabbed the inner lining of my cheek between my teeth and bit down. The skin slipped out and I grabbed it again.

Kristin's breathing evened out next to me. What had I done? No answer came.

*In the morning, you need energy for the treadmill. You are going to have to forget about Kristin and get some sleep.*

"Babe," I said.

Nothing.

"Honey?"

She grunted and shifted in the bed. "I was asleep."

"Babe, can't we please talk about this?" I said. "I can't sleep."

"I was asleep." Her words growled out through gritted teeth as she lay on her side facing the wall. The only thing that linked us now was darkness.

"I don't get why you are mad." I tried for the millionth time. "Please."

"Good night, Jim."

"Honey…"

"Let me sleep." She pulled the covers higher up on herself and left me with the dark room and her breathing again.

My stomach twisted and turned and wretched. I almost threw up, and I sat up quick to stop the feeling. My vision blackened. The dark room came back into focus, and I decided I liked the complete blackness better.

Kristin slept solid, each of her peaceful breaths proving how little she cared about our marriage, about me.

I tried hugging her from behind the way I would if there hadn't been a fight. What was the fight about anyway? What did I miss? I may as well have been cuddling a bag of dirty clothes, so I gave up and rolled onto my back. Hours clicked away, and my inner cheek grew raw.

I got up and moved to the bathroom mirror where even in the dark, I could see the disgusting flab that kept me from being perfect. It rounded out my sides and my gut in front of me. The blood pounded hard into my head and I pressed my fingertips against my eyes. I combed my fingers back through my hair twice.

Through the dark, I could see the lump in the bed that was Kristin. The alarm clock's red numbers said 11:45. Tomorrow was going to be hard if I didn't get some sleep.

*How are you going to do the treadmill with no sleep?*

How would I write? How would I work? Brighid needs me to be up for her.

*Let's not lose track of what is most important here.*

I shoved out my lower lip and sighed. My breath rushed hard against the bottom of my nose. My heart brutalized the inside of my rib cage, and I moved to the inner bathroom and shut the door.

The light switch in there was always temperamental, and it wouldn't turn on for me that night so I stood in the phone booth sized room alone with the toilet. Why wouldn't she talk to me?

Tears came like bullets, and my body convulsed into sobs that sucked deeper and deeper at the air in my lungs until I was doubled over trying to breathe. I hugged my legs and pressed my forehead against the wall. My chin touched my knees.

*You couldn't have brought your knees this close to your face a while back.*

I couldn't catch my breath and I was scared that the staccato rasps would wake Kristin and put me in deeper shit than I was already in.

Awareness left me. All I knew were the tears on my face, the sobs in my breath, and the feel of the bathroom wall against my forehead.

This was stupid to be wallowing in self pity, and I knew it, but I couldn't stand up. My legs refolded themselves when I tried to push myself to a stand, and the action made breathing that much harder. A vision of the night in Boswell's when I first met Kristin flashed across my memory, and a new wave of sobs ripped through me. I pictured her walking toward me and forever next to her mother at our wedding. Forever?

It got cold in the bathroom, and I hugged my legs tighter against the chill. I hand walked myself up the wall to a standing position. My stomach heaved, and I turned to the toilet, but nothing came. I supported myself with both hands against the top of the toilet's tank. My breath came easier now, and I grabbed big gulps of air through my mouth and listened as the rhythm of my breathing normalized.

Standing upright, I palmed the tears off my cheeks and went back to the bed. Sleep took me at last with only the fear that I would wake up in the morning.

# Chapter 33

I sat across from them like I had countless times before. Emmeline had heated something from home, and Gabrielle bought soup from the lunch line. I had a Chicken Marsala lean cuisine, and by the time Gabrielle joined Emmeline and me at the table, I had eaten half the chicken breast and slipped the rest of the black tray of food back into its cardboard box.

"That's all you're going to eat?" Emmeline said.

*None of her fucking business. Tell her. It's not for her to decide.*

I nodded. I had a ration of excuses. I had eaten at an office party earlier. I had had a big breakfast. This chicken tastes funny. My stomach is upset. Emmeline had heard them all before. Her truth-serum eyes didn't help matters much.

"Jim you are way to skinny. You weigh less than I do. Remember when we used to joke we would pass each other as I gained the weight?" Emmeline was leaving for maternity leave at the end of the workday. This was her goodbye lunch with Gabrielle and me.

I smiled—partly for the old joke and partly because she said I was skinny.

"Your face looks old," Gabrielle said.

*Jealous.*

"Ya think?" I said.

They both nodded. "The skin is showing folds like a loose mask."

I shrugged and smiled again. We were on my favorite topic— weight loss in general and specifically mine. The mirror wouldn't show me what these two saw, so it was nice to be able to hear some nice things about myself. I pushed the lean cuisine box back and forth between my hands on the tabletop.

"You do know you could die from this, right? You do know this can kill you?" Gabrielle said. Emmeline nodded and looked down onto her pregnant belly that pushed the limits of a pink maternity top.

*Oh come on. You know Gabrielle. She is always saying things like that. She's never been put on a project here at work that wasn't the most impossible job with the worst people to work with. She's a doom's day wisher.*

"I'm not gonna die." I laughed at the idea.

"Karen Carpenter didn't plan on dying either." Gabrielle said. Emmeline still avoided eye contact.

*Oh sure, here we go. Everyone knows Karen Carpenter. They always invoke the Karen Carpenter thing. Maybe that chick just wasn't as good at this as you are, did anyone ever think of that?*

"I'm not like her."

"But you are heading that way."

*Bullshit.*

"No, I'm not."

Gabrielle sighed, pressed her lips together, and shook her head back and forth.

"I just wish," Emmeline said, "That whatever it is in your life that you don't think you have control over, that you could just give that control over to God. There are lots of things in my life that I know I can't control and I know that God will see them through for me." Tears formed in the bottom of her eyes, and she looked up to try and stop them from falling. They fell, and now I had upset my pregnant friend again.

"Emmeline, I am getting a new therapist. I already have an appointment."

*And what did she mean there were things you didn't have control of? You are in complete control. Ask her that.*

We have been over that before. It's just a difference of opinion.

"This has been going on too long, Jim," Emmeline said.

I smirked.

The subject changed to work and how Gabrielle was having a hard time meeting whatever deadline hung over her head. The two of them went back and forth about the projects they were working on until it sounded like a contest to see who had to work with the most unreasonable people. I couldn't relate to this at all.

At the end of lunch, I gave Emmeline a copy of *One Truth at a Time* and signed it to her.

"What am I supposed to do," she said, "read this to the baby?"

I knew for sure at that point she was sick of me and all my bullshit. She would never call it bullshit though, being a Christian and all. I left lunch and Emmeline and I never spoke again.

Standing in the kitchen, Kristin threw her arms around me the way she used to in the early days. It was a nice long meaningful embrace that seemed to go on past the awkward point where the hug turns more into a slow dance with no music. I pulled her closer to me and felt her do the same. Brighid must have been busy because she would normally worm her way into the hug by now.

"Wow," I said.

"Hmm?" Kristin said, her head still pressed against my chest.

"Look how far your arms can go around me. I can remember when they weren't able to reach this far…"

She shoved me away, turned from me, and walked up the stairs.

"What's the matter?"

"If you don't know, then that is part of the problem," she said. The bedroom door shut behind her as I reached the middle of the staircase.

The knob wouldn't turn in my hand. "Kristin?" I said, and I knocked.

She opened the door and walked away from it. "What is the matter?" I said, "We were hugging and then you freaked out."

"That's just it. We were hugging." She turned away from the bathroom mirror to face me. "I am so fucking sick of anorexia."

"Hon, I have an appointment with a new therapist and with luck, this one will make a difference for me. I am working on it. I know it's a problem."

"Do you know," she said, "that all my friends do is ask about you? It's always 'How's Jim doing?' or 'Is Jim okay?' I'm sick of answering it."

"I am sick, Honey."

*No you aren't. You just have really good diet ideas.*

"You're not sick. You are in love with anorexia and you choose to be how you are."

"That's not how it is, Babe. I have these urges. Really strong urges. They're like…"

"Urges…Fuck that. I have urges too," she said. "We've been over this."

"In sickness and in health," I thought to myself, but she didn't believe anorexia was a disease anyway. She wasn't one to let the facts get in the way of her argument. It didn't matter what the medical field said. She had it figured out that I was doing this on purpose.

"Even Jason asks how you are," she said. Jason was her oldest friend. "No one talks to me without bringing you up. There is no escape for me. There is no me time."

"I'm sorry. Like I said, I start with a new therapist next week."

"Oh and your last one worked so well. You are a weak person. You know how I can't stand addicts and weakness."

"That's not how this is."

"Well, that's how I see it." She checked herself in the mirror one more time. "I'm going to use the computer."

"Kristin…"

"This is not a good time to talk to me." She left me standing next to the empty bed in the middle of our empty room.

The office was a bit more clinical than Dr. Porter's. This one was in a strip mall and was built to be a medical office as opposed to being built to be a house and converted over to office space. It felt weird going to a therapist with a storefront between a TCBY and a Postal Connection store, but I guess technically you could meet anywhere.

I sat in the waiting room of chairs against the walls of a small rectangular room. The predictable small table stacked with magazines interrupted the flow of chairs here and there.

Three pages into the forms and questionnaires they had me fill out, I got bored and my handwriting got worse. Visions of Dr. Porter standing and ranting at the end of a session fought to convince me I'd be better off just walking out of there.

*You are too fat to look anorexic.*

I looked down and checked my gut and pinched my sides. That was a strong possibility.

*This therapist is going to laugh at you when she sees you and you claim to be anorexic. You are the fattest anorexic that ever asked for help. Get out of here before you embarrass yourself.*

The papers were finished and I walked them up to the receptionist with the feeling of walking in a spotlight that adolescents know.

"Thank you…" she checked the name on my papers, "…James. Peggy will be with you shortly."

"Thanks." I read until my name was called. A woman with glasses and a bit of a hippie aura about her stood in the door that led to the offices. My relief was immediate. I could relate to free spirits much easier.

"I'm Peggy."

"Jim." I said, and we shook hands. She led me back through the hall past closed office doors and around the corner to a half open door that she ushered me through.

"I'll be back with you in just a second," she said.

I took a seat and let my eyes wander the office for clues about Peggy. A fountain purred over aesthetically positioned rocks in a corner. A photo on her desk showed twin teen girls. I didn't recognize any of the books on the bookshelves, but on a table near the door was a thick volume by Adrienne Rich.

I sighed hard. I had seen Adrienne Rich speak years ago at San Jose State. During the question and answer portion of the presentation, a teacher that I admired asked her about her time in Robert Lowell's creative writing class.

"He said my poetry was good," she said, "which I took as a compliment even though it came from a white male."

I got up and walked out of her talk at that time. I shared that same story with another instructor at San Jose State. When I accused her of being a man hater, he said she was a friend of his and he assured me that she wasn't like that.

It stuck with me forever though. She rode on the wave of political correctness that made the white males the lower class instead of striving for true equality. To me, she was no different than the governor in Alabama in the 1960s.

So with her book in an obvious position of being recently read in Peggy's office, doubt flooded me.

"Sorry about that," Peggy said as she shut the office door and sat in her swivel chair with a fresh pad of legal paper in her lap.

I nodded, letting my head bounce up and down more than was necessary.

*Your gut is sticking out. Good luck convincing her you have anorexia. You should be ashamed for wasting this woman's time.*

I crossed my arms in front of my stomach and waited for Peggy to talk.

"I want you to know," she said, "that for the first month or so, we won't even be talking about food or anything. I'm not going to start asking you to eat more, so you can just relax. Think of this as a get to know you sort of period."

I moved my gaze from its fixed position across the room and met hers to see if she was serious. She didn't drop her eyes the way a liar would. "Okay," I said.

"So in the form you filled out, it says you saw Dr. Porter for a while. What was that like?"

I shrugged.

"He just didn't work out for you..." Peggy raised the tone of the last word for that expectant feeling.

I smirked and returned my arms to the protective position across my stomach. "He said I didn't have anorexia because men don't get anorexia."

"And what do you think?"

"I don't know."

"Do you have anorexia?" She said.

*No.*

I cocked my head to the side and thought.

*She is going to tell you that you are too fat to be anorexic.*

Peggy didn't mind the silence and waited for my answer.

"Yeah," I said, "I think I do."

"Well, like I said, we're really not going to talk much about that in these first sessions, and I am definitely not going to tell you to eat more or exercise less or anything else. All that will be further down the road."

That set my mind at ease and I relaxed a little in the chair.

"So what are some things you are interested in?" She asked with her pen at the ready above her legal pad.

"Working out. Diet." I said.

She made a note and nodded. "What do you like about that?"

With a smirk, I rolled my eyes a bit to the left in thought and crossed one leg over the other. "I like the success I feel when I have a good treadmill session or when I don't eat any unnecessary food in a day. I like the lower numbers on the scale."

"Okay, so aside from those things, what is important to you?"

I shrugged.

"Well, you are married, right?" Peggy said.

"Yeah." I said, and I looked at her. "Well, yeah, I mean of course my family is important to me."

"You have a good marriage?"

"Yeah, it's great."

"Kids?"

"I have two stepkids and a daughter that we had together, but you know, they are pretty much all mine. I've had the two older ones since they were 3 and 5."

"You have a good relationship with them?"

"Yeah."

"Okay, so you care about your family. What about stuff that is just for you?"

I looked at her.

"You know. Like what is there that you like that is just yours—that doesn't have to do with anyone else?"

Do people have things like that? I wondered and thought of Kristin with her trips to the nail salon every 2 weeks. That was her though. "The treadmill is pretty much all I do for myself that is all mine."

"Okay." She made a note on the pad she had in her lap. "How about as a kid? Did you have any interest as a kid?"

"I was on the swim team. I coached it too actually. And I used to write songs on my guitar and play in a band. I played some coffee houses by myself as well. Oh, and I still write...like fiction—not songs anymore."

"Do you still sing?"

"Not really." I was getting tired and I looked for a clock to see if my hour was up, but she didn't have one that you could see. I shifted in my chair, careful to keep my stomach covered up.

*You can cover that gut all you want. She can see it, and she knows you're a lousy anorexic at best—and that's all you are.*

"So what about your writing? Fiction, you said, right?"

I nodded. "I have 2 books out, and I'm working on a time travel story right now."

"Out like published?"

"Well yeah, but they are self published. I mean anyone with the money could have a book or two out these days. The Internet sites I use as publishers," I made the quote motion with my fingers, "make it pretty affordable and easy."

"So you don't consider your books an accomplishment?" Peggy said.

"Well, sure I suppose they are, but really...They're no big deal. Anyone with the cash can do what I do. Bookstores won't usually even carry my stuff because it's what they call print on demand. The online places have them though...Like Amazon and whatever."

She scribbled some more down on her notepad and flipped the page. "What else did you used to do?"

"That's really about it."

"Do you have any interest in being in a band again?"

"Not really." I shook my head and eyed the Adrienne Rich book.

"Why not?"

"I'm just past that. I'm not big on going back."

She made a final note on her pad and set it on the desk behind her. "I think we should meet twice a week at least at first. Are mornings or afternoons better for you?"

"Whichever is fine," I said, "Probably mornings."

She set me up for two days later at 8 am with the warning that she is sometimes about ten minutes late for that appointment. I took the cue and left the office on the road to recovery?

# *Chapter 34*

"How did therapy go?" Kristin always knew when I had an appointment and that they lasted about an hour, so my cell always rang before my car left the parking lot. In some cases when the appointment went late, there would already be missed calls and voicemail as soon as I turned my phone on.

"It was fine," I said.

On this particular evening, I had seen Peggy at 4, and even though we already had the cell phone talk, she brought it up again after treadmill.

"What did you talk about?"

I shrugged. She wanted me to have a tape recorded memory of any conversation I had when she was not around. I was often asked to recite conversations I had with my mom on the phone or at her house if Kristin didn't go with me. It created a feeling of having to live through things twice. "Just about me and whatever." I hoped that would kill her interest.

The commercial faded to another commercial and I fixed the pillows on my side of the bed for better leaning. Leaning against the wood headboard killed my back. It even hurt to lean against one pillow. Wooden chairs were unbearable as well. I had to sit on some sort of pillow. My car was getting uncomfortable against my ass too.

"You didn't talk about me at all?" she said.

"A little." That was an example of stupid honesty.

"What did you say?" She shifted to her side and faced me.

"Just you know, that we have a good marriage. That I love you. That you are supportive. Stuff like that."

"How did I come up?" she said, during what had to be the longest commercial break of television history.

"I don't remember, Hon."

"Did you bring me up or did she?"

"I don't know."

"Jim Kohl, you must know that," she said.

"Nothing bad was said about you, sweetheart."

"Are you sure?"

"Yes. What bad could I say about you?"

*Arguing and intense conversations like this will raise the heart rate and burn calories.*

"I'm just afraid…Never mind, it's stupid," she said, pulling the covers up closer to her stomach.

"What? What are you talking about?"

"No. I told you. It's stupid."

"What is on your mind, baby?"

She sighed and folded her hands in her lap. "What if after all this counseling and therapy and stuff, you find out that I am the cause of your problems?"

"Oh honey, that's not going to happen. You're great for me. I love you."

*Having sex is the equivalent of at least 150 sit-ups.*

"I know you do, but what if somehow your therapist talks you into believing that I drove you to anorexia?"

"Peggy isn't like that. She just asks me questions about me and what I think and whatever. She never really tells me much of anything."

"Really?"

"She tells me about her kids and stuff a little, but that's about it."

"I just get worried," she said.

"Oh baby, there is nothing to worry about." I rolled over to her and cuddled up against her while the TV babbled in the background and consciousness gave way to sleep.


Kristin's birthday was coming up. We had just had Mother's Day, where I bought her as much as I could. Now I wandered Target alone trying to find something I may have missed or something she may have mentioned since Mother's Day. I could never buy a good enough gift for her. The cards in the store never expressed enough love.

The red logos and vests passed me on my search, and I knew that no matter what I ended up getting, I'd lay awake nights worrying that it wasn't the right thing, that it wasn't good enough, and that I wouldn't make her happy.

"Are you sure you really like it?" I would say, for the tenth time in an evening.

"Yes Honey…It's great."

"Cause you know, we can take it back if you want…"

"I love it Babe."

She could never convince me though and I would drive myself insane with it.

I cinched my belt a little tighter as I felt my jeans sliding down. My shirt billowed as I walked the aisles begging fate that the perfect gift would materialize. At the end of the candle aisle, I saw Heather, who was the administrative assistant in the part of the Lab where I worked before I took Caroline's place.

She made eye contact with me, I smiled, and she walked right past.

"Heather?" I said.

She turned back and looked with no light in her eyes.

"Heather, it's me…Jim." I showed her my work badge.

"Oh. Yeah. Oh my God. Jim. How are you doing?" The shock she showed pleased me.

"I'm doing okay. I've lost some weight. I guess I'm hard to recognize."

"No. No it's not that," she said, "I'm just all spaced right now. I have to get some stuff together for the wedding. We're finally getting married." She smiled. She and her boyfriend had a baby a few months back.

"That's awesome. Congratulations." The conversation wasn't going the way I wanted it to, and I don't remember much about what she said after that. She invited me to the wedding and I said I'd make it. I didn't. We walked away saying we would keep in touch. We didn't.

I continued through Target keeping an eye on the clock on my cell phone so I would make it back to work on time. I flipped through the CD racks and wondered if Heather really had so much on her mind or if I was unrecognizable. I would have my answer in a couple more days.

The Lab had about 6 main entrances when I worked there. You could go in through any one you wanted, but most people would drive in through the one that was closest to the building where they worked.

I arrived at my normal gate about 7 one morning and showed my badge to the guard at the gate.

He looked at me and he looked at the badge. "Can I see your license please," he said, "because this picture doesn't look like you."

"Sure." I undid my seatbelt and leaned to the left to free my wallet. I flopped it open to show my license.

"Can I get you to take the license out, please."

With a nod, I slid the license out from behind its plastic screen and handed it to the guard, who examined both pictures and me. "I'm going to need you to pull over to the side there. The license doesn't look like you either. I'm going to call my supervisor and have him take a look."

"Okay," I said. I parked my car where the guard told me and entertained myself with the idea that I was a spy trying to sneak into the Lab. I laughed at what a hassle this was just to go in and sit at a desk and fix punctuation. Within a few minutes, a security car pulled up behind me and a different guard with mirrored glasses walked up to my open window.

"How you doing?" His hand rested on the butt of his holstered pistol.

"Pretty good," I said, "How are you?"

"Doing all right. Can I see your badge and license please?"

"The other guard has them," I said.

"Okay. Sit tight, and I'll be right with you."

In my rearview mirror, I watched them hand my badge and license back and forth and talk about me. The second guard eventually walked back to my car with both of them in his hand.

"James, it looks like you have lost a lot of weight."

"Yeah I did." I almost said I had been sick.

*You are not sick. Even Kristin tells you that.*

"Well, I understand about weight loss, but you have to understand our point of view. You don't look like either of these pictures."

I nodded.

"I'm going to need you to turn around here and go to the badge office and get a new badge before we can let you in today."

"Okay," I said.

"You may want to think about getting a new license picture too because if you get pulled over, you don't look like that picture either."

"Okay." In my imagination I stormed the gate to a hail of gunfire and bullied my way into my office where I would take my computer hostage and have a lengthy negotiation, ending in my imminent death or imprisonment.

Instead, I just went to the badge office. I smiled as I stood in line knowing that I would get to show my progress to the woman behind the counter. She sent the two people ahead of me on their way, and motioned for me to come over. "Hi. Yeah, the guards said I need to take a new picture because I don't look like this one." I set the fat-faced badge portrait on the counter in front of her.

She glanced from the picture to my face and said, "Wow, they are right you don't look like this anymore." She let her eyes travel from the picture to my face one more time. "Wow."

"Yeah, I lost a lot of weight." I tried to sound casual, but really could she have noticed a cooler thing about me? I doubt it. There is no better feeling in the world than being recognized for your accomplishments.

"I would say so," she said, "Can I see your license too please?"

I grappled my wallet out of my pocket and pulled the license free again. She didn't make a comment about the license picture, but that was okay. It didn't lessen her reaction to the badge picture, and the license picture was thinner than the badge one anyway.

"Stand on the black pad for me please."

I knew that this black pad was a scale, so now she would know my weight as well, which I was sure would impress her. She took my picture and issued me my new badge.

At Dominique's eighth grade graduation, her Aunt Nancy was standing right next to me when we were all smiling and taking pictures of her in her cap and gown.

"Where's Jim?" Nancy said.

"He's right there next to you," her husband said.

It was the closest I ever came to being invisible. It was nice that someone asked for me when they thought I wasn't there. It was nice to be wanted, but it was a lot nicer to be too thin to be recognizable.

# Chapter 35

Peggy talked me into going to see a nutritionist and referred me to a woman named Sally that worked in the main Kaiser office.

"This is not to make you gain weight," Peggy said, "This is just to make sure you are eating enough to stay alive. You do want to stay alive, right?"

"Yes, of course."

She had arranged a rush appointment for me after one of our 8 am sessions that focused on my value. Evidently, when I did resumes and other bits of writing for people for nothing, and then Kristin got to hear the thanks firsthand while I got Kristin's off the cuff, "Oh yeah...They said to tell you thanks" I was allowing myself and my efforts to be devalued.

That part of the Peggy session spun through my head as I drove across town to the Kaiser office.

"You know what phrase I have really grown to hate," I told her at one point, "A phrase that just really makes my skin crawl?"

"What's that?" Peggy said.

"Do me a favor...I hate to hear it, and even saying it right now makes me sick."

"Sick how?"

"Sick like...It just kind of...deflates me. Like it sucks. It's hard to put it into words." I made an ex in front of my body with my arms with my hands near my legs.

"You know if someone asks you to do a favor, you could say no," Peggy said.

"With Kristin, it's not so easy."

"Why?"

"Because that is the kind of thing that is going to start a fight," I said. "She'll get really mad."

"But it upsets you to say yes."

I nodded.

"Why is her being upset more important than you being upset?" Peggy set her notepad on her desk and waited for the answer.

I worked my bottom lip between my teeth and glanced around the room at her daughter's picture, at her fountain, and at her full bookcase. "I have no idea."

I still had no idea as I sat in the waiting room of the Health Education office where Sally, the nutritionist, worked. There was a sign in front of me telling me how important it was that I quit smoking. It showed a graphic horror story of a lung blackened by years of tobacco.

"Are you Jim?" She was blonde, with short hair, and a touch older than me.

"Yeah."

"Sally Greenwall." She offered her hand and I stood to shake it.

"Nice to meet you," I said.

"You too. My office is right over there." She motioned to an open door just past the receptionist counter. "I'll need to weigh you first. If that is all right?"

"Sure." I started to take off my jean jacket and clear my pants pockets of my keys, change, and wallet. Stepping on a scale with clothes on was bad enough, but I didn't need the extra weight.

*She's going to tell you that you aren't thin enough to be a problem. Your weight is too heavy for an anorexic. You are a poser—a fake—and you are wasting this woman's time.*

"Of course," I said, "this weight is with my clothes on, so really I am lighter than this."

"Understood," Sally said. She made a note of my weight and led me into a small room with a table cramped in the middle that served as her desk. The room had the feel of a kid's clubhouse. "So you know why you are here, I imagine?"

"I guess. I'm not going to allow myself to gain weight."

"You don't have to if you don't want to. I just want to talk about what you eat now, and see what you'd be willing to do."

"I'm not willing to eat a whole lot," I said. I didn't want this woman to hate me, but I knew that she and I had opposing goals.

"Do you make yourself vomit?"

"No." I was so offended. Bulimia, to me, was cheating.

"Do you use diuretics?"

"I don't know what those are, and you probably shouldn't tell me."

"Fair enough," she said. "How much water do you drink?"

"Water is pretty much all I drink besides coffee. I don't drink that much of it—especially if it is close to a weigh time."

"What is close to a weigh time?"

"Like…Three or four hours before I plan on weighing…I'm guessing though."

*The lady makes a good point. You should probably watch the time before weighing more closely.*

"And how many times do you weigh every day?"

"Two or three. On the weekends sometimes more."

"And you do it so often?"

"To be sure," I said.

She nodded like she understood and made a note. "Let's go through what you do eat each day…Do you eat every day?"

"Yes."

*Failure!*

"That's good," she said, "So take me through what you eat on a given day." Her pen poised at the ready above the pink sheet of legal sized paper that she had clipped in a file folder with my name on it.

"I have a little cereal in the morning."

*Five flakes, but it's best she doesn't know that. This is no time for honesty.*

"Okay," she said as her pen jumped to life, "And for lunch?"

"Half a Lean Cuisine."

*That was too much information. What did I just say?*

"Half?" She said.

I nodded.

"Okay. Dinner?"

"That is the tough one because there are people watching me. I eat whatever we're having and I just try to not overdo it."

"Would you say you eat a normal portion?"

"Maybe a little less than that, whatever that is." My bones pushed against the hard chair and I tried to find a comfortable way to sit.

"How about snacks? Do you have any snacks during the day?"

"I have some spinach leaves about 3 pm." I really should try and get rid of all snacks. I looked at the floor.

"Anything else?"

"Not really no." I shook my head and shifted in my seat.

"Okay. You're not eating enough, but I'm sure that is hard for you to hear."

"Yeah."

"I don't want to talk you into doing anything you aren't ready for because I know if I ask you to do a bunch of stuff you don't feel comfortable with, that really you won't do it anyway."

She really understood.

"How much do you exercise?" she said, setting her pen down on the table.

"Thirty minutes on the treadmill every day. Right now I have it set at 5.6 miles per hour at a 10 degree slope." I knew she had to be impressed with numbers like that. In 4 more tenths of a mile per hour, I would be maxing out the speed on the treadmill. The slope was already maxed.

"Can I get you to skip a day in between using the treadmill?"

"No."

"Okay," she said. "Like I said, this is about finding what you are and aren't willing to do."

"Well, I definitely can't do that."

"Got it. No problem. I should mention that our goal here today is not to make you gain weight. I just want to see you eating enough to keep yourself alive."

*Like you are anywhere near death. You have so much you could still lose. This is crap. Walk out of here.*

Why did everyone think that death was even a possibility? "Yeah. But I'm not gonna die."

"That is good to hear. Would you be willing to eat a half cup of cereal in whole milk?"

"No. Whole milk makes me gag. It's too thick."

"How about the 2 percent?"

"No. I'll do it with skim milk," I said.

"Will you pour more milk in the bowl than you need and drink it down after the cereal is gone?"

I paused, wondering if this was some sort of trick.

*She is like some sort of car salesman that is working you by making you pile up a bunch of what seems like insignificant agreements. Then she'll hit you with the big one, and you'll lose all your progress and control.*

"Is that something you feel comfortable with?" Sally said. Her face didn't have the slick look of a salesperson.

"Yeah, I think I could do that," I said.

"You could?"

I nodded.

"Great," Sally said and she wrote it on a piece of paper. "I'm worried about your protein intake though. Would you eat a protein bar?"

I weighed the possibility and thought of the calorie count on the bar I stashed and pretended to eat in the drawer at work. "Nah, I don't think so."

So on it went like Dr. Seuss's *Green Eggs and Ham.* Would you could you, eat some meat? Try it, try it, it's a treat. In the end of the negotiation, I agreed to the following:

The cereal and drinking the milk all the way down.

Two table spoons of nuts at 9 am.

The whole Lean Cuisine.

Another 2 tablespoons of nuts at 3 pm.

Dinner.

"Can the nuts be salt free?" I asked.

"Sure…Why?"

"Because it was high blood pressure that started this whole thing in the first place."

"Yeah, that's fine. With or without salt—your choice."

"Right on."

Sally gave me a copy of the eating plan we agreed on. I held it in my hand like a huge bill I couldn't afford before folding it into my jacket pocket. Even there, the list seemed heavy. "And this won't make me gain weight?"

"Not with the amount of treadmill you do, no, it shouldn't. If you start to gain and you feel like restricting, call me and we can work something out."

"Okay." We stood, and she ushered me through the door. "You know," I said, "Do you have pamphlets or anything that can help people understand anorexia? My wife just doesn't get it."

"I think I do, yes." The smile in her voice made her hard to be angry with, even though her ultimate goal was to see me gain weight. She went behind the receptionist desk and rummaged through drawers and cabinets while I leaned on the patient's side of the counter. "You know what, it looks like we are out of them, but I can print you up a couple. They'll be in black and white though."

"That's fine." I took the papers, thanked her again, and went out the door to my car.

*You are going to get fat. You don't need someone telling you how to eat healthy. You know how to diet. Look at the progress you have made. Now you are going to eat nuts twice a day? Do you have any idea what the fat content of nuts is?*

Yes I do.

*And the calories too. I can't believe you would agree to eating nuts. You are going to destroy all we have worked so hard for.*

She said I wouldn't gain weight as long as I keep up with the treadmill.

*You can never miss a day of treadmill again.*

I know.

*Not ever.*


I took the day off from work because of the two morning appointments. It would have taken me another hour to get to Livermore, and I would have only had time to work half a day anyway. I did have to drive Brighid there that morning and pick her up later though, since that's where her school was.

At the house, I made some coffee and headed up to my writing room to call Kristin and let her know how the appointments went. The computer booted up in front of me as the phone started to ring.

"This is Kristin," she said, sounding like I had called in the middle of something huge.

"Hey, Honey."

"Hey babe. How was therapy?"

"It was good, I guess, you know." I swiveled back and forth in my black leather office chair.

"What did you talk about?"

Was this the best time to bring this up? She was 100 miles away and busy at work, but she had asked. She had to know sooner or later or the discovery would be useless anyway. "I did figure out one major thing today."

"What's that?"

I pushed myself up from the chair and headed down the hall to our bedroom. "I feel bad when I do people's resumes and stuff all the time. It makes me feel used. Most times, no one even thanks me; they thank you."

"But they are grateful," she said.

"Yeah, baby, but I don't hear it from them. I only hear it from you, and usually I have to ask to even hear that." As the words came from my mouth, I couldn't remember a time since I met her when I actually said something that I knew she wouldn't want to hear. I was saying how I felt—even though I knew it was unpopular. I could almost feel the rusty strain of reality reorganizing itself.

"Okay," she said, in that pregnant tone that stretches out the vowels to hide the true feelings behind the word.

"What?" I said. I lay down on the bed to avoid being knocked to the floor with whatever she was thinking.

"Nothing," she said.

"Kristin…What is the matter?"

"Nothing…Jim." She had a way of making my name sound like a curse.

"I don't get what you are pissed about," I said.

"I mean. You know, I want you to be over anorexia and all that, but that doesn't mean I want you to become a selfish prick. People ask you for help on resumes and with writing because that is what you are good at. It takes you at most an hour to do what some people would never be able to do. It's like when Uncle Art comes over to help with the pool."

I not only remembered thanking Uncle Art in person, but I remembered paying him as well. Despite the fact that there was no true analogy here, I didn't point that out because she was already mad enough. I stayed silent.

"That is what people do. They help each other with things they are good at. But I guess you are gonna do whatever you need to do, but I'll tell you this. I'm not staying married to some selfish asshole. I did that once already."

"All right. Okay. Forget it," I said.

"No that's okay. You gotta do what you gotta do. I'll just tell people no when they ask me for your help from now on."

"Honey, it may not be forever that I feel this way. I just need some time…"

"Whatever…I'm telling people no," she said. "Anything else?"

I saw the anorexia pamphlets on the bed and picked them up. "I have an eating plan now, and I also got you some information on anorexia so you can kinda see what I am going through."

"I don't want to understand anorexia."

I grabbed my lower lip between my teeth and let the papers fall from my hand.

*You are nothing if not an anorexic.*

The phone call ended somehow, and I slapped my cell phone shut. I closed my eyes and hoped to God I weighed less the next day.

# Chapter 36

With the phone call over, all that was left was the empty house and me. I had already written that day, and I had the house to myself so infrequently that I just enjoyed it. Then it was time to eat.

We had a can of mixed nuts leftover from some party or another. I grabbed that and a tablespoon from the drawer to measure out my snack. If I had dug a little deeper into the drawer I probably could have found an actual tablespoon. I just used one of the bigger cereal spoons and covered the concave surface of it with nuts, poured them on the counter, and repeated the process.

I ended up with about 8 nuts. I couldn't be concerned with whether that was truly 2 tablespoons or not because whatever it was, it was what I was comfortable doing.

I ate the nuts one at a time and chewed them more than I needed to before swallowing. Right about nut number 6…

*I can't believe you are eating that stuff and you didn't even check the label first. All you are doing is sitting around the house today, and you are putting all that into your body?*

I'll do the treadmill later.

*You're going to eat these nuts and sit around until later when you do the treadmill—if you even do it—and in the meantime these nuts are going to serve no purpose and add weight and fat to your body. Look. You can already see a difference.*

I checked my gut and pinched the fat there. It was true. Sally said that this eating plan wouldn't make me gain. She said this was just about staying alive.

*Of course she's going to tell you things like that. But you know better than that. You know about careful eating. You've come this far without Sally. You dropped your blood pressure, and where was she? You know what you need to do, so do it.*

The two last nuts sat on the white kitchen tiles.

*Come on. No one will know.*

I stared at them until it looked like they floated above the counter's surface. They were all that was left, and the rest of the room turned to melted film—the thick syrup of dream liquid.

*What is 2 nuts in the trash? You know you'll feel better. We can't do anything about the ones you already ate, but it's not too late to do right with these.*

I shook my head to refocus the world. I pinched my side again and checked the fatty skin hanging down beneath my chin.

*If you want to weigh in the 140s again by tomorrow, then eat the nuts.*

It's not a fair world when the only choices are fat or thin. It's a trap, this life. I leaned hard with my hands flat on the counter. Do I want to be better, or do I want to stay like this?

*What is better? Fat or thin?*

I thought of Peggy and all her hard work with me so far.

*You are nothing if not an anorexic.*

I picked up one of the nuts and looked at it between my fingers. I remembered a time when I would shove a handful of these into my mouth without even thinking about it. Was that crazy, or was this?

I shook my head, closed my eyes, and popped the last two into my mouth.

Three hours passed quickly, and it was time to eat my Lean Cuisine. I was still full from the nuts, but a deal's a deal. I had to at least give this eating plan a try. Sally had been so nice and patient with me.

I split the plastic over the frozen meal, thinking of thawing frozen cavemen and giving them life. The microwave hummed. I wondered how I would ever fit this meal down. The nuts sat in my stomach like a lump.

When the oven beeped, I pulled the meal from it and let it cool on the kitchen counter for a couple minutes. There was little else I could do to stall now, so I got a fork from the drawer and went at the meal.

It was an enchilada in suiza sauce. Taste wise, it was one of the ones I enjoyed in the days when taste mattered. The Mexican spices, recently freed from suspended animation, didn't mix well with the lump of nuts still clogging my guts up. Halfway through the enchilada, my guts heaved and I had to fight to keep the food down. There is no way in the world that anyone needs this much food in a day.

*Then you know what to do.*

The garbage can was positioned so all I had to do was slide the black tray off the end of the counter and it would all be a memory.

*So do it, if it's so easy then.*

But Sally said...

*And who the hell is she to you? If you finish eating that thing, you are going to have to speed up the treadmill, and you nearly have it maxed out. You don't have the money for a faster treadmill.*

I had to cover my mouth as my esophagus fought to unswallow what was already on its way down. Sweat beaded on my forehead, and the room blurred behind my tears. Food shouldn't go down as hard as cheap whiskey.

I finished it though. There was no sense of accomplishment, but the relief was good enough. I rested on the couch until my heart slowed.

Later that afternoon after I already had Brighid home and the two older kids were home from school and in their rooms, I lay on the bed in my own room. I could see Brighid down the stairs working over a sheet of homework, and I figured this would be a good opportunity to call Kristin.

"Hey, Baby," I said.

"Hey." Her reply was short, so she was either still mad about the whole resume thing, or something at work irritated her.

"How's it going?"

"Fine. I'm bringing my mom home with me."

"That's cool. Why?"

"Because I want her with me."

"Oh okay," I said. I never had a problem with Cooky being over. "I ate, so far, everything I was supposed to eat. But my God, my body tried to reject that Lean Cuisine."

"Tell my mom," Kristin said.

"Hello," Cooky said.

"Hey Cooky. I'm on a new eating plan."

"A new plan?"

"Yeah, I had to see a dietician today."

"And how is that going for you, mejo?"

"Pretty good, but I had to really work at keeping my lunch down."

"Just do the best you can, mejo, as long as you keep trying, you'll be fine."

"Right on, thanks."

"Here's your wife."

"Okay."

"What?" Kristin said.

"I don't know," I said, "I didn't ask to talk to you. Your mom gave you the phone back. How does traffic look?"

"Normal," Kristin said.

"So you think you'll be home around 7:30 or something?"

"Maybe."

"Oh okay, well, I guess I'll talk to you later then."

"Bye." She hung up. I kept the dead silent cell phone against my ear. Nothing is as silent as a cell phone after an argument.

And what the hell was the argument, anyway? More than likely, I'd find out later. Later would suck.

"You do realize that you are killing yourself and destroying this family, right?" This was the sucky later I knew was coming.

"I'm not killing myself."

"Yes you are, Jim."

How many times would we fight over this? "I'm seeing a therapist and I am on a new eating plan, Honey. I will be fine."

"Well, I don't know if this family can hold together while you are getting better. And I don't know that you are getting better. You are so skinny, Jim. Your ass looks like a Sharpei."

"A what?"

"A Sharpei," she said, "It's one of those dogs with the flaps of skin around its face."

"Like a bulldog?" I said.

"Yeah, kinda like a bulldog, but Sharpeis are bigger, and a lot of times they have flaps like that on the body too."

I didn't bother asking why she just didn't compare my ass to a bulldog. I guess it was the body thing that the Sharpei has.

"If you die, this family will be gone, Jim." The dog discussion was over.

"Honey. I am not going to die."

She told me again how she listens for the tapping of the keyboard when I write to make sure that I am alive and checks me for breathing in the middle of the night. She went through the bit about how her friends always ask how I am and how she is sick of hearing it. "You need to be the center of attention."

"That's not true," I shook my head as if that would prove my point. "I have a disease, babe."

"We've been through this before. You know how I feel about this. Do you know that you have made it impossible for me to enjoy my own weight loss?"

"Why?" I asked.

"I looked forward to having this surgery for such a long time, and now that I am finally getting thin—for the first time in my life—I can't even enjoy it because I have to worry about you every minute."

"Sorry." She must really love me if I am more important to her than her own weight loss. "I'm really sorry, Hon. I didn't mean for it to be this way."

"And I have to tell you...Today when you were saying how your body was rejecting the food. That completely pissed me off. That's why I had you talk to my mom. Do you have any idea how bad that is that you have got yourself to that point?"

"But Honey. That is a step in the right direction. I have an eating plan, and I'm following it."

"Barely."

"What is that supposed to mean? I only just got the plan this morning." I sat on the bed and rested my back against the headboard. She didn't sit.

"How much do you weigh now?"

I felt my face redden and the urge was to blurt out that I had made it into the 130s, but she wouldn't have shared my joy.

"145?"

I didn't say anything.

"Lower?"

"A little bit."

"140?"

The numbers must have shown like a digital readout across my forehead.

"You're in the 130s? Jesus Christ, Jim. That's just...I just...Fuck."

"Honey, I'm starting an eating plan. Where are you going?"

She left me sitting on the bed and headed toward the loft and the computer.

"Babe?"

I shrugged. Her anger always hurt, but it's not like she had never been mad at me before. I had things to do anyway. It was treadmill time. Everything would feel better after a good 30-minute burn. I changed clothes and grabbed a small sweat towel from the pile of laundry overflowing from our blue hamper.

I could've just gone straight down to the treadmill where I knew the welcome would be warm, but the fan light in the loft where Kristin sat grabbed my attention when I reached the top of the stairs. I should go talk to her.

*Bad idea.*

But I would feel better if we could talk this out before the treadmill and definitely before we went to bed.

*She's going to stay mad and trying to talk to her is just going to make it worse. Go exercise. You'll feel good about you.*

My marriage seemed more important than the treadmill at that moment, so I made the mistake of going to the loft.

"Hey, Honey."

"Hey."

The computer screen had a website with what looked like holocaust survivors standing naked against a wall. You could see all their bones, their skin hung off them like a rapper's pants. Kristin and I couldn't even finish watching *Schindler's List*, so I didn't see how she could look at this site. "What are you doing?"

"What does it look like?"

I looked closer at the screen and saw it was an anorexic site. "I don't look that bad," I said.

"Almost." She kept her eyes on the screen and scrolled as she read. Maybe she was trying to understand.

"Well, I'm not going to get that bad."

"We'll see."

I could've reassured her that I was on the right path. I might have told her that I loved her and that no diet was more important than she was. An apology may have been the right move. Instead, I said, "I'm going to go do the treadmill now."

"Of course." She clicked to another page of the anorexia site.

"What does that mean?"

"What the fuck do you want from me, Jim. You're badgering me."

"I want us to be okay."

"Well…" She tossed her head to the side and stopped whatever words were on deck to spout from her mouth.

"Well what?"

"Just go do your fucking treadmill."

"Would it make you happy if I didn't do the treadmill?"

*Have you lost your mind? You know what you've eaten today.*

"I don't give a shit." She huffed a sigh and shook her head.

I could have stopped to wonder how we grew so far apart, but really I needed to work out, so I left her sitting at the computer.

I woke in the middle of one night and saw a woman walk from the bathroom and stand in front of the mirror. She leaned in close to look at herself and rubbed a finger across one of her eyes. Figuring it was Kristin, I rolled over to find Kristin asleep next to me. I sat upright in bed, and the woman was gone. After thinking, I realized that the mirror woman had long blonde hair, and that Kristin has dark hair. A ghost? A hallucination brought on by malnutrition? I don't know, but it wasn't the last time I would see her.

# Chapter 37

If the receptionist in the mental health office knows your name by sight, you probably have a problem.

"Hi James. Here for Peggy?" There it was. I wasn't invisible to her like I was to my own friends like Heather in Target. Invisibility had its allure.

"Hey, how're you doing? Yeah." I set my Kaiser card where she could reach it.

"Oh I don't need that, James. Twenty dollars."

I gave her a twenty, and started away from the counter.

"Did you want your receipt?" she said.

"No...No that's cool. Thanks."

"Okay, have a seat and I'll let Peggy know you are here."

I sat and opened whatever book I was reading at the time and lost the room to the fiction. In a few pages, Peggy called me in.

"How have you been?" she asked, as she led me down the hall and to the right where her office was.

"Fine. How about you?"

"Doing okay," she said, shutting the door behind us.

I took my normal chair and made an ex with my arms in front of my stomach.

"Did you see Sally?"

"Yes."

"How did that go?"

"Pretty well, I think." I looked around Peggy's office while I thought. The fountain she had always grabbed my attention. "She was really nice. She didn't force me to eat anything I didn't want to."

"But you were able to come up with an eating plan?"

"Yeah."

"How are you doing with it?"

"All right." I told Peggy what the plan was and how my body rejected the food a little on the first day.

"How about since then?"

"The food has been going down all right," I said.

*You eat too much.*

"I've pretty much been able to stick to the plan," I said. "Not always, but pretty much most of the time."

"What does that mean?" Peggy had her notepad in her lap and her pen cocked and loaded.

I shrugged. "It means that most of the time I stick to the plan, but there are times when I can't."

"Can't?"

I pressed my palms against my eyes and pulled my fingers down my cheeks. "Like with the nuts that I'm supposed to have twice a day. That is an enormous amount of nuts. Sometimes I just can't eat that much."

Peggy made a note and nodded. "So what do you do with them then?"

"Usually, I throw them away, but sometimes I put them back in the can."

"Do you prefer one to the other?"

"Not really. Throwing them away is a bit of a rush."

She nodded and made another note. "Because the ones in the trash—you'll never have to eat those?"

"Yes."

"Were you ever anorexic before?"

I thought about it and searched my memory for the truest answer I could find. "I guess maybe I was heading that way once before."

"Tell me about that."

The soft gurgle of the fountain grabbed my attention and a shadow passed by Peggy's window. "I was just starting out. I was a new teacher and I had my own apartment. I started going to a gym, and I would walk the treadmill every day for 45 minutes. For lunch, I would have an apple and a bagel. For dinner, a veggie burger or whatever, you know. I can remember getting to the point where I would be counting out the number of fat free chips I could have in a weekend."

"Based on the label?"

"Yeah. I'd usually count out about a half a serving and I remember the feelings of guilt, failure, and self-loathing if I succumbed to the temptation and ate a chicken burrito or something." I had forgotten I had lived like that for a time.

"Were you weighing a lot?"

"Each day at the gym, yeah."

"And how low did your weight get that time?"

"160, I think." I shuddered. "I would hate to be 160 now."

"You are less than that now?"

"Yeah. I'm 135." I looked for the astonishment on her face, but there was none. She nodded and made a note as if I hadn't just given her the most amazing news of her day.

"And what happened that time?"

"What...what do you mean?"

"How did you get out of it that time?"

"Oh." I smiled. "I met Kristin, and you know, when you fall in love and all that. You eat out more and whatever."

"And you decided she was more important than working out?"

"Yeah. Cause I used to get up at like 4 am to go to the gym, and it was much better to stay in bed with her. Nicer."

Peggy took that in. "And never before that time? And never until this time?"

"Not really. No."

"You bring up the weight numbers a lot. It seems to be a pretty big part of it for you."

"Yeah."

"Are there any other numbers involved with this?"

"The speed on the treadmill...the slope I have it set to."

"How about as a kid and through your life...Have numbers been a big part of things for you?"

I rested an ankle on my knee and rested the side of my face in a cupped hand with my eyes shut as if that would help me think. "Well, I mean, on the swim team, of course, you compete against yourself to try and better your own time in a given event. And then when I was younger, I was on a football team and there was a weight limit I always had to worry about."

"Weight limit?"

"It was like a safety thing so kids wouldn't get hurt. The problem was, I was really tall for my age and so to weigh 95 pounds was a pretty big worry for me. Each week before the game, we would have to weigh in, and I'd be stripped down to my underwear to make weight. Like the lighter guys, some of the running backs and whatever, they'd just hop on the scale in full pads and there'd never be a problem."

"Pretty humiliating," she said.

"Yeah, it sucked," I said. "Do you think that stuff has anything to do with it?"

"We're just trying to get the full picture. There's not just one thing that has made you anorexic. But that kind of stuff...the fixation on a certain weight at a young age and the self-competing stuff from the swimming could definitely be a piece."

"Hmm," I said. Memories jabbed around my skull and fought for my attention. It had to be near the hour. I was exhausted.

"Did you bring up the editing and the resume stuff to Kristin?"

"Yeah."

"How did that go?"

"She said I was a selfish bastard."

"Ah...Pretty critical then, huh?" Peggy said, making another note and flipping the page on her pad.

"You could say that, yeah." I said. "In the end though, she said that she wouldn't ask me to do any of those things anymore, but that she wouldn't be married to a selfish prick."

"I think it's good for you that you stood your ground on this. If it was really making you that unhappy, then it really is for the best that you don't do those things—unless you want to."

I nodded and looked down at the floor.

"You know, Jim," Peggy said after letting the room fill with silence for a minute, "We've talked about rebuilding your life in here a little, and I just want you to know that when we have rebuilt it, it will not be as it was before you went into anorexia."

I met her gaze.

"Really," she said, nodding.

Soon, I was only seeing Peggy once a week. Once we had all the "getting to know you" stuff out of the way, the one hour a week intense talk was all I needed. I continued on with the nutritionist's eating plan, but I would restrict on that at least once a day. How much I restricted soon became a regular part of the discussion in therapy.

I had sharp pain that would come and go at the base of my rib cage on the left hand side. I imagined it was probably my kidneys, but it may have been just the sensation of the bone jutting into my skin. I had no way of knowing, really, and I wasn't about to go to a doctor and get bad news.

My vision blackened if I stood too fast, and standing too fast was getting to be pretty relative in my case. Every day when I got out of bed I would need to do it slower, or face the blackness. I didn't mind the blackness. It was a sign of victory and of progress just as much as a lower number on the scale was.

Joyce and Frank came to visit us from San Jose. The best part of the visit would be them seeing how thin I was and the jealousy I know they would feel for my self control and ability to diet. It was a Saturday when they came up with their 2 kids, and I stocked the house with food for the grill. Kristin had me buy coconut rum and stuff to mix it with. We also had a couple bottles of red wine and some beer.

They rang the doorbell just before one, and Kristin and I went to meet them. Hugs and handshakes were passed around as easily as the booze would flow later.

"How was the drive up?" I asked Frank as we headed out to the backyard with a couple beers.

"Not too bad," he said.

Joyce and Frank had just bought a house in San Jose that was a fixer upper. Frank was slowly fixing the place up a little at a time and learning quite a bit about electricity and plumbing in the process.

We sat at the table on the patio and talked about books. "Have you read the Gunslinger series by Stephen King?"

"Just the first one," I said, "I actually had it as a book on tape on the treadmill. I've been through a lot of books that way lately."

"The first one was good," he said, "but they get even better from the second one on."

He didn't take the obvious bait I had left out regarding the treadmill. Did I not look thin to him? "That's cool," I said, upending my bottle. It was good having him here. Few of my friends could talk about books. The pool pump churned in the background and filled in awkward silences.

*You need to work harder on the treadmill if Frank isn't even noticing how you look.*

I know.

In a little while, Kristin and Joyce joined us on the patio with some sort of concoction in their hands in our plastic pool cups. Joyce was a little more interested in matters of weight loss. We had already had a talk about it when Kristin was in the hospital. She had to have noticed.

209

The four of us talked about the kids and about whatever. We always laughed a lot when we were together.

"Bubbah, are you going to start the barbecue soon?" Kristin said.

"I don't know."

"I'm not really hungry yet. Are you guys hungry?"

"Not yet, but I'm gonna be," Joyce said. "I hate being hungry."

"I love it," I said.

"Not me," Joyce said, "It gives me a headache, and I get dizzy."

"Me too," I said.

"Then how can you like it?" Joyce said.

"You're missing what he's saying," Frank said, "You guys both have the same symptoms, but Jim interprets them as a good thing."

"Yeah," I said, motioning to Frank with the open end of my beer bottle. "I need another one." I got up and headed for the house.

"See if Brighid wants to swim," Kristin said.

I didn't want to, but since when did that matter?

I spent the next half hour following Brighid and the kids around the pool while Kristin talked with the adults.

"Bubbah, do you want to start the grill now?"

"Okay," I said, glad to be getting out of the cold water. Standing in front of the gas grill warmed me almost as fast as my normal hot shower and blanket wrap.

Kristin brought out a large Tupperware bowl of meat that she had marinated over night, and I covered the grill with it. The bowl sat on the grill's right hand side serving tray, and on the left was a metal container covered with foil for finished meat. Cooking the food gave me control over how it was prepared. I bought boneless and skinless chicken breasts for myself. Steak was way too fatty.

The sizzle and sputter and smoke from the grill defined summer. I'd poke more meat out of the Tupperware bowl and keep things moving from right to left.

To my horror, I found the chicken breasts underneath the steaks.

*You know what that means.*

"Kristin?"

She sat with Joyce and Frank about 20 feet from me at the table where I had started the afternoon. "Yeah?"

"You marinated all the meat together?" I already knew the answer. The evidence was right in front of me. All night long, fat seeped out of the steak, through the marinade, and into the chicken breasts. My food was poisoned.

"Yeah," she said, as if it were no big deal.

I grabbed my inner cheek between my teeth and sawed back and forth. What could I do now? She'd never let me get by just eating salad. Too many people are here to try and fake eating it. Someone would see. They would know.

*Just slice a small corner off of one of the chicken breasts. That way, no one can say you didn't eat and you'll be minimizing the damage.*

Will that work?

*Come on...Have I ever steered you wrong? Leave the chicken on the grill a little longer than it needs to be there too. Maybe you could burn off some of the fat that way. Not enough so you could eat a whole piece, mind you.*

I understand.

*Cause you know those denim shorts you are wearing? The ones your stepson grew out of? If you eat more than I say, you'll never fit in those again.*

Those shorts were a crowning achievement. I couldn't lose them. They were size 28 waist, and I had room to put my hand in the waistband while wearing them. I wiped sweat from my forehead, grateful for the extra heat from the grill.

In the metal tray that held the cooked meat, I did my best to make sure the chicken and the beef didn't touch. It was too late though. The best I could hope for was to get by eating a small amount.

"Okay, Hon, I'm all done over here," I said, wrapping the foil over the top of the meat.

She got out of her chair with Joyce and Frank right behind her, and the 4 of us went inside to get food for the kids and then ourselves.

Wine and beer flowed during the dinner bringing on the laughter of true friends. It was hard not seeing Joyce and Frank often. Our house made the move worth it, we told ourselves. We tried every chance we got to convince them to move to Modesto as well.

After dinner, I cleaned up, opened another bottle of wine, mixed some drinks for Kristin and Joyce, and sat in the living room. Kristin unsnapped her bra and pulled it out of her sleeve. "Will you put this up in the room Bubbah?"

The wine swimming in my head made the request feel like it was too much. I put the bra on over my T shirt instead.

"Don't do that," Kristin said.

"How come?"

"Take it off," she said, "Let's go out by the pool. It's hot in here."

The four of us got up, and for me the room rocked from side to side a little. It was all fun and warm—a nice alcohol evening. Joyce and Frank stepped out onto the deck and down to the patio first. Kristin was about to step out the door when she grabbed the collar of my T shirt. "Take that fuckin thing off."

I grabbed the front of the bra, ripped it off like I was about to take advantage of myself, and hurled it over my shoulder.

"Go put it in the room."

"We can just leave it there," I said.

"Jim..." her tone thickened.

I rolled my eyes back and almost lost balance from the effort before I crossed the room, got the bra, stumbled up the stairs, and shot it rubber band style toward the mountain of dirty clothes we had by the TV.

The kids were busy in the family room trying to figure out what DVD to watch when I went out the sliding glass door to find Kristin standing on the steps of the pool, the water up to her knees, as she leaned on and hugged Frank.

Joyce stood in the water a few feet away with her drink on the pool's edge. I looked back to Kristin, who leaned against Frank with no indication that she would open her eyes, and figured Joyce was my date for the evening.

Frank shrugged when I made eye contact with him. He looked like his main focus was making sure Kristin didn't fall over backward into the pool and drown.

"Know what?" Kristin said, the words slurred by alcohol and because the side of her face was smashed against Frank's chest.

"What?" Joyce caressed the top of the water with her hands and then reached for her drink.

"I'm not wearing any underwear." Kristin erupted with laughter. Only she was drunk enough to see the humor. She wobbled with the effort, and Frank had to tighten his grip and shift his weight to stop them both from ending up underwater. "Where's my drink?"

"It's gone," Frank said, looking down at her in his arms. This was okay. I trusted Frank. Joyce didn't seemed phased.

"That dinner was really good," Joyce said. She sipped from her drink and then set it down by the pool's edge.

"Thanks," I said, "It's all in how you stand by the grill."

She laughed.

"I think you need to go up to bed," Frank said, looking down at the top of Kristin's head.

"No...I not tired..." Kristin said.

"I think you are," Frank said.

"Okay," Kristin agreed.

Frank helped her up and out of the pool and she dripped and shivered in the cooler evening air. "Do you want to take her up?" Frank asked me.

"I want Frank to do it," Kristin said.

I flipped my hand toward Kristin and raised my eyebrows.

"I'll be right back," Frank said.

As the sliding glass door shut behind them, I noticed Kristin's still full drink on the patio table where Frank and I had begun the afternoon. I walked over and emptied it into the bushes.

I walked back to where Joyce was standing and pinched my gut.

"There is nothing there, Jim," she said.

"Yeah there is. Look." I picked up the bottom of my shirt and showed her how much I could pinch.

"It's all sunken in. Your whole stomach is sunken in."

I looked down and held my flesh between my fingers. Why was she lying to me? To spare my feelings I imagine.

*She doesn't know what she is talking about.*

"It's all sunk in."

"No," I said, shaking my head.

She looked up at me from in the pool and for an instant our eyes met, neither believing what the other was saying and both wishing they would.

"There's nothing there, it's all sunken in."

The sliding door broke the trance my skin between my fingers had me in, and Frank joined us again in the backyard.

"Just for the record," he said, "She was right…She wasn't wearing any underwear."

"Anyone else and I'd be pretty pissed off," I said. I trusted Frank though. He wasn't the one whose motives needed questioning.

# Chapter 38

I weighed 130 pounds on Kristin's birthday. She always wanted a big thing for her birthday. We booked a bus to Reno with a bunch of family and friends.

"We're going on a weekend bus trip to Reno," I told Peggy. "It's usually a pretty fun time. We can drink on the bus, and whatever. Makes the ride up there pretty quick."

"You're going to be okay with drinking," Peggy said.

I nodded.

"How about eating while you're there?"

I sighed. "Well, I'm worried about it to be honest with you. I mean, all they have up there are buffets and stuff like that. But I figure one weekend…"

*One weekend is way too long to be eating the way you are thinking. You'll gain on that trip and ruin all your progress. You better skip your nuts today, or at least throw away part of your Lean Cuisine.*

"…I'm just going to try my hardest. Uh…Not to stress about it. I mean, I can always get back on the eating program on Monday, right?"

*Monday will be too late. The damage will be done.*

Peggy nodded.

"What?" I said. Would the damage already be done?

"Have you ever heard of people with terminal cancer—they do what's called take a vacation from the disease. They basically go away for a few days and pretend like they don't have it."

I looked at Peggy like I had no idea what language she was speaking.

"They do," she said, "They just spend a few days living as if the disease isn't there and then at the end of the vacation, they go back to it as if it were a job they had left."

I pinched at the flap of skin underneath my chin and then crossed my arms over my stomach.

"This could be your vacation from anorexia," she said.

*You are nothing if not an anorexic.*

"Yeah. Right on." I nodded.

"Just leave it behind, act like it's not there, and when you get back—face it then. How long will you be gone?"

"We leave Saturday morning and come back Sunday afternoon."

"See, so it's just one day. You could probably do this, don't you think?"

"Yeah."

*No.*


"I don't want to hear about anorexia on my birthday weekend," Kristin said, as she changed out of her work clothes. "Not even the word."

"Peggy and I were just talking about that today," I said. I explained about the vacation from anorexia.

"I'm serious Jim. Tell me now if you're not going to be able to do this for me. I don't want you going if anorexia is going to be a part of the trip at all. I mean, I want you to go...But not anorexic Jim. Just Jim." She stopped what she was doing and looked at me as if doing so would hammer her point flat.

"I'll do the best I can," I said.

*You are nothing if not an anorexic.*

"I don't want the best you can do. I want an absolute guarantee that anorexia won't be part of this weekend."

"I don't know if I should go," I said.

"Jim Kohl...It's my birthday weekend."

"I know, Honey. But I can't be sure that anorexia will never come up."

"You can't even do that for me? One fucking day?" She stormed across the bedroom and started rinsing out the Jacuzzi tub.

"I'd like to be able to tell you that and have it be true," I said, "but the fact of the matter is that I don't know for sure that I can have it not even come up. I mean look at me. Some people who haven't seen me for a while are gonna wonder."

"Are you kidding me?" She raised her voice over the running tub water. "There isn't one person we know that doesn't know what is going on with you. Not a day goes by when someone doesn't ask me how you are doing. It's become like part of my fucking job."

There was one scenario only that wouldn't piss her off. "Okay then."

"Okay then what?"

Okay then, your majesty? "I won't bring up anorexia over the weekend."

"Promise?"

"Yes."

"Okay."


The bus was set to pick up a bunch of people in San Jose and the rest of the people in Stockton. We bought a bunch of beer, vodka, and bloody mary mix for the bus, and we also stocked up on chorizo and egg burritos so everyone would have breakfast.

"Why don't you meet up with us in Stockton?" Kristin suggested to me.

"Why?"

"Just so you can kinda be in charge of getting everyone together up there," she said.

This was to minimize her contact with me. I'd become a liability to her and an obstacle standing between her and fun. If I met up with the bus in Stockton, there would be two hours where she wouldn't have to think about me. "I don't really want to do that."

"Kay, fine. Come with us to San Jose then."

"Us" was Kristin and her friends Melanie and Rachel. Early on Saturday, we loaded into Kristin's SUV and made the 100 mile drive from Modesto to San Jose. The bus was supposed to meet us in the parking lot of the company where Kristin worked.

*There is no way you can make it without anorexia coming up. You will ruin your wife's birthday.*

We unloaded the supplies and piled them to wait for the bus in the warming morning sun of June. The ice glistened and clicked in the tub of beer.

Some of the people coming on the trip I hadn't seen in a year or more. I ran through the invitation list in my mind and got excited for each person to show up—dying for them to tell me how thin I looked.

Marco, a coworker of Kristin whose daughter I used to tutor, showed up to do some work at the office and stopped to talk with Kristin. Kristin had posted me next to the party supplies, so I was a few feet away from where the rest of the people gathered.

"Your birthday, huh?" Marco said.

"Yep." Kristin said. "We're heading up to Reno for some partying and gambling."

"Great," Marco said, smiling, "Well I hope you guys have a great time and win some money. Where's Jim?"

"He's right there." Kristin pointed over to me.

I waved and smiled.

"Oh my God," Marco said. His smile collapsed. "Oh my God, I didn't even recognize him."

It had been a while since anyone had said I looked great.

*They're jealous.*

Exactly what I was going to say.

*Plus, you still have some weight to lose.*

Yeah. That too.

As new people showed up, I'd walk from my post long enough to say hi. Finally, Martin showed up and I had someone to stand by the supplies with.

"I get your problem," he said, "but I have it the opposite way."

"Not supposed to even bring up anorexia on this trip, man," I said. I looked at Kristin, but she was busy with friends.

"Okay," Martin said, "When's the bus supposed to get here?"

"About 15 minutes ago," I said.

"Bubbah, what time is it?" Kristin called to me. Her group looked my way as I dug into my pocket for my cell phone.

"9:45."

"Fuck! Where is the bus?"

"I don't know, baby."

The stress hit me pretty hard that the bus simply wouldn't show. Kristin's birthday would be ruined, and it would have nothing to do with me and my disease—I mean my choice, as she would say. All this beer and food would go to waste.

Ten minutes later, the bus arrived and I had one less piece of worry crushing my mind.

"Load the bus, Bubbah."

The request stung, but I grabbed the first of many things that needed to go and lugged them across the lot, up the stairs, and to the back of the bus. I turned to go get another armful, dodged Martin, who had one of his own, and came face to face with Kristin.

"Don't put the burritos there. That's where the mixed drinks stuff should go. And the ice chest needs to go on the floor a couple rows up. We don't want to have to be climbing over the ice tub to get to the burritos, and it can't be so close to the bathroom door or we won't be able to get in there."

"Where do you want the burritos?" I said.

"A couple rows up from where you put them. Or if you push the ice tub over to the side," she motioned to the side she meant, "then the burritos can go in the back seat on the other side."

"Okay." Sweat beaded on my forehead and I hadn't even begun the job.

A bunch of guys started helping and the bus was packed, things were set where Kristin wanted them, and we boarded the bus. The beer and mixed drinks started flowing before we left the parking lot. Jason, one of Kristin's oldest friends, worked as the bartender just across the aisle from Martin and me.

We sat with our beers and watched the road pass outside the window. It would be a 2-hour drive until we met the people joining us in Stockton, and maybe another 3 hours after that before we reached Reno. The only way to tolerate such a long ride was with beer, so I made sure I always had one in my hand. In an hour I was on drink 4 or 5 and was feeling pretty relaxed.

"You better slow down." Kristin had made her way down the aisle of the bus.

"What?" I said, knowing damn well what she meant.

"The beer. You better pace yourself."

Between the beer, how to pack the bus, the fact that I had to pack the bus, the guard duty over the supplies in the parking lot, the suggestion that I get on the bus in Stockton, and the rule about anorexia...

*You are nothing if not an anorexic.*

Yes. I know...This last request with the pile of others was too much. "Don't tell me what to do," I said.

Her face reddened, and she turned and stormed back up the aisle to her seat near the driver. I knew I'd pay for that later, but for now I opened another beer. If I never sobered up, I would never have to deal with her. All the beer calories that I was letting into my body was taking a vacation from anorexia. Peggy would be proud and Kristin should be happy.

"What the fuck, dude," I said, "It's the Reno bus trip. We're supposed to be drunk on the bus."

"I don't know," Martin said.

"She makes all these rules all the time. I'm not even allowed to talk about anorexia, and she acted like that would be damn near impossible for me or something."

Martin shrugged, smirked, and drank his beer.

"So dude, do I look thinner to you than the last time you saw me?"

"Yeah," he said.

The bus pulled off the freeway and into Stockton where the rest of the party waited in the parking lot of a Save Mart. I decided to climb off the bus for a stretch and to meet the rest of the people. Uncle Art and Tia Mary would be there, among others. Kristin stood at the base of the bus's stairway. I turned the corner and faced her just as my wedding ring slipped off my finger.

It had been really loose, and in my buzzed state, I forgot to walk with my hands in a half-fisted position. It clinked on the bus's stairs. Kristin's face growled as I bent down to pick it up.

Angela was a coworker of Kristin's that lived in Modesto. I had never met her, but Kristin told me that she had beaten anorexia. Angela tried to explain it to Kristin. "The second you eat food, you feel like you have to run it right off. You have this strong feeling like you have to run around the block three or four times."

Back when Kristin told me that, I almost felt like she was beginning to understand and maybe even think it wasn't a choice. When I saw Angela in that Stockton parking lot, I approached her.

"Angela?"

"Yes."

"Hi. I'm Jim, Kristin's husband."

"Oh hi!" She shook my hand.

"I wanted to thank you for talking about anorexia with Kristin," I said.

She looked around as if looking for a way out. I later learned that her domineering boyfriend didn't know she had ever had it and she wanted to keep it that way. My buzz held me there even though she wanted an escape. "Sure," she said, folding her arms across her chest and shifting her weight from side to side.

"I think it really helped her begin to understand me a little. You know I have it, right?"

She nodded.

"Can you tell by looking at me?"

Her eyes moved from the ground up to my face. "A little bit around the eyes," she said.

I nodded, saw Uncle Art, and relieved her of my company.

"Hey Uncle Art!"

"Hey, mejo." We hugged like we always did. "God damn, Jim, you better eat something."

"I do eat."

"You sure?"

"Yeah. Do I look thinner than when you last saw me?" I already had the confirmation I needed from Martin, but that was a couple of beers ago. It's safest to check often.

*Now you're thinking right.*

"Don't know about thinner, but you're still too skinny." He looked me over, and shook his head.

"So not thinner then?"

Kristin came up, so I had to change the subject. She hugged and kissed Uncle Art. "Bubbah, can you go into the store and get some…"

Doesn't matter what she asked me to get. The point was, I was listening and I did what she asked. It was her birthday weekend, and I knew from the past that if every request was not met with the pleasure of serving, I would pay for it in many ways for many days. I found Martin, and we headed into Save Mart for her errand.

"We should get some better beer while we're in here. A stash just for us."

"Okay," he said.

The bus ice tub had some Corona, and mostly Budweiser, and I preferred things a bit more European. Along with whatever it was Kristin sent us for, I picked up a 12 pack of Newcastle that Martin and I kept with us at our seat for the remainder of the ride.

"You need to slow down," Kristin told me again when the bus had reached some unidentifiable stretch of highway.

"It's the bus trip, man."

"Jim Kohl." Her eyes sterned up on me.

From there, things got hazy.

I woke in a hotel room. The sun was still up, and within a few seconds I realized we arrived in Reno. Kristin lay beside me. I pinched my gut to check for weight gain. I seemed okay, but I knew I'd better check again.

*You should have brought the scale.*

Now you tell me.

The density in my head made the walk to the bathroom last forever. A glimpse of myself in the mirror was more than I wanted to see.

*This vacation is going to ruin you.*

When I came out of the bathroom, the TV was on, Ronald Reagan had died, and Kristin sat up in the bed.

"Hey honey."

"Hey," she said with her eyes on the TV, "can you go downstairs and get us some coffee?"

*All walking burns calories.*

"Sure."

After pulling on my clothes and an elevator ride…

*You should have taken the stairs.*

I stood in line at the small coffee stand near the gift shop of the Reno Hilton. Kids pressed their fingers and faces against the window that displayed the pastries. They had the right idea.

"Can I help you?"

"Two medium coffees. And an apple fritter too, please."

*Are you out of your mind? That is the first step toward being fat. You break the discipline, and it makes it all that easier to break it again.*

I pulled my wallet from my back pocket and was glad to see that I still had some money. I didn't remember checking in, going up to the room, or getting into the bed. Alcohol had spared me the experience. This was Kristin's birthday weekend though, and as sick as I felt, there was no way I could let it show.

At the stand near the entrance to the line, I grabbed some powdered creamer and sugar for Kristin's coffee and took a bite from my apple fritter.

*It's not too late to spit it out and throw the rest of it away.*

I finished eating the apple fritter before the elevator arrived to take me back to the room. "Shit!"

Panic swirled in me as the elevator doors shut. I didn't know my room number. My cell phone wasn't attached to the belt loop of my shorts. I stood stupid, a white Styrofoam cup in each hand, and stared at the numbered buttons hoping for a triggered memory.

The doors opened up on the 5th floor, and I saw a telephone sitting on a small table beside a large mirror. As the new passengers boarded with cups of change for the casino, I squeezed past them and headed for the phone.

"Front desk?" a woman's voice said.

"Hi. Um, I need to know which room Jim Kohl is in."

"We can't give that information, sir."

Of course they couldn't. They had to protect me from psychopaths like me. I stammered.

"I can connect you to the room," she said.

"That would be great!" This woman was a true professional. Kristin answered the phone, told me the room number, and I got back on the elevator.

Balancing the cups of coffee in one hand, I knocked on the door. Kristin opened it and went back to the bed as the TV went on about the dead president. I handed her coffee over and sat next to her on the bed. "Thanks," she said.

It was clear I was in trouble, but I wasn't sure why. "Hey, I had an apple fritter downstairs," I said, sipping from the small opening in the lid of my cup.

"Good for you," she said.

Her excitement was less than I had hoped for. Didn't the fact that I ate an entire apple fritter show that I was taking a vacation from anorexia? "What's wrong?" I asked. I knew she was no fan of Ronald Reagan.

"You have already ruined my birthday," she said, eyes still on the TV highlights of speeches he gave and suits he wore.

"What do you mean? I ate an apple fritter." The worthlessness of that accomplishment left me hollow.

"All I asked for was one weekend when you didn't bring up anorexia. That's it. It's all I wanted for my birthday. And there you were, drunk on the bus, going on about it, crying about it. Talking about how it could kill you and you can't stop." She shook her head and tightened her lips against each other.

"I'm sorry, Hon. You know, I told you that I might not be able to do that. That it might be hard."

She turned to face me. "I told you to stop drinking because I knew this would happen. I told you to slow down, but you just acted like I was being a bossy bitch."

"I would never call you a bitch."

"And then everyone on the bus is suddenly worried about you. They're all asking if you're okay. They're asking if you are seeing anyone about your problem. The whole fucking bus is suddenly about you. Just like I fucking told you I didn't want it to be. I already fucking told you that I am sick and tired of everyone always asking if you are okay and if you're eating." Her face reddened and she set her coffee on the bedside table.

"I'm sorry." It sounded as stupid as my pride over the apple fritter. It was stupid. I had ruined her birthday. "I should have stayed home."

"Yeah, see there you go making yourself the victim again. If you didn't come, I'd be looking like the biggest bitch on the planet leaving my sick husband at home."

This was not the time to point out that she had finally referred to anorexia as a disease. "I don't know what to say."

"You should go take a shower. We are meeting everyone for dinner in a little while."

# Chapter 39

"How did it go up in Reno?" Peggy said.

"I fucked it up." I slouched in the therapy chair.

Peggy raised her eyebrows in an invitation to elaborate.

"I couldn't do it." I shook my head, shrugged, and folded my arms across my gut. "I couldn't go the weekend without anorexia being a part of it, and I pissed Kristin off. She said I ruined her birthday."

"Did she seem to have any fun at all on the trip?"

I caught my lower lip between my teeth and glanced toward the ceiling. "I think on Saturday night she did. She kept drinking those appletinis, and got so wasted she said she couldn't feel her face. We were in one of those little lounges where a band was playing, and she started thinking every appletini in the place was hers. So like she was grabbing people's drinks right off their table."

"Jesus."

"I know."

"Did she remember any of that?"

I shrugged. "Then she started sitting in random guys laps and whatever."

"How did that make you feel?"

"Like an asshole."

Peggy nodded. "Is she still mad?"

"I think so, yeah. She may always be. I promised I'd not bring up anorexia, got drunk on the bus, and then anorexia was center stage."

Peggy made a note or two. "I'm sorry it turned out that way."

"Me too," I said, "I think if I had stayed sober, I could have pulled it off. It would have been fake though. It's all I think about."

"Anorexia?"

"Yes. Losing weight. Making sure I am not gaining weight."

"How are you doing on the eating plan?"

"I'm following it." I pinched the fat on the side of my gut that Kristin said was just extra skin. "There are times when I eat less though."

"What do you think makes you restrict like that?" Peggy said. The computer monitor behind her blackened and went into screen saver mode.

I rolled my shoulders. "Just sometimes what I am supposed to eat feels like too much. So maybe I'll skip one of the nuts snacks or toss out half my Lean Cuisine. And like in Reno...I wasn't able to really ever enjoy anything I ate because I knew it was going to ruin my progress."

"Did you weigh more when you got home?"

"No," I said. "But until I got to the scale and knew that for a fact, there was a lot of stress. The whole bus ride home, I worried about it."

"I've told you this before," Peggy said, "but remember that you have to eat 500 calories more than you need to survive for 5 days in a row to gain 1 pound."

"That's what they say, yes." I grabbed the inside of my cheek between my teeth.

"You don't believe that?"

"Not really. No. I mean, it's not that I think you are lying to me—I believe that the doctors all say that and whatever. But it's a hard fact for me to believe, I guess you could say."

"So what all did you eat in Reno?"

"Oh, you know. I went pretty crazy at the breakfast buffet. I had a lot of sushi too."

"But you didn't like it?"

"It tasted good," I said, "but the stress it caused was far worse and it just wasn't worth it to me."

*Stress does burn calories though.*

Yeah, I know.

"Let's talk a little bit about your family growing up. What was that like?"

"Fine," I said.

"You feel like you had a good relationship with your parents?"

"Yeah. Not when I was 13, but pretty much the rest of the time, yeah," I said, "Lately, I kind of wonder how I came out of that family though."

"What do you mean?"

"Well, like we all went back to Philadelphia—my mom, dad, sister, and me—and while we were there, I noticed how different I am from them."

"How so?"

"I think they are all really good at living in this world, and I don't see myself as having the things that this society values together as much as they all do." Peggy looked puzzled, so I went on without prompting. "You know, like financially and just making decisions that assimilate well with how our society is set up. I don't think like they do."

"Do you think that is a bad thing?" Peggy said.

"I think that I would have an easier time with things if I could think like they do."

"Do you think that they could have written the books you have written?"

I shrugged.

"Just because you don't think like they do…That isn't necessarily a bad thing."

"My books are all self published. It's not like a real publisher picked them up or anything."

Peggy made a note on her pad. "Growing up, do you think that the difference in thinking affected anything?"

"My parents were good parents. There was nothing wrong with how I was raised."

"I'm not saying there was. I just wonder if the way you saw the world versus the way they do, and your sister too right?"

I nodded.

"I'm just wondering if this difference had any impact on how you grew up. It's not that they did anything wrong…It's more like since your mind is setup a certain way whether or not your perception of things had an impact, if you see what I mean."

"I don't see what you mean," I said.

"You're pretty self critical. You just a second ago said that your books weren't that big of a deal because a real publisher didn't pick them up." She was reading from her notepad. "You also recognize that there is a difference between how you think and how the rest of your family thinks, and you assume that the way you think is the wrong way."

I agreed.

"How far back do you remember this negative self perception?"

I paused and thought. In football, I was the one that had to strip down. In swimming, I won, but my body was never good enough. I was never cool enough in school. I never sang well enough. My books weren't good enough for a real publisher. I wasn't as smart as some of the other kids in the gifted class. I couldn't memorize comma rules, and I was too dumb to think Tolkien was any good. "Forever," I said.

"Did you ever tell your parents about these feelings?"

"On occasion, yes. I would occasionally have meltdowns. And there was…There was a suicide attempt at 20."

"What did you do?"

"I tried to drink myself to death in a single night. I drank a huge—like maybe a gallon—of Bacardi 151, and I still woke up the next morning. I tried to start fights with my best friends that night so it would be easier on them when I was gone."

"So you really had it kind of planned out."

I nodded.

"And what was your parent's reaction to this?"

"They didn't like to hear about it. They didn't know what to do. My mom said I shouldn't feel that way about myself. It's nothing they ever dealt with—these feelings that come on for no reason. My mom would often say, 'I don't know what to tell you.'"

"What did that mean?" Peggy said.

"Probably just that. It meant I was describing feelings and thoughts that were so far out from her experience that she didn't know what to say."

Peggy looked like she needed more.

"It's like my mom didn't see me as a kid with problems. She thought of me as this great kid. So to hear me describe myself the way I saw myself…I may as well be speaking a foreign language to her, you know?"

"Does she still tell you that she doesn't know what to tell you?"

"At times, yes."

"How does that make you feel?"

I searched the room. The computer screen saver had turned off and the screen was blank. Other than the pile of client files, the room was like any other office. "Like I am beyond help," I said.

At a different session, Peggy and I continued this romp through my past. I didn't see what any of it had to do with now, but she was the therapist, and I had to trust someone because I sure as hell couldn't trust myself.

*I never steered you wrong.*

That's true.

"The last time you were here, you talked about how your mom would always tell you that she didn't know what to tell you," Peggy started.

"Yeah."

"When she did tell you things, like way back, what sticks out in your mind that she did say?" Peggy looked at me with her normal pad readied in her lap.

I thought for a moment. Being asked a question like that can knock you back a little just trying to get a handle on what answer was expected. If you are sitting with a therapist trying to figure out what they want to hear, you are cheating yourself.

What did my mom say? What was my childhood like? Aside from my weight and treadmill speed, I couldn't think of a thing. I had grown up living with both my parents the whole time. She must have said something to me at one point or another.

*You were nothing before you were an anorexic. You are nothing if not an anorexic.*

It came finally. "She always wanted me to build character."

"What does that mean?"

"Like she would want me to do things that would make me a better person, I think. I guess. I never really thought that much about it; I just kind of knew what she meant—or I thought I did." I wrapped my arms tight around myself and looked at the floor.

"How would you go about doing that? What does a better person do?"

The question needed answering, but we were delving into things I didn't want to face. My character had been built. Once a house is there, no one gives much thought to how it was put up.

I did know the answer though. I knew how to build character. "It meant," I said, thinking over the words before they came out of me, "It meant to put others' interests before my own at all times."

"At all times?"

"Pretty much, yeah."

"Can you give me an example?"

"Like it would build character to hang out with a kid that I didn't like at all simply because my mom and his mom made some sort of agreement that I should walk to school with him. It would build character to make any kind of sacrifice for another. Like if I had a birthday party as a kid, and there were only enough prize bags for my guests and not for me, I would have to give up my prize bag so I could build my character."

"Do you still believe that today?"

"I don't know."

"Well, you mentioned you would always do people's resumes and such for them even though you really didn't want to. Do you think that could be part of that kind of thinking?"

Peggy hadn't asked an easy question since the first couple weeks of sessions. My mind, exhausted, searched to see if that was an accurate statement or not. I didn't know how long this session had been going, but I wanted to go home and sleep. "Now that you mention it, yeah. That makes some sense, actually. I pretty much would do anything to make Kristin happy—even if I really didn't want to. And I know that it made her happy when I did her friends favors."

"Would you say," Peggy said, "that you have a hard time saying no to people?"

"Yeah."

"All people, or just Kristin?"

"People in general, but especially Kristin. I want to be a good husband and I want to make her happy."

"At the expense of your own happiness?"

"Yes."

"Because it builds character?"

I laughed. "I don't know. Maybe that's it. I don't know." I knew I felt unappreciated and if I even got thanked for the work I did on people's resumes, it was usually second hand thanks and an afterthought at that. Maybe I had given all I had. Maybe I had a limit. The idea had never occurred to me.

# Chapter 40

*The same or better. First you need to use the bathroom and push as much junk out of yourself as possible. Then we'll weigh—you gotta be the same or better than the day before.*

Yeah. The same or better—I know. I sat on the side of the bed, waited for the room to return from the blackness that blocked my vision, and stretched.

*The steps to the bathroom are calories spent. Walk as fast as you can no matter where you walk. Make the most of every movement. Every movement is burned calories.*

*You sure that's as much as you can go? Shake your leg while you are sitting there. Every movement counts.*

I sat on the toilet, bouncing my leg up and down on the ball of my foot. In a few moments, I would be heading across the bathroom to the scale. The light from the small room with the toilet through the cracked door would be good enough to see the digital number.

*Walk to the scale. This is it. You're either good or bad—valuable or worthless. Step up on the scale and let's see what you're made of. What's the number?*

130.

*Really? 130 point what?*

130.8—crap.

*We were point 7 yesterday, and as I recall your legs hurt and you got off the treadmill 2 minutes early yesterday. Remember what you told yourself? You said it would be fine because it's not like you were training for the Olympics or anything. Now look. You need to listen today. Forget what everyone else is telling you. You better make up those lost 2 minutes on the treadmill.*

I better make up the 2 minutes on the treadmill.

*Now.*

I got in my exercise clothes and headed down the stairs to the garage, walking as fast as I could. The point 8 had burned a hole in my mind, and I saw it even with my eyes closed. It was the beginning of bad things. My gut already hung over my shorts more, and I could pinch a handful of flab.

*You could have walked to the treadmill faster. No water today while you work out.*

Yeah. A failure heat crept up my neck, and panic made it hard to breathe. I needed to get down…

*To the 120s. That would be success.*

Yes. I cranked up the treadmill to 6 mph, and set the slope to 10%, maxing out both of the settings. When the sweat came, there was slight relief, bit it was too little too late. My weight had already climbed. That tenth of a pound had to come off again.

*Wipe your body down and weigh yourself again after this— before you write.*

That's the plan, yes.


The workout sweat stuck my T-shirt to my body, and I peeled it off on my way up the stairs.

*You should have taken the stairs faster.*

The shirt fell heavy from my hand into the mound of dirty clothes next to the TV. I scraped a hand towel against my body as if the extra pressure would take the fat off. My skin stung a little from the rough towel after two complete body scrapedowns.

*Get on the scale.*

It sat in the corner where the bathroom vanity area met the wall. The light still broke from the cracked open bathroom door.

Kristin breathed slow and regular in sleep. If she woke and saw me on the scale, she would think it was my first weighing of the day. Weighing once was not a problem, but more than once…

*Stress burns calories.*

I stepped onto the scale and closed my eyes while it picked a number to show. "Please make it better."

130.8—Shit.

I looked at the number and it never got better. Hot tears came, and I stepped off. My stomach knotted into acidic cramps.

*That eating plan you are on is too much food. You need to cut something out of that. Two snacks with nuts a day? Come on! You know how much fat is in there. The calories are off the charts too. No one needs a snack anyway. You could probably get by with none of them.*

Yes.

It was time to write.

*Walk the hall to your office as fast as you can. Once you get that computer turned on and it starts booting up, go downstairs at the same pace. You can move faster that that.*

I'm trying.

*This isn't about trying, this is about doing.*

In the kitchen, I ground up the coffee beans and filled the maker with water.

*As long as you are moving, you are good. Even the simple movement of coffee preparation is better than nothing. And actually, even your heart pumping is good movement, but what we need is above and beyond that.*

I paced the kitchen while the coffee percolated. Once enough was in the pot to fill a cup, I poured it and headed back to the stairs, thankful for the two story house but wishing there were more stairs to climb.

*Take them fast. Remember the scale.*

I sat at the computer and opened up the rough draft file of my book, *Through the Fog*. It took a few seconds to read the page I had finished the morning before so I could get my bearings in the story and start typing. Typing was movement.

*But it's not enough movement.*

There weren't a whole lot of aerobics you could do at a computer desk.

*Shake your legs or even flex and unflex the muscles throughout your body.*

I could do that.

After an hour at the keyboard, it was time for my shower. I pictured the fat and calories burning off me in the hot water as I kept moving, if only shifting my weight from leg to leg.

Kristin was sitting up in bed when I stepped from the shower. "Daddy, can you make me some espresso?"

*Perfect! Another excuse to go down and up the stairs.*

I longed to step back on the scale, but not in front of Kristin. The extra trip up and down the stairs may make a difference, but I couldn't check.

*Just check anyway.*

Not in front of her.

*You need to know.*

Maybe while she is in the bathroom. I ground the espresso beans to the required fine powder and started up the maker. It cooked through and scented the house in thick carmelly black while I poured myself some cereal.

*That is too much.*

There were not enough flakes of Special K to cover the bottom of the small bowl. I pinched out some of the flakes and returned them to the box for another day.

*Still too much.*

Five flakes remained after I pinched the second time. They floated like lost islands in a sea of skim milk. I chased them around the bowl with my spoon until they were gone and drank down the milk like the nutritionist said. Kristin's espresso was cooked, and I added the required raw sugar and vanilla syrup.

*You know what that means. Up the stairs again. Then at the top, walk in and give Kristin her coffee and head back down the hallway to get Brighid up. Keep moving. Your weight is high. You failed.*

Coaxing Brighid out of bed took some time and patience. While she woke, I got her clothes for the day ready. This involved crossing her room from one side to the other a couple times to find a shirt to match her pants.

*If you're just standing in front of her closet looking for clothes, nodding your head can burn some calories and it beats standing still.*

Yeah. I nodded. "Come on, get up baby," I said.

Brighid stirred herself to a sitting position and took in the room through bleary eyes.

"Ready for the shower?"

She gave a slight nod before setting her feet on the floor and standing. She lumbered behind me as I sprinted the hall back to where Kristin sat on the bed, watched the Weather channel, and drank her coffee.

Brighid was still young enough at the time to need a lot of help in the shower.

*Keep moving.*

Exactly. We got her in and out of the shower in minutes, and then I helped her get dressed and did her hair.

*Now what? You can't afford to sit. Remember the scale? You'll be sitting all day at work.*

"Bubbah," Kristin called to me from the shower, "Can you get me a towel?"

*You lucked into that one. The linen closet is way down the hall by Brighid's room.*

"Sure," I said.

*Good God, did you see yourself from the side in the mirror? It's a miracle you still fit in your clothes. You're fatter than before. I'll bet you can't fit in those 28 waist shorts that used to be Lorenzo's anymore.*

I got the towel and wiped the sweat from my forehead with the back of my hand. After another power walk down the hall, I put her towel on the edge of the tub close to the shower door so she could reach it.

*I'll bet you can't fit in those 28 waist shorts that used to be Lorenzo's anymore.*

Those shorts were in the second drawer from the bottom of my dresser. I linked a finger in the bronze handle on the brown drawer and pulled it open. There they were—folded in half on top of a pile of T shirts. Sweat formed on my forehead, and I gnawed at my lower lip as I reached for them. I shook them once as if doing so would make them fit for sure. With a hard swallow stuck lumpy in my throat, I held them down and slipped one leg into them and then the other.

"What are you doing?" Kristin stood in front of me with her hair up in a towel turban and the towel I just brought for her wrapped around her upper body.

*Nothing.*

"Nothing." The shorts slid up and over my hips. I buttoned them with enough room left to slide my hand down the waistband. The shock thrilled me. It was like holding a pair of doll clothes in front of you and then being able to fit in them. All reason and logic were defied by my fitting in these shorts. The guy I saw in the mirror would never be able to fit in them.

"You're wearing shorts to work?" Kristin had her hands on her hips.

"No." I slid my hand into the shorts and made a fist against the denim waistband. My full fist fit against my skin—another bit of magic.

*Your weight is up. Don't you forget that.*

"Then what do you have them on for?"

I shrugged, slipping them off and putting them back in the drawer.

"There's no way you should fit in those anyway," Kristin said, "Lorenzo outgrew them."

I turned from her and went into our walk-in closet for my work clothes with a smile across my face.

*Your weight is up. Don't you forget that. You probably have those denim shorts stretched and that's why they fit. You better find the biggest pair of pants in this closet to wear to work today.*

"Bubbah, which shoe?" Kristin had her proposed outfit for the day draped in front of her and one of each of the pairs of shoes she was considering on her feet. From experience, I knew that the first proposed outfit was rarely the winner and any shoe choice at this stage of the morning would be premature, but I gave an opinion anyway.

"That one," I said, motioning to her right foot.

"You think?" she said,

"I like it, yeah." I said, looking back to make sure. I cinched my belt to the tightest hole and buckled it.

*Yeah, but those pants are 34 waist. They're also old so the waist is probably looser than 34.*

The pants barely fit around me.

"Look at your pants. The waist band is folded in on itself and the top of them puffs out like a balloon." Kristin's face burned with anger when I turned to look at her.

"What?" I looked down at my waist line. She had to be messing with me.

She huffed in disgust and went about getting herself ready.

I took to the stairs again, hoping that great globules of fat fell off my body with each step. I had to get the weight down again by tomorrow. I couldn't take another day of unrest. The self loathing was too much.

In the kitchen, I got Brighid's lunch together, put it in her backpack, and then got the food that I was supposed to eat throughout the day. I didn't need to pack my nuts because I had a jar in my office.

Up the stairs again with a smile on my face.

*You should have spent extra time on the treadmill today. This up and down the stairs is just regular living. To lose weight, you need to go above and beyond the normal day stuff.*

Kristin stood in front of the bathroom mirror perfecting her makeup. Brighid sat on the bed watching TV. "Come on, Brighid," I said.

She grabbed the remote control, turned off the TV, and rolled off the bed.

"Bye, honey," I called to Kristin.

"Bye." She didn't look away from the mirror. I was in trouble as usual, and I didn't know why.

Facing the 90 minute commute to Livermore was agony alone, but knowing that for 90 minutes my movement would be so limited added a whole other dimension of hell on a day like this. Even after getting to work, I'd be stuck at a desk all day. Taking small walks more often than necessary would be my means of survival.

That pinching pain on my left side started up about halfway to work.

*Tightening up and loosening your muscles burns calories.*

True enough, and that was something I could do while driving.

We pulled into Brighid's daycare before it was open, so she climbed into the front seat with me so we could play stuffed animals.

*Even these little movements are good. Of course, it's not too much more than normal day stuff, but moving is better than not.*

That morning, stuffed Grumpy was picking on Lizzie Maguire, and reminding her that she stinks. Lizzie told on him, and Grumpy got a time out, but he didn't apologize because, after all, he is "a jerk, remember? Duh!"

A car pulled into the dark parking lot and took a space a few over from ours. "Is that my teacher?" Brighid said.

"I don't know yet."

It was her teacher. I gave the familiar shadowed figure a head start and waited until she had triggered the last of the motion sensor lights in the school's hallway before I got out of the car.

*Always move as fast as you can.*

I helped Brighid out of the car and helped her slip on her backpack. "Come on." I took her hand and led her across the parking lot. She laughed as she dragged behind me, and I felt irritation build because she wasn't keeping up and as a result was slowing me down.

"Come on," I said again.

We got her to the room. I said goodbye and headed down the hallway at a power walk. A thin slime of sweat moistened my forehead.

*Good.*

Yeah.

The lab guard let me in and I drove the short two blocks to my building, power walked to my office, and then power walked to the small kitchen down the hall to store my Lean Cuisine in the freezer. No one else was in the building yet—unless some people with the clearance for the back were there. They never knew if I was around or not anyway.

*Now would be the perfect time to walk around the block.*

My computer booted up in front of me as I twisted from side to side in my rotating office chair.

*Take that walk. No one will know. If you wait too long, someone will see you.*

I entered my username and password to logon to the system and open my Windows account.

*Your weight was up. All this fidgeting at your desk is okay, but it's not the same as a good walk around the block.*

There was nothing urgent in the morning e-mail.

*Time is wasting.*

It would be good, actually, to get my blood moving a little. It's not that long around the block here.

*Now you're talking.*

I got up from my desk and headed back into the brisk morning air. My muscles pulsed from the quick walk as I sat back in my desk chair again.

*Once around was not enough.*

I opened a bottle of water and the document that I was in the middle of editing. My breathing was shallow and quick. My eyes darted across the screen to find the place on page 59 that I left off on the previous work day. I settled in for a day of grammar correcting.

Beneath my desk, I shook my right leg up and down, using the ball of my foot as a pivot point with the floor.

*You'll need more than that to get the weight down. Walk the block again.*

I scrolled to the next page in the document.

*Walk the block again. Do you really think this document is more important than your body? You're allowing yourself to be fat. You are a failure. You are nothing if not an anorexic.*

One of the guys from the back knocked on the side of my door and came in with a document that had an image that needed altering. I heard myself say, "That's cool. I probably won't be able to get to it today, but I'm guessing I'd have it by...Thursday or Friday?"

*You will get fatter. It's the only option. You have yourself in therapy for recovery. That really means fat. There are two choices—fat and thin. You are choosing fat. You are a failure.*

"Friday would be fine," the man said, and he walked from my office on the way to the restricted area.

*About walking that block...*

I stood and walked out of my office door. The women that worked across the hall were not in yet. Kim hadn't stopped by on her way to her office yet. If she came by and I wasn't here, she might figure out I took that extra walk.

*So what?*

Yeah...I don't know.

The printer in the main area of the lobby sputtered to life and started spitting paper. No one had seen me yet, but standing with no point in the hall just outside my door would look bad. For a destination, I headed to the men's room.

The mirror showed me the ugly, fat truth.

*Now are you ready to take that walk?*

Yeah.

Kim came from my office as I stepped from the men's room. "There you are," she said.

"Hey! How ya doing?"

*Get rid of her. You need that walk.*

Kim stayed for a while and we talked about whatever. She looked up at my wall clock and said she'd better get up to the office before her boss got in. We made tentative plans to go to Wal-Mart during lunch.

*You blew your chance to take that walk. It's too late now.*

I'll be walking around Wal-Mart at lunch.

*You could have walked then and now. Your weight was up. You are a failure.*

The can of nuts loomed on a shelf to the right of my workspace. The time to eat them had passed. The sight of the can made me gag. I didn't need a snack.

I worked through the morning and found a convenient breaking point when I saw it was nearing the time that Kim and I would go.

"Did you eat yet?" she asked, as she came into my office.

"Yeah." Half of my Lean Cuisine sat hidden in its original package in the trash can in the kitchen.

We got in her car and went to Wal-Mart where she filled the cart with things for her girls. My job was to run items to the scanner if there was a question of price. The more items I scanned, the more I moved, the more calories were burnt.

*You still missed out on that extra morning walk.*

Since I had skipped my morning nuts, and I had only eaten half of my Lean Cuisine, skipping the afternoon nuts was no problem. I had done well.

*But you could have done better.*

# Chapter 41

"What do you really love to do?" Peggy asked.

The question felt weird because by now she had to have known me well enough to know the answer. I checked her look to see if she was kidding, but she sat in her chair, adjusted her glasses, and looked at me like she really wanted to know.

"Diet and exercise," I said.

*Good answer.*

Peggy nodded as if she expected that answer. "What did you used to love to do?"

It was like getting slapped. I sat stunned and looked at her, then I looked around the room but found no help on her bookshelf or on her computer's screen saver.

"Before you got sick," she said, "before anorexia, and maybe even before you were married, there must have been some things that you loved to do."

I had a memory flash of sitting at a table in San Jose State's student union café with a notebook open, scribbling out song ideas. Writing was still part of my life, but did I love it?

*You know it doesn't feel as good as a lost pound.*

There was more to that memory than just telling the story. "I used to really love music," I said.

"Good," Peggy said, making a note on her pad. "What kind of stuff did you listen to?"

"I loved the Grateful Dead." I paused in thought for a second. "I still do. I even go and see what's left of them when they come around."

"Great. What else?"

"Mostly loud and simple rock. I loved the Ramones...and Joan Jett, I really liked Joan Jett."

"This week, I want you to spend some time reconnecting with this music. I think it would be a good thing for you," Peggy said.

I mulled this over on the drive home. I knew, somewhere, that I had Joan Jett's greatest hits CD. I had lots of Ramones, but I had been listening to them lately. It wouldn't feel like a reconnection if I put them on. The Grateful Dead were the same way.

Joan Jett—it had been a while.

The next morning after I wrote, I fished around my CD box until I found the Joan Jett CD. I glanced over the song titles and visions of the old videos came to mind. "I wonder if she is still playing," I thought.

Once we were in the car, the CD kicked on as she proclaimed that she didn't give a damn about her bad reputation. I remembered how much I loved her guitar sound and how it roared when many others fizzled with mock distortion.

"Do we have to listen to this?" Brighid said from the backseat.

"Yes. My doctor said it's good for me."

"Your doctor?"

"Yeah. Peggy."

"Peggy said?"

"Yes, Brighid," I said with a sigh.

"Okay, okay... You don't have to yell."

At work, the curiosity got the better of me, and I looked for her website. There she was, looking not a day older than when I last saw her open for Robert Plant in about 1988.

Reading through her message board told me that she did still tour and that she often hangs out after shows to talk to fans. She allowed people to take pictures at her shows. For me, it's an important thing that the artist does so much and cares so much about the fans. She was almost Grateful Dead like in that regard.

She was coming to Reno, which was only about a 3 hour drive from Modesto, and she was playing a Friday and a Saturday night. Kristin loved Reno, so I figured it would be a pretty easy sell to get her to one of those shows. She liked Joan Jett too, so that was even better.

I thought back to the first time I heard Joan Jett. I was on a bus for a field trip to Sacramento when I was in 8$^{th}$ grade. My friend, Greg, had her debut album on tape, and we listened to it through a Walkman with dual headphone jacks. The thought of me then brought tears to my eyes, but I wasn't sure why.

I edited through some documents that day, ate my snacks and my lunch, and kept checking her website and message board every couple of hours.

"Babe do you want to see Joan Jett?" I asked her over the phone on her way home.

"Sure, where is she playing?"

"Reno." I smiled into the receiver knowing this would please her.

"Even better. It's on a weekend?"

"Yeah."

"Sounds good. We can talk about it more when I get home."

This would be good for us. Maybe I could make up for ruining her birthday if we went away for this weekend like a couple.

The sound of Joan Jett's voice and that crunching guitar mattered to me. I could have it and enjoy it on my own terms. Her music had been part of the soundtrack of my youth, and now here it was again like an old friend who steps back into your life and picks up conversations with you where you left them 20 years ago.

I loved my family, and I loved diet and exercise. If my life were a pie chart, my family would be about a quarter of the chart, and diet and exercise was the bigger slice.

Now Joan Jett was taking some of the slice away from diet and exercise. She mattered because her music reminded me of my passions before I was sick. She helped me begin chipping away at anorexia and replacing it with things in my life that I could love, have control over, and that were mine.

That night Kristin and I were in front of the computer looking at Joan Jett tickets for the Reno show. I was excited, not only for the live show and the gambling, but for the time away with just Kristin.

"She is playing two nights there," Kristin said, sitting in the computer chair while I hovered by her shoulder.

"Yeah," I said, "at the Nugget."

"I think the Saturday show would be better, don't you? Then we wouldn't have to take time off work."

"That sounds good."

"You know what," Kristin said, "that's right by Melanie's birthday. Get me the phone. I'll see if she wants to go."

I sighed as I walked the hall to get the cordless phone from our room. It was never enough to just be with me it seemed, but I was probably just feeling sorry for myself.

*Walk back to her a little faster.*

"Here you go." I handed her the red and white cordless phone. She took it, switched it on, checked for a dial tone, and dialed.

"Hey Melanie...You want to go see Joan Jett...Joan Jett....Up in Reno...Near your birthday." Kristin's lips curled into a smile. "Jim and I are getting the tickets now—we'll get you one. Okay...okay...Bye."

"Order four of them," Kristin said.

"Four?"

"Jason will probably want to go."

"Don't you want to at least call him and ask him before we spend the money?" I said.

"He'll want to go. Just order four." She said.

I ordered four tickets while she left a voicemail for Jason asking if he wanted to go. Jason was a good guy, and a lot of fun, but I wanted this trip to be about us as a couple.

*You ate too much today, you know that, right?*

Yeah.

*I hate to even think about the scale tomorrow morning.*

Me too.

# Chapter 42

I was already tired when I showed up to Peggy's office for a session. My book was open in my lap, and I looked at the words without seeing them.

"Hi Jim," Peggy called from the door that led back to the individual offices.

"Hey, how're you doing?"

I followed her back to the normal room and took my seat in my usual chair. She shut the door behind us and got her notepad and my thick file. "So how is the music? Did you reconnect?"

"Yeah. I did. I even have Joan Jett tickets for September."

"Wow, she still plays?"

I nodded. "We're going up to see her in Reno at the Nugget. She looks exactly the same from the pictures I've seen."

"That's really cool." Peggy said. "You and Kristin are going?"

"Yeah." The words sat festering at the back of my throat. Did I really need to say them though? "And her friends Melanie and Jason."

"Are they a couple?"

"No." I laughed.

"You don't sound that excited that these other two are going with you."

"I'm not."

"Then why are they going?"

Peggy had a real skill of waiting for answers, and I pushed it to almost the limit on that one. "Because she wanted them to go."

"Why don't you want them there?" she said as she added more to the mountains of notes she'd accumulated about me.

"I wanted a trip with just us—as a couple."

"Did you tell Kristin that?"

"No."

"Why?"

"Because she wanted these people to go," I said.

"And you made that sacrifice for her."

I nodded.

"Because it builds character?"

"I suppose. That's pretty bad, huh?"

"It's not really bad or good. It's what you did, and really all you did was what you were taught to do. But I think with Kristin, that may not be the best approach. I think you're past your limit, but you never knew how to set one."

"And that's why I'm anorexic?"

"Partly." Peggy adjusted the glasses on her face. "What would have happened if you had told Kristin that you didn't want the other people to go?"

"She would have been mad."

"Mad how? What would that have looked like?"

I smirked and thought of the best way to describe that. "She would have not wanted to talk to me. She would have said I was self centered, I imagine, for not including Melanie on her birthday. Then I would have given in anyway because I really wanted to go and it would have come down to her way or no way."

"I see," Peggy said.

"So, you see, it just saves a lot of time and headache to do what she wants from the beginning."

"Yet, you are not happy by the outcome."

I hid my gut with my arms. "Not entirely, no," I said, "But at least I'm going to see Joan Jett."

"Is that really enough consolation?"

"I don't know." Exhaustion started beating in against my brain. I couldn't see a clock, but my feeling was the hour had to almost be up and the truth was I had just sat down.

"Can you talk about the feelings regarding this whole situation?"

"Well…It never seems to be enough for her—for just the two of us to do something."

"How does that feel?" Peggy was in a digging mood.

"Like I'm inadequate. Like I'm not good enough or fun enough to be around alone," I said, "I really wish it could be the two of us going, but like I said, I'm happy to at least be going."

"Because it builds character to feel that way."

"I suppose so," I said.

"Is there any connection between this situation and eating that you have noticed?"

"Actually, yeah," I said, "I remember being nagged by that voice right about the time I saw how the trip was going to go." I put my hand to the diagonal rear of my head approximating where the nagging impulse seemed to come from.

Peggy scribbled manically and then let her pen rest at the ready. "What other times does that voice show itself?"

"The most common time is if my weight is up from the day before—or even from the last weighing, whenever that was. If for some reason, I have to short change myself on the treadmill it comes then as well. And of course, if I eat something I shouldn't or eat more than I should of something that is okay to eat."

"What are your safe foods now?"

"The things Sally has me on. The Special K, the nuts twice a day, the Lean Cuisine." There were few topics as exciting as my diet. This I could talk about all day. The exhaustion from earlier was gone.

"So how are you doing on that?"

"Fine," I said.

"Is it ever too much?"

"What?"

"Is the food that you are supposed to eat ever too much?" Peggy said.

"Sometimes."

"And what do you do when that happens?"

"I eat less."

"So you are still restricting, just not all the time?" Peggy said.

"Yeah. I guess that is true."

"Can you generalize about the kinds of things that trigger the urge to restrict?"

"Just the times I'd mentioned. Like if I weigh too much in the morning, I might pinch the top off my cereal and stick it back in the box. To be honest, most days I am probably eating less cereal than I am supposed to. I'm supposed to have a cup of it, and I usually feel safer with 5 or 6 flakes."

Peggy gave no reaction to my flake count, which I found disappointing. "So in times of stress, would that be a fair assessment?"

"Yes," I said.

"And the stress could be something like doing one of those building character things you were raised to do, or it could be from the anorexia itself?"

I nodded.

Peggy made some notes. "I think it's good that you are so excited about Joan Jett. Anything you can do that you think is fun, you know, that you feel is really yours and on your own terms would be good for you."

I smiled at that idea. "But you know, it's not like Kristin took control. I gave her a certain amount. My anorexia isn't because I feel robbed of control."

"You may have, and you probably did because that is what you were raised to do, but she has gone beyond the limits. Whether you let her or not is irrelevant."

I let that sink in for a bit.

"Another thing I think would be good would be to be actively mindful of the things that trigger the desire to restrict. When you feel like you absolutely have to restrict, make a note of what brought on those feelings."

"Actually write it down?"

"Yeah. You can just add it to your daily mood and food log," Peggy said. I had been keeping that kind of journal since I started therapy and e-mailing daily entries to Peggy.

"Okay. I could do that." I nodded my head and let my eyes wander around the forest trees printed on Peggy's office wallpaper.

"So that's your homework then. Try and find things that are yours that you enjoy and be mindful of what makes you want to restrict."

"Yes."

*You are nothing if not an anorexic.*

I know.

# Chapter 43

My teenage stepdaughter, who had been making a series of poor life choices, had reached the very end of my tolerance. I was short tempered with her most of the time. She was smoking, shoplifting, drinking, and who knew what else and she was 15. Maybe I was just undernourished, but I couldn't have a conversation with her without yelling lately.

I would feel bad after yelling because I knew it wasn't doing any good. If anything, I was making everything worse, but at the time of my explosions there didn't feel like there was an alternative. When we would ground her for doing something, Kristin would forget she was grounded and let her do whatever she wanted to do, so there were no consequences. Maybe I was really angry about that, but whatever the reason, I had stopped being a pleasant person to be around and the house had stopped being a pleasant place to be.

My phone rang at work, and I saw on the caller ID it was Kristin. "Hey honey," I said.

"Hey," she said. She sounded excited, and I started to feel excited too. "Joyce called me."

"Right on. What's up with her?" I said.

"You know how she won that cruise to the Bahamas?"

"No," I said.

"Oh, I thought I told you. Anyway, she won this cruise to the Bahamas. It's a 2 week cruise in September. She was going to go with Frank, of course, but he can't go. So she invited me."

"Wow," I said, "When in September?"

"I think she said around the 20th or something."

"We have Joan Jett on the 23rd," I said, "And you invited Melanie for her birthday and everything."

"Well…Maybe she said we would be getting back on the 20th. I'm not sure. But I really want to go."

"It's free, right?" I said.

"It is, but it's going to cost us $300 to change the name of the ticket from Frank's to mine."

"That's not free then," I said.

"But still for $300 I'd be able to really go places and see things I have never seen before. You've been to Hawaii as a kid. I never had the chance to go anywhere. I really need this vacation, Jim."

I bit my inner lip and slapped my desktop with the phone cord.

"This is a once in a lifetime chance, Jim," she said.

"Well, I...I really don't see a problem with it except that we already have plans in September, and you've invited 2 of your friends to go to Reno with us. Plus, we're supposed to see Joan Jett." That didn't carry the weight for Kristin that it did for me, but it was central to my thoughts.

"I'll check with Joyce on the dates again, but you have no problem with it if it doesn't interfere with the Reno trip, right?"

I paused. This pause turned out to be a defining moment in my life. "Yeah that's fine," I said, "But make sure it's not during our trip, okay?"

"Okay. Cool. Thanks." She hung up.

Within minutes, I had an e-mail that she forwarded from Joyce assuring me that the trip would actually end the day before the Joan Jett show. I could pick up Kristin from the airport one day, and we could leave for Reno the next. My one stipulation was met.

*The whole time she's gone, you can eat as little as you want. She won't be here to see.*

I know.

*You could do the treadmill 2 times a day if you wanted.*

Sounds good.


Kristin got home from work and I followed her upstairs while she changed. "I am so excited about this trip," she said.

I forced a smile.

"I've never been on a cruise before. I hear they are amazing." She tossed her work blouse and bra onto the dirty clothes mountain to the left of the TV.

"I've never been on a cruise," I said.

She pulled an oversized Mickey Mouse nightshirt over her head. I sat on my side of the bed with my back against the headboard.

"And Joan Jett was the 29th right?" she said.

My face boiled. From the corner of my eye, I saw the blonde ghost pass across the open bedroom door. I'd seen her check herself in the mirror that one night, and she showed herself in times of great stress. "It's the 23$^{rd}$."

Kristin stopped on her way to the bathroom and did her best shocked face. "I thought it was the 29$^{th}$?"

I shook my head. "I told you the 23$^{rd}$."

"Oh…cause…I'm not coming back until the 27$^{th}$."

I grabbed my inner cheek between my teeth. "The e-mail you forwarded from Joyce said you'd be home on the 22$^{nd}$."

*The way you are sitting right now, it's easy for anyone to see how out-of-control fat your gut is.*

"On the way home, she called me and she told me she was wrong. That we wouldn't get back until the 27$^{th}$. I don't know why I was thinking Joan Jett was the 29$^{th}$." Kristin acted like I should believe this.

"Joyce just told you whatever she needed to tell you so that you would go with her on the cruise," I said.

"Don't start getting crazy like this is some sort of a plot against you," Kristin said. "You're always thinking the worst of people."

"I told you about 4 times that the show was the 23$^{rd}$ this afternoon. I have an e-mail assuring me you'll be home by the 22$^{nd}$. Then on your way home from work, suddenly it's the 27$^{th}$. You don't see how I could think that you guys planned the date misunderstanding?"

"Yeah, everyone is totally out to get you," Kristin said.

*Your gut is sticking out. Suck it in.*

I covered my stomach with my arms. "Not everyone," I kept that one under my breath and Kristin chose to ignore it. She finished her walk to the vanity area of the bathroom before talking again.

"You know what really pisses me off about this whole thing?" she said, "I was just telling everyone today about how cool you were and how you were understanding about me needing this vacation. About how you can appreciate my needs." She turned to face me. "That was all bullshit, wasn't it?"

"I said from the beginning that it was cool as long as it wasn't at the same time as our Reno trip." I could see from her face that my request was never under consideration. "You said that it wasn't. Now you come home and you say it is, and you're still going."

"This trip is very important to me," she said.

"More important than I am," I added.

"You chose your family over me when your mom invited just family to Philadelphia. You didn't even stick up for me. You don't think of me as family, or what?"

"My mom wanted just the 4 of us to go back and bury my grandmother's ashes. It was a funeral. You have to let people have funerals the way they want to have them."

"Oh, and how long over the 4 days that you were there did you actually stay at the grave? Ten minutes?"

I didn't know how this discussion was suddenly about my mom, but somehow it was, and I didn't know what to say. This trip to Philadelphia had long been a sore spot to Kristin. She said that I should have told my mom that I wasn't going without Kristin and that she would never go anywhere that I was not welcome.

The trip to Philadelphia gave her license to break our plans now and choose another trip over the one we already had planned. This was the second time she had cashed in this chip because we were supposed to go on a trip to Reno earlier in the year as well, but she turned it into a girls only trip because of Philadelphia. I would be paying for Philadelphia for the rest of my marriage.

"Not every family does a 4-day death parade when someone dies, Honey."

The argument continued, but in the end she was going on this cruise. "I don't think you understand how badly I need to get away from anorexia," she said. "I can't have a conversation with anyone who knows you where they don't ask how you are doing. It always has to be about you, and I think that's why you are doing this."

"This is a disease, Kristin."

"But you like it. You like losing weight, you like barely eating, and you like working yourself to exhaustion on the treadmill. It's not like it's cancer where we could fight it together—you are having an affair with anorexia."

I looked at her like she was speaking French.

"You do, don't you? You like your disease." She made finger quotes and dragged the word disease out longer than it needed to be.

"I am working on getting better," I said.

"I don't see any difference." She looked me up and down.

"It takes time."

"Yeah…well, I need to see some results." She stormed back to the end of the bed.

"This isn't what we are talking about," I said, scooting myself up to a better seated position on the bed.

"Oh sorry. What is it that we are talking about then, Jim?" She stared at me until I covered my stomach with my arms again.

*You should have skipped one of those snacks today.*

"Nothing," I said. "Never mind."

She sat on the foot of the bed, and I moved my feet up and away from her. "This trip has everything to do with anorexia. I have never been able to go anywhere, and I have been putting up with anorexia for almost a year. Your anorexia has ruined my own weight loss for me. I wasn't even able to be excited about my gastric bypass because of you. You are too tired for sex, and you make me feel undesirable. I need to get away."

"What about Joan Jett?" I said.

"Take Dominique."

I nodded.

"You'll still go with Melanie, right?"

"Melanie is your friend," I said. "I'll just take Dominique up."

"You're just gonna ditch her on her birthday?" Kristin said.

I looked from the wall that had held my attention to Kristin to see if she was kidding. She wasn't. I wanted to say that I wasn't the one ditching her on her birthday, but I didn't. I didn't have it in me. We would have this same fight a few more times before the actual cruise, and I would use that line later, but it had no effect.

"Fine, we'll go up with Melanie." I rolled my eyes and pinched my side looking for fat.

*Skip your morning cereal all together tomorrow.*

Kristin nodded.

"What about Jason?" I said.

"Oh, he probably won't go because I'm not going, but I'll ask him," she said.

I wanted to ask what about the money we already spent on his ticket, but I knew it would be irrelevant to her and a small price to pay for her cruise dream vacation away from me and anorexia.

# Chapter 44

"She's going to take a cruise without me," I said. I took my normal seat in Peggy's office.

"A cruise?"

"Yeah, for 2 weeks."

Peggy looked like she didn't really know what to say. "How are you guys able to afford that?"

"It's free. Her friend Joyce won it, and Joyce's husband can't go." I went through the whole thing and the arguments that followed while Peggy listened and made an occasional note.

"Have you noticed any eating problems?"

"Well, you know, in times of stress, it is easier to restrict because it gives me relief. So yeah, the urges to restrict are pretty strong right now. And of course, the more weight I lose, the more she feels like she needs to get the hell away from me."

"You're staying with the kids?" Peggy said.

I nodded.

"All three?"

"Yeah."

"We should focus on how you are going to get through those 2 weeks without completely relapsing," she said. "You're already wanting to restrict because of it, and if you start that…That's a very slippery slope."

"I know. Plus, with her gone, there will be no one watching what I eat."

"Yeah, exactly," she said. "So what kinds of things can you distract yourself with when she is gone?"

Being hit with the direct question left me floundering to find an answer.

"Is Joan Jett ruined for you?"

"What? No…no…never."

"Okay so you still have her show coming up—you'll just be going with your stepdaughter."

"Yeah."

"And Kristin's friends."

I nodded.

"Do you want to go with them?"

"It's not so much that I don't want to go with them as it is she set it up so they could go and now she's not going," I said, "And one of them will probably flake anyway."

Peggy made a note. "What if you just told Kristin you weren't going to go with her friends?"

"I did. She said I was ditching Melanie on her birthday."

Peggy laughed.

"I know," I said. "She made it seem like I was being the asshole."

"But you're going to go with her friends, right?"

"Yes."

"Because it...what was the phrase?" Peggy flipped back a few pages in my file, "Because it builds character."

"I imagine so, yeah." I looked down at my shoes and checked my waistband for gut spillage.

"Did your mom ever make it clear when you were finished?"

I raised my eyes up until they met Peggy's. "Finished?"

Peggy cocked her head to the side for a moment before speaking. "At what point will you be finished building this character you are building? I mean, is it a forever thing? Is there a time when your character is built and all the self sacrifice can stop?"

"Geez, I never really thought about it."

Peggy nodded. "You'll probably still go to Reno with her friends because you said you would and because you feel bad for them because Kristin ditched them just like she ditched you, to use her words. But really, I think it's about time you stop doing things that put yourself out. It's not black and white between generous and selfish, and if you are being generous but it's making you miserable, then it defeats part of the purpose of being generous in the first place. The feeling of altruism, which is supposed to make you feel good, gets twisted around and you do what makes you feel bad so that others can be happy. Do that too much and..."

"You get anorexia?"

Peggy shrugged, "Or alcoholism, or any number of problems. It feeds a cycle of devaluing yourself. Like when you were doing those resumes for no thanks. You're...how old?"

"Thirty-four."

"Yeah, see your character is built. You can stop building it now. You did a good job, but there comes a time when the project

255

is just…" Peggy made circles with her hand as if stirring the words from thin air, "…complete."

"You think?"

"Yes." She let a silence stretch. "You already said you would go to Reno with her friends, but you don't have to if you don't want to. Really." Another long silence for processing followed.

"Okay," I said.

"Do you really believe that?"

"I don't know." I knew that when I didn't want to do resumes anymore, Kristin let me know that I was a selfish prick and that there was no way she would be married to one. I didn't believe I could live without her. "Kristin will say I'm selfish."

"Kristin made plans with you and two of her friends and broke the plans when a better opportunity for her came along," said Peggy.

I sat in the long silence and thought again. "But this is a once in a lifetime opportunity, and you know, she grew up in a poor household and she never really got to go anywhere."

"Where have you gone since you have been married?"

The list was rather short—Disneyland, Reno, San Diego for a wedding, and that Philadelphia trip that I was not even allowed to enjoy. "Not too many places. But see, she really feels like she needs to get away from anorexia."

*You are nothing if not an anorexic.*

I know.

"I think you really need to find some things that you want to do when she is gone. She is taking this trip for herself, so you should do some things for yourself."

"Like what?" I said.

Peggy shrugged, shook her head, widened her eyes, and tossed one of her hands into the air, "Anything you want."

I thought for a second. "I do have some PTO. I could take a couple days off while she is gone."

"There you go," Peggy said. "And what will you do on those days?"

"Probably see a movie. Or maybe read in a coffee shop or something. I used to always read in a coffee shop for hours when I was single and I had free time."

"There you go," Peggy said. "The point is, you should do what you want. Aside from diet and exercise."

We both laughed.

Driving home after the session, I knew I could do this, and the next day at work, I put in for 2 days off while she was gone.

"I'm taking a couple days off work when you are on your trip."

This pulled her attention away from the TV even though we weren't in commercial. "What? Why?"

"My therapist said I should." It was great to have doctor's orders for a reason.

The cruise came. I remember being short tempered from malnutrition and a feeling of abandonment. The kids took the worst of that.

"Mom really needed this trip," Dominique told me when I complained about being left for 2 weeks. "It was a once in a lifetime opportunity."

I recognized the rhetoric as learned and ignored it.

Joan Jett was great. Dominique and I went with Melanie and we lost the money on Jason's no show, but that was no surprise. After the concert, Dominique and I went to one of the cafes and we both had dessert. I didn't once worry about those calories.

At the end of the two weeks, Brighid and I drove down to the San Jose airport from Modesto to meet Kristin. She and Joyce came from the gate, and Joyce threw her arms around Frank and kissed him like a couple reunited after a war.

"Hi," Kristin said, and flopped her arm around my shoulders with a little pat—the hug of strangers.

"Hi," I said. With Joyce and Frank being what they were, I felt like the blind date couple on a double date where the woman instantly knew from my looks it would be the longest evening of her life.

I knew that she would be hungry, so I made sure I stopped off and got her some food for the ride back.

She didn't want it.

At the end of the 2 hour ride, she went in and greeted the older kids like she hadn't seen them in a years while I carried her bags from the car to the living room. Suitcases were unzipped, souvenirs were handed out, and thanks was given.

"You'd be amazed if you ever get to go on a cruise, Daddy," Kristin said to me. "It's the most amazing vacation ever. The food, oh my god…" she paused and looked at me, "Well, like you know…when you are better."

We slept and woke up, but things never quite went back to normal with us.

Two weeks later, Joyce e-mailed pictures from the cruise to my private e-mail address. I looked through the pictures to see where they had been, and smiled as I saw all the amazing places and things.

Then a picture displayed of a hot tub with Kristin sitting on a man's lap among the hot bubbles. They looked very happy together. She got away from anorexia, and she couldn't tell the difference between it and me anymore.

*You are nothing if not an anorexic.*

I nodded, and the vision in the picture hollowed me.

*You are such a fat and ugly bastard that your wife had to go elsewhere to find a decent man. You need to really listen from now on. Enough with these snacks and all the shit your nutritionist says to eat.*

"You were just looking for something bad in there," she said when I confronted her.

"It wasn't hard to find."

"I was drunk, and I don't even remember that."

"Well, there's a picture, and I wasn't even there, but I will always remember it," I said.

"I know nothing happened between me and that guy."

"Enough is in the picture," I said.

"Well, you make me feel so undesirable."

"I know the feeling."

Peggy's office closed in on me and I sat with my arms tight around my stomach. "And then she said she was drunk, and she didn't remember that, but she assured me that nothing happened."

Her pen lay on its side on the notepad on her lap, and she clipped it there with her thumb. "What are you going to do about this?"

"Nothing," I said. "I mean, I told her that if I'm ever around Joyce again that this picture and the fact that she e-mailed it to all kinds of people would be the main topic of conversation."

"So what did she say?"

"She said I can't control who her friends are and that's what I'm trying to do, but I made it clear she can go ahead and be friends with anyone she wants and that she can't control what I say to people that are around me."

Peggy nodded.

"So basically, she isn't going to hang around with Joyce anymore. And I realize this is misplaced anger on my part because my real problem is with Kristin, but it's easier to be mad at Joyce than it is at Kristin."

"Why?"

"Well, because I'm married to Kristin and being mad at her makes life harder," I said.

"Are you trying to 'build character' by not being mad at your wife even though she did this to you and to your marriage?"

"Maybe." I hated myself for that being true. "Maybe that's what I am doing. And you know she said that I make her feel undesirable because I'm asleep so early."

"You can't make anyone feel any certain way, Jim. You don't have that kind of power." Peggy lifted her pen to the ready again. "How is your eating going since this?"

"It's been surprisingly pretty good. When she was gone, I even ate a little bit of junk and whatever."

Peggy looked impressed.

"Not too much, though," I said.

*Yes it was.*

"And how about since she's been back?"

"I've pretty much stuck to the eating plan pretty well." I gave it some thought and pictured all the foods I had been eating. "Yeah."

"So no restricting at all?"

"Maybe a little, but not too much. Like I still have the thing where I pinch the top of my cereal off and put it back in the box."

"Every day?" Peggy said.

I considered this.

*Tell her no. Tell her you hardly do it at all.*

"I would say probably most days," I said.

"How many times a day are you weighing now?"

"Four or five."

"Do you think you are ready to cut that down a little? Like, do you think you could commit to weighing once a day?"

My heart beat faster at the thought, yet I remembered a time when I would go months without weighing myself, and it hadn't killed me.

*But it made you fat. It gave you high blood pressure. You are nothing if not an anorexic.*

"I don't think I could do that," I said.

"Okay. Because I think you are at a stage where in order to get to the next level, you are going to have to pick one of the urges and go against them."

Seemed reasonable and as scary as a shit storm.

"Or more than one of them," Peggy said.

I worked my teeth against my lips.

"How about the treadmill? Could you cut that down to every other day?"

You had to admire her determination, and I really wanted to comply and be a good client, but if I tried not to weigh myself, I'd have no idea if I had gained. I'd worry constantly, and the stress of it all would make it impossible to stick to the eating plan that Sally had me on. If I cut back on the treadmill, I would need to weigh more often because my weight would need constant monitoring. Right now, I had the perfect balance. It was like juggling chainsaws and needing to sneeze.

*You will destroy all your progress.*

"How about checking yourself in the mirror? Is that something you could cut back on?" Peggy had her pen ready to make a note as soon as I agreed to a condition.

"Uhm…"

If I checked myself in the mirror less, that would take away one of the tools I used to make sure I wasn't getting fat. That would mean that I would have to weigh myself more, and I certainly wouldn't be able to cut back on the treadmill or things would get out of control in no time.

"How about just the pinching for fat part?" Peggy said, her patience showing no sign of breaking.

That seemed harmless. I'd still have the mirror and unlimited use of the scale to make sure I was safe.

*You're going to lose control.*

"I think I can do that," I said.

"Do you? Great. Now just make sure with yourself that you really can make that commitment. It's no good if you agree to it when you know you can't follow through." Peggy made her note on the pad and looked back up at me.

"I think I can do that. It's kind of an unconscious act though."

"Just need to be aware of it. Replace the urge to do that with a Joan Jett song or whatever. When you feel the urge, distract yourself with another thought if you can. Be mindful of the urges. The more you are and the more you refuse them, the less powerful they will become."

I nodded, not believing a word of that.

# Chapter 45

The rules that governed my anorexia could be chipped away at a little at a time. The process was just unlearning the self-imposed rules that I had viewed as essential to living. I had to show myself that I would be okay even if I didn't follow the rules, but I had to do it gradually.

Once the pinching for fat rule was taken off the list of laws, I could concentrate on only weighing once a day. That was a tough one, and I often broke that rule. The panic would get too much, and I would have to get on the scale just to set my mind at ease. Stripping off my pants and getting into the 27-inch-waist shorts took the place of weighing for a while, but soon, concentrating on one false law at a time, I was able to get to a slightly better place.

"I think I am ready to go to see Sally the nutritionist again," I told Peggy during one session.

"Oh?" she said.

I nodded. "I think I'm ready to start to try and gain a little weight. Just a little."

*You are a complete failure. You never even made it down to the 120s. You are stuck at 130 and you gave up. Loser.*

"What do you think brought this on?"

"I don't know" I said, "All I can tell you is it feels like the right move to make at this time."

"Okay," Peggy said, "I mean it's a good thing so I guess we don't really need to worry about the why and so forth."

"It's just that I am really okay with weighing once a day now, and it took me what—like a month to get here—so I feel like it's time to chip away at the monster a little more."

"Have you thought about just cutting down the treadmill?" Peggy said.

"There's no way I can do that." The thought of it tensed my body in my chair and blurred my vision for a second.

"Okay," Peggy said, "Do you want to make the appointment, or would you like me to make it for you?"

"If you could make it, that would be awesome," I said.

*You're going to be disgusting and no one will ever want you again. Your wife already cheats on you. Now you're going to add fat to the list of repulsions that is you?*

Peggy turned to her computer, jiggled the mouse, made a few quick clicks and offered me a time and day to meet with Sally.

"Sounds fine to me."

"Great. And remember that when you are going through this kind of recovery, you may relapse a bit. This is normal, and you need to accept that you did it and move on with things"

I nodded not really getting what she meant.

"Kim, can you do me a favor?" I phoned her from my office to her office on the other side of the security wall.

"Sure what?"

"This is lame," I said.

She laughed, "Well it is you calling, after all."

With a smile I said, "I really need to eat this banana, but it's hard. So will you please come down here and sit with me while I eat it?"

"Sure."

Within a few minutes she was in my office. She knew all about everything because of all the lunch hours we spent running around Target and Wal-Mart. Kristin was sure I was having an affair with her, but it wasn't true. "So how's everything going? A banana huh? That's not on your normal food list."

"That's why it's so hard," I said. "I just saw the dietician, and we've increased what I'm eating a bit."

"That's a good thing right?"

"Yeah. It's a step towards recovery. Do I look fatter?"

Kim shook her head, but I looked at her eyes for any sign of lying. She always said what she was thinking. "All right, so let's eat this banana, and then we'll go smoke."

I peeled it down, and the two of us talked as I lifted it for bite after bite. It felt like trying to eat a pumpkin straight out of the patch. This had to be one of the biggest bananas from the roughest bunch ever harvested.

"What did Kristin say about that picture from the cruise?" Kim said.

*You don't need this food. You were stupid to have Kim come down here.*

My stomach flexed and tried to reject the banana, but I shut my mouth and my eyes and held it inside of me. I only had one half of it left. "She said she was drunk and that she didn't remember that picture, but that she is sure nothing happened."

"And you've decided to believe that?"

"What else am I supposed to do?" I said, forcing more banana into my mouth. My jaw ached from the chewing and the ground up fruit sat and swished around in my mouth, making a suffocating paste before I could finally force it down my throat.

"Tell her it's bullshit," Kim said.

"I did say that." Only a quarter of a banana left. I pulled the peels down a little further and looked at the gargantuan stump that still remained in my hand.

"Did you?"

"Yeah," I said, ignoring Kim's sarcasm.

"And what did she say?"

"She said that if I didn't believe her that it was my problem."

*That banana is more than you need. Throw the rest away.*

"No no no," Kim said, "There's still banana there."

"I'm full?"

"Nice try."

Sweat beads formed at my hairline and I unfolded the peels once more to reveal the thickest most indigestible banana chunk the world had ever known. I raised it slowly to my mouth as my guts retched.

Kim ignored my heroism of keeping the food down. "So that's it then, huh? You're just letting her get away with cheating on you."

"I don't know that she cheated," I said. The battery operated clock on the wall ticked and I threw away my banana peel.

"You sent me the picture. Doesn't matter if she slept with him or not. It shows her on his lap in the hot tub. There's no way of telling what was up under the water there, but that's not even the point. She shouldn't have even been on dude's lap."

"I know," I said, "You're right."

"Damn straight." Kim smiled. "Of course I'm right...Duh!"

"I'm actually more mad at Joyce," I said.

"Why?"

No matter how my answer formed in my brain, it came up weak at best. "I guess because she is the one that sent around the e-mail with the pictures. It's bad enough my wife was whoring, but she sent that e-mail out to over 100 people or whatever."

"Do you and Kristin know all of Joyce's friends and family?"

"No." You could always count on Kim to shoot your bullshit full of holes.

"So then most people that got the e-mail probably think she's a regular whore and not a married one."

"I guess you're right," I said.

"Again...Duh!" Kim laughed, and I joined her. "Plus, did it ever occur to you that Joyce was just trying to tell you what she thought you might need to know?"

"No, cause there were too many pictures there for it to be that kind of thing. The pic I stopped at was like 108 out of 275 or some shit. If she just wanted me to know, she would have just sent that pic and whatever ones after it that may have shown a similar thing."

"Still though." Kim rocked from side to side in her chair and pushed her hands into her leather jacket pockets. "It's cold in here."

"Yeah, I don't know what's up with the AC," I said.

"This building is fucked." Kim had a couple of cigarettes in her hand when it came from her pocket. "Do you want one?" she said.

"Sure."

We went out and stood in front of the building.

"You know, the whole thing's really messed my head up. Now when I hear about a cruise or about the Bahamas, it just makes me mad. It's like cruises are ruined for me for life or something." I used her lighter and handed it back. "Thanks."

She nodded, dragged on her own cigarette, and let the smoke go. "That's stupid thinking, you realize."

I almost snapped my neck turning to look at her.

"You're mad at everyone and everything except the person that did something to you here." She dragged again and held the smoke inside a little longer before it poured out through her nose.

I dragged and exhaled while watching my reflection in the building window. "Ya think?"

One of her eyebrows cocked up high enough to be mistaken for her hairline.

"I guess you're right."

"Duh!" Kim ashed and took a quick drag. "Did you not get the memo? I am always right."

265

"Well, I can't be mad at Kristin for this. It would wreck my marriage."

Kim threw her head to one side and shrugged a bit. "How would it wreck your marriage?"

"Well, she really needed to take this trip. It was about getting away from anorexia and all."

"So it was about getting away from you." Kim motioned to me with her free hand and ashed again.

"No." That was ridiculous. If I hadn't been sick, she never would have wanted to go on that vacation without me. Would she?

*You are nothing if not an anorexic.*

"It was about getting some space and sorting things out in her mind." I nodded as if I believed that.

"I saw the picture of her thinking things through," Kim said.

I laughed.

"You're buying her bullshit," Kim said, taking the final drag and flicking the last ash from her smoke before stamping it out under foot.

"Huh?"

"The cruise wasn't about any fuckin' thing except Kristin. She's using your anorexia to justify what she knows, on some level, was the wrong way to behave. If your anorexia was so fuckin' bad, why did she believe that you would be a good person to watch all three of her kids for two weeks while she's off getting wasted and trying out hot tubs?"

"Because I wouldn't hurt the kids?"

"You're not eating healthy. Anything could have happened to you while she was gone. Then the kids are left with who?"

To spare myself another "Duh," I just kept quiet about Kim being right. "Well it's just easier and it helps keep my marriage alive by focusing my anger elsewhere."

"So by lying to yourself, you are saving your marriage?" Kim said.

I stamped out my cigarette butt and held the door for Kim as we went back into the building. "Pretty much, yeah," I said.

"Then why bother?"

Soon, the new food list wasn't such a challenge to me anymore. I was able to eat the new items with minimal protest from my body, and my weight still hovered at about 130.

*You never made it into the 120s. You didn't have what it takes. It's not too late though. Maybe ten extra minutes on the treadmill each day would move you in the right direction.*

Peggy and I negotiated the next piece to attack in one of our sessions. I had already stopped pinching my body, tried to avoid mirrors, cut down on the weighing, and increased my food.

"Do you think I should take the next step?" I said.

"What is the next step?"

"Maybe cutting back a bit on the treadmill."

"Do you feel like you are ready for that?"

My eyes wandered the jungle print wallpaper of her office and returned to her. "I don't really know. Like how much of a cutback are you talking about?"

"Every other day?" Peggy tossed her hand up as if the idea were coming at me to catch or drop.

"Hmmm…" The idea was scary, but if I was going to recover, then maybe I should just take the steps towards recovery.

*You will get so fat so fast that your head will spin.*

"It really is up to you. For this to work, you really need to do it at your own pace," Peggy said.

I had to do the right thing, and the right thing to do is to recover. I had a daughter after all, and I didn't have the luxury of being anorexic and ruining her life. If it were just me, there would be no problem. "Yeah, I can start doing that."

*Stupid.*

"Okay," Peggy said, "As long as you feel ready and you don't feel like you are trying to do too much too fast."

"No, it's cool. It's about time."

*You are kidding yourself and you are going to fail. The fat is already piling up in you deep beneath your skin. Fat pockets are forming and wrecking your body—destroying all the progress you have made.*

"As long as you're sure." Peggy made a note in her notepad.

"Yeah. Not a doubt in my mind."


My cell rang seconds after I turned it back on following my appointment. "Hello."

"Hey, Bubbah. How was therapy?"

"It was good." I guided my car with one hand toward Scenic Road, past the discount cigarette stores and the scrapbooking place.

"What did you talk about?"

I sighed. "Nothing really. Just the normal stuff…You know like how I'm doing and eating and all."

"Did you talk about me?"

"No." The lie was exhausting, but not as exhausting as going through the entire session verbatim.

"Not at all?" She said.

"No, Honey. You didn't come up." The light turned and I inched toward the house, wishing we needed something from the grocery store. "But I think I'm ready to cut the treadmill down to every other day."

Silence.

"Babe?" I said.

"Huh? Oh sorry. I was reading something."

"I said I think I am ready to cut back on the treadmill a little."

"Oh…Okay Honey, well I will see you at home."

I snapped the cell phone shut, turned up the radio, and kept driving. Modesto's flat horizon stretched in front of me. "Somewhere out there, there may be someone that gives a shit."

# Chapter 46

The next morning, my eyes popped open at 2.

*Look at the hump your stomach makes below the blanket. You're stupid to give up any of the treadmill.*

I could stay in bed an hour and a half before I should head to the writing room to work on my book. Sleep didn't come back through, and I watched the red digital numbers count their way through the predawn morning.

*It's not too late to get on the treadmill and still get in a good hour of writing.*

I'm cutting down on that.

*You just said you'd do every other day. You could start skipping tomorrow. What's the difference? You're awake now anyway, and when you go and weigh yourself, you know you'll wish you hit that treadmill this morning.*

No.

*Loser.*

The lump of my gut beneath the covers increased every time I blinked my eyes.

*You failed. You are worthless. You are nothing if not an anorexic.*

Getting back to sleep would be the best idea, but laying on either side or my back didn't bring the soothing path to sleep.

*You are wasting time. You are getting fat. You sicken me and everyone else around you.*

Sleep wasn't happening, so I headed to the writing room and started up the computer and then down to the kitchen to get the coffee going. I opened up the *Through the Fog* file and checked the last couple paragraphs to get my place in the story. The coffee was bitter and perfect writing fuel. It wasn't long before the words flowed and made their way down the electronic white page.

*Look at your gut hanging over your boxers.*

Peggy would advise me not to look down. I reached for the coffee cup to keep myself busy when the sentences paused. I hit Ctrl—S more than was necessary.

*Look. You need to see how disgusting you're getting. You need to see your fat.*

I looked down and the bulge was repulsive. I don't know how I let myself get so bad in a day, but I had. I pinched at the flab of skin that pudged out between me and the computer desk. I was a failure. I was disgusting.

The clock at the bottom right of the computer screen showed that I only had 15 minutes before I needed to get into the shower and then start Brighid's day with her. Sweat formed on my forehead. It was too late.

*But it's not too late to do the treadmill tonight. You know you get home before Kristin. You could do the half hour easily before she gets home.*

But I said I was going to cut back.

*That was stupid talk. You're going to let your body and all this work go to waste just because you made a stupid decision.*

It's not stupid. I am ready for this step.

*Oh you are, huh? Then why is your face dripping sweat at the thought of it? Why is that flabby gut of yours the main focus of your morning?*

I pressed against my temples with my fingertips and stared at the computer screen until the words blurred. I breathed deep. The words were not coming anymore that morning, so I went to the shower.

Work was no better. My banana snack didn't chew well.

*If you do the treadmill before Kristin gets home, all will be fine.*

The work day was so slow, and the anxiety built. I needed to get on the treadmill sooner rather than later. The food I'd taken in was already damaging my body.

*You don't need all that food.*

The Lean Cuisine sat in front of me still smoking from the microwave. I carried it back to my office as if it were a piece of contraband.

*Just eat the meat.*

It was a chicken breast doused in some sort of brown sauce. The bubbles in the sauce—were they fat?

*Yes.*

I prodded at one of the bubbles with a plastic fork. It didn't seem safe. Though I knew it already, I checked to be sure my brown office door was shut and locked. Kim wouldn't be able to walk in here and catch me tossing this crap.

If I picked off a small piece of the chicken and shook it before moving it to my mouth, any fat bubbles attached would probably fall off.

*Are you really willing to take that chance?*

I stabbed a piece of the chicken. There was no way I was going to eat any of the potatoes. The brown gunk glazed the chicken and reminded me of snot.

*You don't need to eat the whole piece of chicken.*

I am really supposed to.

*You haven't seen yourself in the mirror today. You didn't weigh this morning. You know how quickly things get out of control. Your gut is pushing the limits of your work pants, and Kristin gave all your larger pants to her brother in law. So when you allow yourself to get fatter than you are, you will have nothing to wear.*

I should have weighed this morning, and for God's sake, I should never have committed to cutting back on the treadmill. At minimum, I should have pulled on the shorts with the 28-inch waist to make sure I could still fit in them.

*You can't.*

The clump of chicken still sat on my white plastic fork. I shook it a couple times and popped it into my mouth. It was colder than I would have liked. My stomach convulsed but didn't push anything up.

*You know it's too late now. Once it's swallowed, there is nothing you can do.*

I plopped the next bite of chicken back into the packaging tray, slid the tray back into the box it came in, and took the whole mess down to the break room to throw it away.

*You still ate too much.*

The next day the treadmill was allowed and I hit it with the intensity of greeting a lost love. It was easier to eat what I was supposed to on treadmill days. My weight didn't balloon the way I expected it to. I pretty much stayed where I was for the first couple of weeks.

The next part of recovery I never expected.

# Chapter 47

I stuck to the treadmill every other day. Most days I ate what I was supposed to eat. Life sucked. The scale showed 131 and then 132 a week or two later, and the old panic shook my heart and wrenched my guts.

*You need the treadmill every day.*

I couldn't though. I made the commitment to Peggy. My body rebelled and fattened up with weight I could see long before the scale showed it.

*You are nothing if not an anorexic.*

While Kristin was on her cruise, Kim had roped me into singing karaoke with our work group at the fall picnic. I had sung in bands before, but at the rehearsals I was shy. My bands had been in high school and college—worlds away from the married family man I was now. That was a closed chapter. My guitar sat in my writing room in a corner.

After 4 or 5 songs at the karaoke rehearsal, I let my voice out a bit next to Kim during "Under the Boardwalk." Kim, who was holding the microphone, pushed it in front of my face.

"Jesus, Jim, why didn't you just say you could sing?" Kim asked as we drove the government car back to the building we worked in.

"I don't know. It's been a long time. I wasn't sure I still could."

A couple days after our karaoke group performed at the picnic, Gary and Dan, a couple guys I worked with showed up at the door of my office. I had done editing work for both of them, but I never had both of them at the door at the same time before.

"Hey Jim." Gary said.

"Hey guys." I pushed my chair back from my desk and swiveled it to face them. It must have been a pretty big document if both of them were here to show me what they needed.

"Hey, we hear you are a singer," Gary said. He leaned against one side of my door and Dan leaned against the other.

I laughed. "I did that whole karaoke thing. I was in bands years ago."

"Well, we hear you are pretty good, and we were wondering if you'd be interested in getting together and making some music.

We've been messing with some songs—stuff like the Stray Cats and things like that."

"I love the Stray Cats," I said.

"Well, maybe we could all get together at lunch and do some practicing."

I couldn't believe this was happening. I could feel the dust shaking off a section of my brain and being that had lay dormant for so long I forgot it was there. Could I still do that? Could I still get up on a stage with a band and do that?

I was ahead of myself though. They might hear me in rehearsal and think I suck and that would be it.

*You can burn a lot of calories on stage.*

"Yeah, I'd totally be into that, man." I heard my voice say. I was an observer about five feet deep in my consciousness.

"Cool, well, we'll be in touch and see what we can work out."

The band went well, or maybe it didn't. I met with Gary and Dan and soon we added a drummer named Mark. It was fun—I guess. I knew I sucked though and it was only a matter of time before they figured that out as well.

My desk at work got cluttered. I hadn't talked to my mom in a few days. I was a crappy son too, so what difference would it make. As that thought squeezed into reality, my desk phone rang.

"This is Jim."

"This is Mom."

"Hey! How you doing?"

"Good and how are you, dear?"

"Oh...you know..." This conversation was tiring. My voice shined and pretended from a tarnished spirit. I wanted to sleep. The phone was too heavy to hold, and the chatter was too much to bear.

My mom laughed, but I wasn't sure why. We piddled around the subject—the whole time my voice sounded fresh and alive. Add liar to the pounds of things that are wrong with you, you pathetic loser. A pause in the conversation finally allowed us to get to it.

"Are you taking care of yourself, Jim?"

How the fuck was I supposed to answer that? "Yeah, of course. As a matter of fact, I have cut back on the treadmill. I'm only doing it every other day now." Why did I have to get out of bed?

It's not like anyone reads these stupid-ass documents I edit all day for nothing an hour.

"That's great!"

*No it's not. You're a failure.*

"Yeah," I said. Whatever.

We said a couple more things to each other. My head was heavy. The clock told me it was 9 am, which meant it was still a good couple hours before I could lock my office door and nap my lunch hour away. Wait…She was still talking.

"Yeah…Right on…Brighid's great, yeah…She misses you too. Yeah. Okay…Cool. Yeah. Yeah. All right, I'll talk to you later."

My eyes burned as if tears would fall, but none did. The clicking of my battery operated wall clock counted the seconds toward my eventual death. It was 2005, and everyone living was living in the century they would die in. There's no fucking point.

At lunch, I ate my god damn Lean Cuisine and shut my eyes to the world. The alarm I set for myself went off sooner than I wanted, and there I was with me again. "Fuck."

Kim came down to see if I wanted to step outside with her for a smoke break.

"Do you want one?" Kim said.

"Yes, please. I mean…if you don't mind."

She dug into the inner pocket of her black leather coat, pulled a soft pack out, and handed me a smoke.

"Right on. Thanks" I took the cigarette and her light and lit up. I was soon in the groove and cradled in the yellow nicotine hum.

Kim talked. I talked, but I was nowhere near the conversation. Someone else got dressed as me that morning from the skin out, and a dense cushion of rank, wet cotton separated me from my life. I heard my voice, and I even heard my laugh—right on cue. The cigarette smoldered in my hand. Maybe if I touched the cherry end of it to my arm, I would feel something.

Peggy needed to know stuff like this. My appointment was 4 days away though. Could I make it? Did I want to?

Kim was saying something. I answered her, and the words fell together like a script someone with no understanding of me outlined years ago. When the flame met the filter, I watched Kim crush it out and drop it into the tube ashtray with the large base. I copied her.

The end of my shift was good for the movement and the change of scenery. By the time I made the half-mile drive to Brighid's school, the sun annoyed me, Joan Jett's played out music blared, and I had hit every fucking red light along the way. The car in front of me perched in the center of the road with its left turn signal blinking. No cars came in the oncoming lane, but this guy didn't move.

"Fucking retard convention on the road today," I muttered.

Brighid's small school had 5 classrooms, but of course, the daycare was the fifth one from the god damn parking lot. "Then I have the fucking 90-minute commute to face. Fuck me."

My stomach turned and I had to piss as I took the car off the main road and onto the residential streets where our house was. I had had it with Brighid by this time. I hated the inside of my car. I wanted bed, but there would be homework and someone had to make dinner. The kids were sick of the things I could make but nowhere near as sick as I was of making them.

No one had a worse lot in life. No one sucked more than I did.

The front door was unlocked and Dominique's music thundered from the stereo near the dining room table. She stood at the kitchen sink washing last night's dishes at the staggering rate of half a plate an hour.

I came into the kitchen, and she jumped when she spotted me from the corner of her eye. "Jesus Christ you fucking scared me!"

I didn't bother telling her that playing the music too loud while standing with your back to the unlocked door of the house was like putting up a huge neon sign announcing that she was 15, alone, and a perfect rape victim. She wouldn't have listened anyway. No one did.

Dominique ran over to the stereo and lowered the volume to a normal level. "How was your day?" she said, returning to the kitchen.

"Fine," I said, "How was yours?"

She went on to talk about some drama between her and some of the girls in her school and how she just felt like sometimes she was going to blow up in the middle of a boring class.

I nodded. I had been that kid once.

I cooked and fed the kids and got Brighid ready for bed. Then I put her in bed, and Kristin came home.

"Hey Bubbah," she said, throwing her work stuff aside as she came through the door. "Did you put a couple of those chicken wings in the microwave for me?"

"No, but I will."

"I'm gonna go change."

"Kay." I waited downstairs as the microwave glowed and hummed.

Nothing got better over the next couple days, and I really needed to get in and see Peggy. I had two more days to wait, and the most comforting thought I could entertain was one of me hanging from a self-made noose or sitting behind the wheel of a running car in the closed garage.

*You know how you could feel better. Today is treadmill day. It's not too late to skip dinner.*

"Why are you so down all the time?" Kristin said one evening as we got ready for bed. "You come home, you never want sex, you make me feel undesirable and you sulk around here all the fuckin' time. Is this family not enough to make you happy anymore?"

"It's got nothing to do with anything," I said.

"Then you need to cheer up."

"I'll talk to Peggy about it," I said.

"What the fuck can she do for you that I can't?"

I sighed.

"What the fuck is the matter with you?"

"I don't know, Kristin. I just don't feel good." The invisible muck bubble that separated me from my life thickened around me.

"If you are fucking your *friend* Kim at work, then that is something I need to know."

"That's fucking ridiculous." I said, laying down on my side of the bed.

"And why do you smell like cigarettes?"

I sighed again.

"Cause if I don't make you happy, then we need to talk about ending this."

Tears came hot and fast. "Why is that always the answer with you?"

"I'm just saying that if you're not happy and this family doesn't do it for you, then why bother?"

*Do the treadmill and all the hurt will leave. Eat no more than 5 flakes of Special K and things will get better. You'll be you again. You are nothing if not an anorexic.*

I know.

When all the good things in life annoy you for more than a day, then it is time to call your therapist. I didn't though. I had that appointment coming up, and I wasn't important enough to schedule something earlier. There were crazier people that needed to be seen first. I manned up and waited until the scheduled appointment. It built character.

No song sounded good. The voices blabbing on the radio to fill the space between songs grated on my last raw nerve. TV sucked—but then TV does suck.

Even the writing in the morning brought little joy. My books were always self published and ignored. My point, in this whole life, was?

The treadmill, my best friend in the house, betrayed me. Doing it every other day didn't bring the old rush. It was more like a fling than a love—pointless and hollow, yet fun while I was on it. I promised Peggy that I would stick to the every other day commitment. Had I only promised myself, I could have broken it. My promises to myself were among the few things in this world less significant than I was. Peggy counted on me though. My failure to beat anorexia would be her failure as a therapist, and I couldn't allow that.

I slumped in the chair of Peggy's waiting room looking at the words on the page of whatever book I was reading. The woman behind the glass window knew me by sight and greeted me by name as usual. I was known in a mental health office the way I used to be known at the pool where I was the swim coach.

Worse yet, I had no idea what her name was. That's what a rotten I guy I was—someone I saw as often as her, you'd think I could at least learn her name. Nope—not me. I was too busy on the scale and treadmill to give two shits about anyone else. I sucked on so many levels; I should probably be locked up to better society.

Peggy poked her head out of the door that led to the offices about 15 minutes after my appointment should have started. She had more important things to do, I was sure, so it didn't bother me to wait.

I took my usual seat across from her with my book in my lap.

"So how are you doing?" Peggy said with the familiar pad in her lap.

Tears burned at the bottom of my eyes and flooded my cheeks. "I don't know."

# Chapter 48

"Peggy thinks I have depression and she thinks I should consider taking antidepressants." I let the words hang in the air as Kristin drove the two of us out to dinner.

"What?"

I swallowed to try and hold the tears back. "She said I have depression and that I more than likely have had it all my life."

"Okay," Kristin said with a tone that would have fit better if I had just announced that Peggy thought I could fly. "So what do you think about that."

I shook my head and started in. "I can remember wanting to kill myself all the way back to my teen years. I tried when I was 20—tried to drink myself to death in a single night." The hot tears came back. "I told my mom the next morning. She seemed concerned but told me basically that I shouldn't feel that way. She told me feeling sad or happy was a choice. She told me she didn't know what to tell me."

"Do you want to kill yourself now?" Kristin said. The light turned red in front of us, and she turned to face me at the end of her question.

"Not at this particular moment, no."

"Have you wanted to at any point during our marriage?"

"The light turned," I said, flicking my finger toward the windshield. Kristin stepped on the gas just as someone from behind us blared their horn.

"Fuckin' dildo cheese whack!" she said as she scanned her rearview mirror for suspects. "How long was the light green—a second? Fucking pricks."

"Yeah, so anyway. She wants me to see a psychiatrist and have a meds evaluation." I couldn't tell if she heard me or if she still needed to know who honked their horn.

"What?" Kristin said.

I sighed. "Peggy wants me to see a psychiatrist and have a meds evaluation."

"Isn't Peggy a psychiatrist?"

"No."

"Then what the fuck are you seeing her for?"

"Peggy is a therapist. A psychiatrist can write prescriptions."

"Well, what kind of prescriptions?" Kristin turned the car into the restaurant's parking lot and found a space near the front door. "Am I the parking queen or what?"

"She mentioned Prozac," I said.

"Prozac?" Kristin shut off the car and looked over at me. With a laugh, she said, "She thinks you're crazy, huh?"

*You better find some chicken on the menu. Make sure it has no cheese or sauces. No bread either. Look down for a second, and I'll show you how fat your gut is.*

I laughed, but I kept my gaze out the window.

*Better look down. You're barely able to fit in the seatbelt.*

I pushed my hands against my temples and fingered the corners of my eyes. "I suppose I am. I'm scared though, of the pills. I'm the way I am naturally. This is me." I put my palm on my chest to emphasize the point. "If the pills make me happy all the time, then I will be living a lie. What if they make me float through life without a care as my whole world gets wrecked around me?"

"Don't I make you happy?" Kristin said.

I paused. I knew what I had to say, but I also knew that despite the simplicity of what needed saying, it was one of the hardest things for Kristin to ever wrap her mind around. "This," I said, "isn't about you."

My appointment with Dr. Chen was at 10:30 on a Wednesday. I left work and drove the 50 miles back to Modesto to see her. After the appointment, I would face the drive again, work a few hours, pick Brighid up, drive the commute again, cook dinner, work on whatever issues Dominique had, and get Brighid ready for bed. Lots of shit to do, and there was no way I could get it all done by Brighid's bedtime. I had to race the clock.

I gripped the wheel and shook my head back into the present for a second.

Dr. Chen and Peggy worked out of the same office. "You'll like her," Peggy said. "She's a good person. I really like working with her."

I replayed these reassurances in my mind against the fact that I was heading into an appointment that would change the chemical content of my brain. When you get right down to it, what more are we than our consciousness? What more is our consciousness than the chemical content of our minds? I was a dead man walking—Alice on the edge of the rabbit hole.

The familiar bell jingled as I pushed open the office door. The usual receptionist sat at her desk behind the sliding Plexiglas. "Hi James." She smiled. "Here for Peggy?"

"Dr. Chen, actually," I said.

"Oh." The surprise was obvious in her voice. She knew now that I had graduated from needing a therapist to needing a full-fledged shrink. She feared me now. I let my head droop in shame. "Okay, have a seat, and I'll let her know you are here."

My nerves jangled in my stomach. Peggy had me sign a piece of paper allowing her to show Dr. Chen all the notes she had on me. By now, Dr. Chen would have it all.

I set my eyes on the familiar door where Peggy would normally come and get me. The latch turned and a woman walked out, let the door close behind her, crossed the waiting room in a hasty blue blur, and went through the jingle door on her way out. Only a hint of perfume suggested she was real.

In a while, the latch turned again and a petite woman with long, straight black hair and thin-rimmed glasses peered out of the opening. "Mr. Kohl?" she said, smiling at me.

I stood. "Jim," I said.

I walked to the door where she was and the waiting room smeared in dream like slow motion as I crossed it. I saw my hand extend in front of me for a handshake because that is what people do in this situation.

"Dr. Chen," she said.

"Nice to meet you." I heard my voice say.

"Come on back," she said.

I followed her past Peggy's closed office door to an open one at the end of the hall on the left hand side. She took a seat on the other side of a desk, and I took a chair facing the window. The blinds striped my face with sun, and Dr. Chen adjusted them so I didn't have to squint.

"Peggy gave me your files, and I have been reading through them."

I nodded. She knew everything. I didn't know her at all. I folded my arms across my gut and hugged tight, making sure I could still reach around and have my hands almost meet behind my back.

"I still want to talk to you a little though just to fill in the empty spots."

All the spots are empty. "Okay."

*She can see your gut.*

I adjusted my arms.

"It says in your file that you can remember being depressed, or feeling depressed from the time you were a teenager."

"Yeah."

"Can you tell me a little about that? How did it feel? What were your thoughts like?"

That's never an easy question. You don't have to have depression to appreciate that if someone asked you to describe your thoughts from 20 years ago that it takes some digging.

I pictured my 13-year old self at the neighborhood pool where I was on the swim team having an argument with a friend and punching myself in the face repeatedly and then tearing my shirt. I thought of another time when I punched the back of a chair in my mom's house and ripped it. The rip made me feel worse for doing something wrong and then I punished myself with more blows to my own head.

"In general," I finally said, "My thoughts were pretty self destructive as a teenager."

"What about now?" Dr. Chen said.

"I am anorexic."

*You are nothing if not an anorexic.*

Dr. Chen nodded as if that were enough about my current status. "Did you or do you have thoughts of hurting yourself?"

This is psychiatrist code for suicidal thoughts. "Yes."

"How often?"

"A few times a day."

"Would you say they are obsessive?"

I cocked my head to the side.

"Would you say that they interrupt your ability to live a normal life?"

My palms were sweating and I rubbed them on my pants but returned my arms to their protective position as soon as I was finished. "I don't think so. I think they just are my normal life. I mean, I get up and go to work and all of that. And they haven't been this bad for a while. I didn't really notice them until..." Hot tears formed at the base of my eyes. "...until I started eating again."

Dr. Chen nodded and wrote a note. "Did you ever attempt suicide?"

"Once."

"How old were you?"

"Twenty."

"At that time, did you seek counseling or anything?"

I shook my head.

"What was the reason for that?"

"The reason I tried?" I said.

"No. The reason that you didn't seek counseling at that time."

I shrugged. "I was still living at home. I told my mom about it the next morning. She told me that I shouldn't feel that way about myself because I am a good person. She said it's a choice—your mood is." I looked at Dr. Chen to see if she agreed that moods were a choice, but her face revealed nothing.

"And so now the suicidal thoughts are back?"

"Yes."

"And you noticed them about the time you started eating to recover?"

*Destroying all the work you have done. Ending the progress.*

"Yeah." I pinched at my gut to see how much damage my recovery had rendered this far.

"Tell me what else you have been feeling." Dr. Chen said.

I explained the cold disconnect between myself and my life. I told her about how I could hear my voice making appropriate sounds in conversations, but I didn't feel like I was really a part of it. I told her about the hopelessness in giving up the one thing that gave me value. "I am nothing if not an anorexic."

*Exactly.*

Dr. Chen made a lengthy note on the pink pages of my file. I watched the pulsing light of a dying fluorescent bulb behind the opaque glass in the ceiling. "How do you feel about medication for depression?"

*You hate the idea. All you need is the treadmill. Get off this eating program and we can fix this depression in a day or two. Get back on the scale...*

"I hate the idea of it."

"Why?" I checked her face and was relieved to see she wasn't being argumentative. She had genuine curiosity.

"Because it will change who I am. I am the way I am, and this is the natural order of things. If I start taking pills to change the way I feel emotionally, then I am in essence changing who I am and living a lie."

"That's not really the way they work," Dr. Chen said. She set her pen down on her desk and folded her hands in front of her. "The reason you are depressed, especially with such a long history of feeling depression, is that there are a couple of chemicals missing from your brain. The pills will allow the chemicals to be present at a level where you won't feel as bad."

"That is exactly what I said in not so many words. I am not meant to have these chemicals at that level or I would have been born that way." My logic seemed solid. I wiped the sweat from my hands again and returned my arms to their crossed position on my gut.

"Do you also think," she said, "that if someone has allergies they shouldn't take allergy medicine?"

I saw no connection, and my face showed it.

"If someone is born with allergies, and that is their natural way of being, should they not take allergy medicine because the medicine would have them live a lie? Or would you say that they should take the medicine because it would allow them to have a more comfortable life?"

*You don't need medicine. You need to get back on the treadmill. You need to get back on the scale.*

"I was fine until I started the new eating plan." I looked at the floor. "It started all this and it's the reason I am here right now. I should not have messed with things."

"Do you think you were not ready to start eating for recovery?"

I thought for a moment staring into the corner where the wall met the ceiling. "Ready? We never are." My voice tapered off to almost a whisper.

"Pardon me?"

"I never will be ready, but I am doing it anyway."

Dr. Chen nodded and adjusted her glasses on her nose. "That's fair."

*How is it fair? Why should they decide what you eat and how much you exercise?*

"On the subject of the medication," she said, "obviously, no one can make you take it. And also, it's not an exact science to figure out the correct dose for people. It's kind of a trial and error method."

I wondered what the worst case scenario of the error might lead to.

"There are quite a few of them to choose from now, but chemically they are all based on Prozac. So for me, it makes the most sense to start with Prozac and see how it works and make adjustments from there."

Tears ran down my cheeks.

"You really don't want this, do you?" Dr. Chen said.

I shook my head. "I just don't know...I just can't be sure. It's...I don't know."

"You know you will be under my care especially when we first start this. You'll be checking in with me and with Peggy to make sure you are okay. And if you don't like the way the pills make you feel, we can change them or get you off them completely."

I brushed my forehead with my fingertips and checked them for sweat. I knew Peggy wanted what was best for me. Dr. Chen was a friend of hers, so it was a safe assumption that she probably wanted the best for me too.

And what if it really did work well for me? Plus, I had driven 50 miles in the middle of the workday, and that would be a huge waste of time if I decided to refuse treatment. Dr. Chen had other patients and wasting her day was inexcusable.

Dr. Chen sat patiently behind her desk.

*You just need to exercise more.*

"I guess I'll give the pills a try."

*You need to not eat so much. You need to get back to the plan. It's past time when we should stop messing with the progress.*

"Again, like I said. Peggy and I will be monitoring you, and of course, should you ever feel like you are a threat to yourself or someone else, you would need to call 911 or get yourself to the nearest hospital." Dr. Chen didn't break eye contact as she spoke.

"Is that something you expect?"

"Trial and error, like I said Mr. Kohl. Some pills and some dosages don't work for everyone. Plus, sometimes a patient will experience a bit of an emotional roller coaster of sorts until the meds level out."

*This is far too dangerous. Exercise is all you need.*

I took a second and let the words process. The pile of prescription pads sat beneath Dr. Chen's computer monitor. "Well…What do we do then?"

"Does this mean you are willing to give the medication a try?"

After a pause, I nodded. The sun had moved and the cracks between the blinds behind Dr. Chen were not as bright.

"Well…What if I am really thin right now—well thinner than a normal person maybe by a little." I checked Dr. Chen's face for a sign of agreement or argument and found only interest. "So like, then I take these pills and suppose they make me feel better. But then my weight…my weight…" I swallowed hard. "My weight goes up…" A long sigh escaped my lips. "…and then the dose isn't good enough anymore because of that. Then I have to take more and more pills, I imagine. So pretty soon, all I'm doing is taking pills my whole life."

"It doesn't work that way." Dr. Chen said, shaking her head.

"What doesn't?"

"With relation to weight. It doesn't work that way with these pills because they only interact with the chemicals in your brain. Your brain functions the same, chemical wise, no matter what you weigh."

"Hmm." I said in a staccato blast.

"I know it seems hard for you to believe, but I assure you that is the case."

"I'm just thinking about how alcohol affects you more when you are thinner, you know?"

"Again, this is not the same sort of thing. While we are on the subject, you really shouldn't drink with these meds because alcohol will counteract them."

"Never?"

"Ideally, yes, never. Again, it's like canceling the effects of the medicine. An occasional drink is not a problem though."

Dr. Chen told me about the side effects that could come with Prozac, which included sexual side effects, stomach pains until the body got used to the meds, and weight loss.

"Do you think I need to lose some weight?" I said, my eyes brightened with the idea.

"I didn't say that, Mr. Kohl."

# Chapter 49

The Prozac came in little white and green capsules. The capsules sat in their orange tinted plastic bottle in a white Longs Drugs bag on my passenger seat. I had taken a couple already and waited for an effect.

"The news will sometimes say that Prozac causes people to attempt suicide," Dr. Chen had said, "This is only because some depressed people are on the verge of suicide and they just don't have the energy or the drive to bother. Prozac gives them the energy they need." She had stressed again the importance of calling 911 or getting to an emergency room should I feel that way.

"What if these pills make you think that I don't treat you well?" Kristin asked me that evening.

"Honey, that won't be the case. They'll just stop me from being sad for no reason."

We were on the couch, having our usual commercial break conversation. "Why can't I make you happy? Aren't I enough to just make you happy?"

"It's the chemicals in my brain, babe. It has nothing to do with you or anything else in the world. It's just how I am."

Kristin said nothing and the show came back.

At the next commercial, I said, "The thing that concerns me is that since that is how I am, the pills will make me...not how I am. Like I am afraid they will make me fake."

"So it is a possibility that it will affect us."

"Why would you think that?" I said.

She looked at me from her end of the couch. "I don't know. I don't feel like I know you anymore. You were never sad when we first got together. I don't feel that you would still do anything for me the way you used to. You don't want to do anyone's resumes anymore. You don't seem to want to help at all. You are not as generous as you were."

"I have been sick," I said.

"You know I don't see that as a disease. It's a choice just like any addict. I have no tolerance for that kind of weakness, and I never have. You know that."

Whatever show was on returned from commercials.

"Look, if I start to change in a way that you think is bad for me or for us, then I'll get off the pills."

"Huh?" she said, eyes fixed on the TV screen.

"I said I'll stop the pills if they turn me into an asshole."

"Whatever."

Within the next couple of days, I started to feel the effects. It was quick for me, and despite what Dr. Chen said, I was convinced that the fast effects were due to my low weight.

Kim and I stood and smoked out in front of our building. She was around me a lot, and I figured if someone would notice a change in me in any way it would be her.

The hard part was I couldn't tell Kim that I was on Prozac. The Lab and the government looked down on Prozac and other meds like it when they were considering you for a security clearance. I couldn't mention it at work or I would be subject to the Lab psychiatrist analyzing me to see if I was a security risk.

I smiled as Kim talked. Her daughter, Althea, was in the Girl Scouts, and it was really more drama than it was fun. "It's turned into a club where little girls learn new techniques to out bitch each other," Kim said. "I don't remember it being that way when I was a kid." She took her last drag and flipped her cigarette butt into the parking lot.

"Glad you're telling me this," I said, "I'll think twice about sticking Brighid in the Girl Scouts."

"Totally."

The dark fog I had spoken behind had broken a bit. This conversation, which in all other ways was unremarkable, was my first conversation in maybe 2 years. Anorexia spoke for me for a year and a half, and depression hid me from my life for the last few months. For this talk with Kim, I was really there, feeling alive, and feeling necessary to the conversation and life in general.

The clouds would come and go. Some days would still start out dark and detached. Like the overcast sky in a beach town, the clouds would sometimes burn off about halfway through the day. Sometimes they wouldn't.

"What you're describing is pretty normal for just going on meds," Peggy said. The pad in her lap sat there and she hooked her pen underneath her thumb. "It tends to be ups and downs until the levels finally settle. We'll really know if they work for you in a month or so."

"But I already feel better a lot of the time. I feel like I am right there in my life."

She nodded and smiled. "That's good. How is your marriage?"

Joann, who had been the maid of honor at our wedding, was getting married herself. We were invited to it, and it was the same day that the Dead were playing at the Shoreline for what turned out to be the last time the band reunited for a tour to date.

"You can go to the show with your sister," Kristin said. "I can go to the wedding alone."

Visions of the picture from the hot tub on the cruise swarmed my head. To save my marriage, I had to go to this wedding. To keep us together, I had to be there. "No, that's all right. I'll go to the wedding with you. I already said I would."

"Don't feel like you have to go with me."

"Don't you want me with you there?"

"I do. But I am okay if I go alone," Kristin said. She was doing her makeup and didn't look over to me as she talked.

This kind of thing could easily be thrown in my face later. "I am going to the wedding."

I missed the Dead show to go to this wedding. It was the right thing to do. It built character to put the desires of my wife before my own. Character sucks.

The day of the wedding Kristin was getting her nails done and her hair dyed and styled. I was across the street at Starbucks reading and waiting for her to be finished. I'd been taking Prozac for a couple weeks.

A woman came into the Starbucks and we met eyes for a second. I smiled and so did she.

The reality hit me that she was looking at me because I seemed like a nice guy. It was a casual social interaction with no words, but it was huge to me. It was the first time I could remember meeting eyes with a stranger in public and not immediately assuming they were looking at me in disgust or because I was some sort of freak.

I continued to smile as I went back to reading my book at the small round table where my drink sat. My thinking had changed in regard to myself, but I still felt genuine. My mood was good, and I liked myself enough to want to hang out with me. It was a new mental playground to explore.

"You look awesome!" I said to Kristin as I picked her up from the hair appointment. The girls in the shop smiled as I gushed over her hair and nails.

"Thanks."

The wedding was out on the Delta and we booked a room in what used to be a Speak Easy. The place had been kept up, but still had the look of a place about 100 years old. There was no TV in the room, and very little for us to do with each other anymore.

"Let's go down and get a drink before we get ready for the wedding," Kristin said.

"You mean like a beer?"

"Yeah, or whatever."

*Are you out of your head? You know the calories that are in beer. You know there is going to be all kinds of food at the wedding. Don't be stupid and add insult to injury. There was 110 calories in that nonfat latte you had earlier at Starbucks.*

"Um...I don't know if I want one, but I'll go down with you."

"Why?" Kristin stopped by the hotel room door and jerked around to face me.

"I don't know...I just...I don't know..."

She sighed and said, "Fine." She turned and opened the door. I jumped off the bed and followed her.

"What's wrong?" It took a bit of effort to catch up with her.

"Nothing." Her eyes were fixed on the hall ahead of us and room numbers blurred as we raced down the hall.

"I'm sorry. Fine, you know? It's a good idea. I'll get a drink too. C'mon."

"You don't have to get a fucking drink if you don't want to and don't do me any fucking favors." We turned the corner toward the stairs that led to the bar and lobby area below.

Even being at this wedding was a favor, but I didn't bring that up. "I don't understand why you are so mad."

"I'm not." She headed down the stairs first and never looked back for me.

At the bar, she ordered a tequila sunrise and I got a Heineken.

*You are so stupid. You are worthless and you have no sense of commitment.*

We sat outside at a small table on the hotel's wraparound porch. The cold bottle sweated in the heat of the central valley Delta. The history of the place whispered to you if you listened, but I had no time to do that. I was 2 hours away from heading to a wedding with a woman that wasn't talking to me, and the Dead were probably doing sound check down in Mountain View.

"I don't get why you are mad at me," I said.

"You can't have fun anymore. You can't just kick back and relax."

"Yeah. I know that. But things are getting better." I told her about the lady at Starbucks and she rolled her eyes.

"You should just feel that way automatically. You shouldn't need a pill to feel like that."

"I know." The happiness I had about the smile in Starbucks was cancelled. I sipped my beer.

*You are worthless and weak. You should have stood strong and not ordered a beer in the first place. Do not even entertain the idea of having cake at this wedding. You're pathetic and disgusting.*

I finished that beer. I struggled with the fatty foods at the wedding doused in white creamy sauces. Kristin tightened her lips whenever anyone mentioned to me how thin I was. I didn't eat cake.

# Chapter 50

"It just doesn't bother me as much as it did once," I said.

*You're a liar.*

"How so?" Peggy said.

"I don't know. It's like it's not as strong. I still can hear the suggestions coming—the diet ideas, but I tend to just kind of do the opposite of what they are saying. Like if I start thinking that way…"

*Which way? Say it. Like if you start thinking you're fat and you get a great diet idea?*

My eyes wandered Peggy's office. "…Like if I start thinking I am fat, I go and buy a doughnut."

"That's good. The anorexic thoughts only have power over you if you listen to them. The more you can act against them, the less they will come, the less powerful they will feel."

"It seems so easy when you say it that way," I said.

Peggy laughed. "It seems easy and obvious to you now because you are ready to know it. When you first came in here, if I had suggested such a thing, you would have thought I was crazy."

"Yeah," I laughed too. "That's true, huh?"

"The Prozac has allowed you a little space to sit back and take a good look at yourself. It allows you to be more mindful, and be aware of your moods and feelings. It gives you a couple seconds to recognize which thoughts are not true and which ones are not healthy."

It had been about 2 months on Prozac and I liked myself all right. I didn't feel like I had a care in the world most of the time. I felt okay even in the mirror…a good portion of the time anyway.

The treadmill was broken. I had burned out the motor, and even when I had cut my exercise to every other day, the poor thing didn't stand a chance against my 6 mph at a 10 degree slope half hours. I let it lay dead in the garage.

At Wal-Mart with Kim at lunch, I would look at the treadmills as we headed to the girls' clothes section to shop for her daughters. I priced the treadmills out, but I never bought another one.

The scale went out in the garbage maybe a month later.

Now and then I'd panic and feel out of control. How much did I weigh now? What was my number?

*You know what you need to do.*

I battled the thoughts daily. They would come, and for health reasons, I couldn't buy a donut every time. I'd have to recognize them as a bad thought, resolve not to act on the thought, and redirect my thoughts somewhere else.

*Run. Run around the block. You are starting to look like you did, do you want me to show you in the mirror?*

"That's not true. I didn't lose all that weight in 2 months, and I am not gaining all that weight back in two months. It doesn't happen like that. Reading a book sounds good right about now, or maybe I'll check my e-mail."

And so it went. Every day was a new day. Every challenge was a new challenge. It was a whole new way of living and getting by, and I was starting to like it.

Prozac gave me a whole new life where I could rebuild and rediscover myself. If I didn't want to do something, I really didn't need to. I didn't have to build any character anymore.

I was allowed to be me, and I had the strength to do it.

I could smoke if I wanted. I could stay up or go to bed or go to sleep. I could clean the house. I could fold the towels and tell Kristin if she didn't like the way they were folded, she could fold them herself.

I could eat.

The world didn't have nearly the amount of rules that I thought it had, and it was a scary and exciting time. I never had to do anything I didn't want to do aside from pay taxes and die someday long in the future.

"You don't have my heart anymore," Kristin told me while we sat one day in the dining room at the expensive table she picked that still wasn't paid off.

"What?"

"I love you, but I am not in love with you anymore."

"Geez babe, that's kinda harsh."

"I can't help it. It's just the way I feel. You have changed too much. You're not the same guy I married—the guy that would do anything for me. The guy that was so sweet and generous. That guy is the guy I loved." Kristin looked out the glass doors that led onto our small back porch while she talked as if she could see the guy she was in love with out there somewhere.

"I'm still the same guy," I said. "I've been the same guy the whole time. There was nothing left of me for a while, but I am rebuilding. I am a new and better Jim. I am a stronger Jim."

"You are not a better Jim." Kristin said. "Don't you remember all the times you would go to the store and I would ask you to get me a surprise? You would always come home with something. That was the fun part—to see what you would pick."

I looked at her and waited for her to go on.

"Now..." she said, "Now when I ask you to get me a surprise, you sigh and act like it's a major imposition."

"Well honey, what am I supposed to get you at Longs?" I said.

"There are things there. There are things everywhere if you care enough to look for them. But mostly when you are in a store, you are with your friend, Kim. You're probably fucking her."

"Kristin..."

"Jim."

I rolled my eyes. The clouds crossed over the sun outside and dampened the light coming through the glass porch doors. My gut called out to be pinched for a fat check, but I stopped myself.

*You know you want to. You know you have to.*

"Every night," she went on, "I pray to God that I will fall back in love with you. I pray like crazy for that, but it just doesn't seem to be working. Like I said, you don't have my heart anymore, and I'm not sure if you ever will again."

I combed my fingers through my hair and said, "I still love you."

"I still love you too. I'm just not in love with you. Your anorexia and the trip to Philadelphia with your parents did a lot of damage in this relationship. You make me feel undesirable. You'd rather get up and write than stay in bed and fuck me."

"That's not true," I said, but it was true. Seeing her in the guy's lap in the hot tub so that she could feel desirable had made her undesirable.

"Yes it is true," she said. I didn't argue this time.

"All right, so what do I need to do to earn your love back?" It sickened me even as I said it. I wanted to run hard and long around the block until I collapsed. Visions of spinach leaves and 5 flakes of cereal in an ocean of fat free milk swarmed my imagination.

"I don't know that you can," she said.

I didn't. We tried in counseling and we tried doing things like getting new wedding bands to symbolize a new start. Kristin even bought me a small plastic heart that symbolized me earning her heart back. I carried it in my pocket for about a month. Out of depression and out of anorexia, I was finished letting someone control each aspect of my life. Kristin was right that the cured and new Jim was incompatible with her. The marriage ended in June of 2006.

# Afterward

When I was in recovery, Dominique sat across the room from me on the green couch and I lounged in the blue easy chair. The TV babbled, but neither of us paid attention to it.

"Do you know what the worst part of anorexia was?" I said, stretching and resting the back of my head in my nested fingers.

Dominique's face twisted into a look of confusion and disgust. "All of it?" she said.

I laughed. "Yeah…Yeah, I guess you're right."

"I mean, dude. It's a disease," she said.

"Yeah." My mind showed me images of hours on the treadmill and more hours trapped in the mirror seeing the fat that would never leave. I shook the memories from me.

"But what were you gonna say?" She said.

I huffed a laugh at the ridiculous point I was going to make a few moments ago. "Always being so cold."

Am I cured? Are we ever really cured of anything?

Even as I sit and type this today, safe in a new relationship and separated from my great diet ideas by 4 years, I can look down and see too much gut. It's never over. I have triggers to this day that will make me panic and pinch my gut or check the skin beneath my chin. I don't own a scale, and when I go to the doctor's office I refuse to get on one unless they absolutely promise me that I will not know the number.

As more time passes, it gets easier. While writing this book, I got on a treadmill a couple times, and my mind immediately started playing some of the old games detailed in these pages. I really should never use a treadmill again anymore than a recovering alcoholic should just have one beer. Kristin was right in that anorexia was like an addiction, but Kristin was wrong in that it is a disease.

*You know I'm still here. You know what you need to do. You are nothing if not…*

I will never be cured, but I will always, with luck, strength, and love, be in recovery. The thoughts come, but I am not my thoughts. I am separate from them, and they are no more a threat to me than the pages in a novel or a bad dream.

14187055R00178

Made in the USA
Charleston, SC
26 August 2012